Eduard von Hartmann

Philosophy of the Unconscious - Speculative Results According to the Inductive Method of Physical Science

Vol. II

Eduard von Hartmann

Philosophy of the Unconscious - Speculative Results According to the Inductive Method of Physical Science
Vol. II

ISBN/EAN: 9783337069162

Printed in Europe, USA, Canada, Australia, Japan

Cover: Foto ©Thomas Meinert / pixelio.de

More available books at **www.hansebooks.com**

THE
ENGLISH AND FOREIGN PHILOSOPHICAL LIBRARY.

PHILOSOPHICAL INQUIRY is essentially the chief intellectual study of our age. It is proposed to produce, under the title of "THE ENGLISH AND FOREIGN PHILOSOPHICAL LIBRARY," a series of works of the highest class connected with that study.

The English contributions to the series consist of original works, and of occasional new editions of such productions as have already attained a permanent rank among the philosophical writings of the day.

Beyond the productions of English writers, there are many recent publications in German and French which are not readily accessible to English readers, unless they are competent German and French scholars. Of these foreign writings, the translations have been entrusted to gentlemen whose names will be a guarantee for their critical fidelity.

"THE ENGLISH AND FOREIGN PHILOSOPHICAL LIBRARY" claims to be free from all bias, and thus fairly to represent all developments of Philosophy, from Spinoza to Hartmann, from Leibnitz to Lotze. Each original work is produced under the inspection of its author, from his manuscript, without intermediate suggestions or alterations. As corollaries, works showing the results of Positive Science, occasionally, though seldom, find a place in the series.

The series is elegantly printed in octavo, and the price regulated by the extent of each volume. The volumes will follow in succession, at no fixed periods, but as early as is consistent with the necessary care in their production.

THE FOLLOWING HAVE ALREADY APPEARED:—

In Three Volumes, post 8vo, pp. 350, 406, and 384, with Index, cloth, £1, 11s. 6d.

A HISTORY OF MATERIALISM.
By Professor F. A. LANGE.
Authorised Translation from the German by ERNEST C. THOMAS.

"This is a work which has long and impatiently been expected by a large circle of readers. It has been well praised by two eminent scientists, and their words have created for it, as regards its appearance in our English tongue, a sort of ante-natal reputation. The reputation is in many respects well deserved. The book is marked throughout by singular ability, abounds in striking and suggestive reflections, subtle and profound discussions, felicitous and graphic descriptions of mental and social movements, both in themselves and in their mutual relations."—*Scotsman*.

THE ENGLISH AND FOREIGN PHILOSOPHICAL LIBRARY.

Post 8vo, pp. xii.—362, cloth, 10s. 6d.

NATURAL LAW: An Essay in Ethics.
By EDITH SIMCOX.
Second Edition.

"Miss Simcox deserves cordial recognition for the excellent work she has done in vindication of naturalism, and especially for the high nobility of her ethical purpose."—*Athenæum.*

In Two Volumes, post 8vo, pp. 268 and 288, cloth, 15s.

THE CREED OF CHRISTENDOM:
ITS FOUNDATIONS CONTRASTED WITH ITS SUPERSTRUCTURE.
By W. R. GREG.
Eighth Edition, with a New Introduction.

"No candid reader of the 'Creed of Christendom' can close the book without the secret acknowledgment that it is a model of honest investigation and clear exposition, conceived in the true spirit of serious and faithful research."—*Westminster Review.*

Third Edition. Post 8vo, pp. xix.—249, cloth, 7s. 6d.

OUTLINES OF THE HISTORY OF RELIGION
TO THE SPREAD OF THE UNIVERSAL RELIGIONS.
By C. P. TIELE,
Dr. Theol., Professor of the History of Religions in the University of Leiden.

Translated from the Dutch by J. ESTLIN CARPENTER, M.A.

"Few books of its size contain the result of so much wide thinking, able and laborious study, or enable the reader to gain a better bird's-eye view of the latest results of investigations into the religious history of nations. . . . These pages, full of information, these sentences, cut and perhaps also dry, short and clear, condense the fruits of long and thorough research."—*Scotsman.*

Third Edition. Post 8vo, pp. 276, cloth, 7s. 6d.

RELIGION IN CHINA:
Containing a Brief Account of the Three Religions of the Chinese, with Observations on the Prospects of Christian Conversion amongst that People.

By JOSEPH EDKINS, D.D., Peking.

"We confidently recommend a careful perusal of the present work to all interested in this great subject."—*London and China Express.*

"Dr. Edkins has been most careful in noting the varied and often complex phases of opinion, so as to give an account of considerable value of the subject."—*Scotsman.*

Post 8vo, pp. xviii.—198, cloth, 7s. 6d.

A CANDID EXAMINATION OF THEISM.
By PHYSICUS.

"It is impossible to go through this work without forming a very high opinion of his speculative and argumentative power, and a sincere respect for his temperance of statement and his diligent endeavour to make out the best case he can for the views he rejects."—*Academy.*

Post 8vo, pp. xii.—282, cloth, 10s. 6d.

THE COLOUR SENSE: Its Origin and Development.

AN ESSAY IN COMPARATIVE PSYCHOLOGY.

By GRANT ALLEN, B.A., Author of "Physiological Æsthetics."

"The book is attractive throughout, for its object is pursued with an earnestness and singleness of purpose which never fail to maintain the interest of the reader."—*Saturday Review.*

Post 8vo, pp. xx.—316, cloth, 7s. 6d.

THE PHILOSOPHY OF MUSIC.

BEING THE SUBSTANCE OF

A COURSE OF LECTURES

DELIVERED AT THE ROYAL INSTITUTION OF GREAT BRITAIN, IN FEBRUARY AND MARCH 1877.

By WILLIAM POLE, Mus. Doc. Oxon.

Fellow of the Royal Societies of London and Edinburgh; one of the Examiners in Music to the University of London.

"We may recommend it as an extremely useful compendium of modern research into the scientific basis of music. There is no want of completeness."—*Pall Mall Gazette.*

Post 8vo, pp. 168, cloth, 6s.

CONTRIBUTIONS to THE HISTORY of THE DEVELOPMENT OF THE HUMAN RACE.

LECTURES AND DISSERTATIONS

By LAZARUS GEIGER,

Author of "Origin and Evolution of Human Speech and Reason."

Translated from the Second German Edition by DAVID ASHER, Ph.D., Corresponding Member of the Berlin Society for the Study of Modern Languages and Literature.

"The papers translated in this volume deal with various aspects of a very fascinating study. Herr Geiger had secured a place in the foremost ranks of German philologers, but he seems to have valued his philological researches chiefly as a means of throwing light on the early condition of mankind. He prosecuted his inquiries in a thoroughly philosophical spirit, and he never offered a theory, however paradoxical it might seem at first sight, for which he did not advance solid arguments. Unlike the majority of German scholars, he took pleasure in working out his doctrines in a manner that was likely to make them interesting to the general public; and his capacity for clear and attractive exposition was hardly inferior to that of Mr. Max Müller himself."—*St. James's Gazette.*

Post 8vo, pp. 350, with a Portrait, cloth, 10s. 6d.

DR. APPLETON: His Life and Literary Relics.

By JOHN H. APPLETON, M.A.,

Late Vicar of St. Mark's, Staplefield, Sussex;

AND

A. H. SAYCE, M.A.,

Fellow of Queen's College, and Deputy Professor of Comparative Philology, Oxford.

"Although the life of Dr. Appleton was uneventful, it is valuable as illustrating the manner in which the speculative and the practical can be combined. His biographers talk of his geniality, his tolerance, his kindliness; and these characteristics, combined with his fine intellectual gifts, his searching analysis, his independence, his ceaseless energy and ardour, render his life specially interesting."—*Nonconformist.*

Post 8vo, pp. xxvi.–370, with Portrait, Illustrations, and an Autograph Letter, cloth, 12s. 6d.

EDGAR QUINET:
HIS EARLY LIFE AND WRITINGS.
By RICHARD HEATH.

"Without attaching the immense value to Edgar Quinet's writings which Mr. Heath considers their due, we are quite ready to own that they possess solid merits which, perhaps, have not attracted sufficient attention in this country. To a truly reverent spirit, Edgar Quinet joined the deepest love for humanity in general. Mr. Heath . . . deserves credit for the completeness and finish of the portraiture to which he set his hand. It has evidently been a labour of love, for the text is marked throughout by infinite painstaking, both in style and matter."—*Globe.*

Second Edition, post 8vo, cloth, 7s. 6d.

THE ESSENCE OF CHRISTIANITY.
By LUDWIG FEUERBACH.
Translated from the Second German Edition by MARIAN EVANS, Translator of Strauss's "Life of Jesus."

"I confess that to Feuerbach I owe a debt of inestimable gratitude. Feeling about in uncertainty for the ground, and finding everywhere shifting sands, Feuerbach cast a sudden blaze into the darkness, and disclosed to me the way."
— From S. Baring-Gould's "*The Origin and Development of Religious Belief,*" *Part II., Preface, page xii.*

Third Edition, revised, post 8vo, pp. 200, cloth, 3s. 6d.

AUGUSTE COMTE AND POSITIVISM.
By the late JOHN STUART MILL, M.P.

Post 8vo, pp. xliv.–216, cloth, 7s. 6d.

ESSAYS AND DIALOGUES OF GIACOMO LEOPARDI.
Translated from the Italian, with Biographical Sketch, by CHARLES EDWARDES.

"This is a good piece of work to have done, and Mr. Edwardes deserves praise both for intention and execution."—*Athenæum.*

"Gratitude is due to Mr. Edwardes for an able portraiture of one of the saddest figures in literary history, and an able translation of his less inviting and less known works."—*Academy.*

Post 8vo, pp. xii.–178, cloth, 6s.

RELIGION AND PHILOSOPHY IN GERMANY:
A FRAGMENT.
By HEINRICH HEINE.
Translated by JOHN SNODGRASS,
Translator of "Wit, Wisdom, and Pathos from the Prose of Heinrich Heine"

"Nowhere is the singular charm of this writer more marked than in the vivid pages of this work. . . . Irrespective of subject, there is a charm about whatever Heine wrote that captivates the reader and wins his sympathies before criticism steps in. But there can be none who would fail to admit the power as well as the beauty of the wide-ranging pictures of the intellectual development of the country of deep thinkers. Beneath his grace the writer holds a mighty grip of fact, stripped of all disguise and made patent over all confusing surroundings."—*Bookseller.*

Post 8vo, pp. xviii.—310, with Portrait, cloth, 10s. 6d.
EMERSON AT HOME AND ABROAD.
By MONCURE D. CONWAY.
Author of "The Sacred Anthology," "The Wandering Jew," "Thomas Carlyle," &c.

This book reviews the personal and general history of the so-called "Transcendental" movement in America; and it contains various letters by Emerson not before published, as well as personal recollections of his lectures and conversations.

"Mr. Conway has not confined himself to personal reminiscences; he brings together all the important facts of Emerson's life, and presents a full account of his governing ideas—indicating their mutual relations, and tracing the processes by which Emerson gradually arrived at them in their mature form."—*St. James's Gazette.*

Seventeenth Edition. Post 8vo, pp. xx.—314, cloth, 10s. 6d.
ENIGMAS OF LIFE.
By W. R. GREG.

"What is to be the future of the human race? What are the great obstacles in the way of progress? What are the best means of surmounting these obstacles? Such, in rough statement, are some of the problems which are more or less present to Mr. Greg's mind; and although he does not pretend to discuss them fully, he makes a great many observations about them, always expressed in a graceful style, frequently eloquent, and occasionally putting old subjects in a new light, and recording a large amount of reading and study."—*Saturday Review.*

Post 8vo, pp. 328, cloth, 10s. 6d.
ETHIC
DEMONSTRATED IN GEOMETRICAL ORDER AND DIVIDED INTO FIVE PARTS,
WHICH TREAT

I. OF GOD.
II. OF THE NATURE AND ORIGIN OF THE MIND.
III. OF THE ORIGIN AND NATURE OF THE AFFECTS.
IV. OF HUMAN BONDAGE, OR OF THE STRENGTH OF THE AFFECTS.
V. OF THE POWER OF THE INTELLECT, OR OF HUMAN LIBERTY.

By BENEDICT DE SPINOZA.
Translated from the Latin by WILLIAM HALE WHITE.

"Mr. White only lays claim to accuracy, the Euclidian form of the work giving but small scope for literary finish. We have carefully examined a number of passages with the original, and have in every case found the sense correctly given in fairly readable English. For the purposes of study it may in most cases replace the original; more Mr. White could not claim or desire."—*Athenæum.*

In Three Volumes. Post 8vo, Vol. I., pp. xxxii.—532, cloth, 18s.; Vols. II. and III., pp. viii.—496; and pp. viii.—510, cloth, 32s.
THE WORLD AS WILL AND IDEA.
By ARTHUR SCHOPENHAUER.
Translated from the German by R. B. HALDANE, M.A., and JOHN KEMP, M.A.

"The translators have done their part very well, for, as they say, their work has been one of difficulty, especially as the style of the original is occasionally 'involved and loose.' At the same time there is a force, a vivacity, a directness, in the phrases and sentences of Schopenhauer which are very different from the manner of ordinary German philosophical treatises. He knew English and English literature thoroughly; he admired the clearness of their manner, and the popular strain even in their philosophy, and these qualities he tried to introduce into his own works and discourse."—*Scotsman.*

In Three Volumes, post 8vo, pp. xxxii.—372; vi.—368; and viii.—360, cloth, £1, 11s. 6d.

THE PHILOSOPHY OF THE UNCONSCIOUS.

By EDWARD VON HARTMANN.

[Speculative Results, according to the Inductive Method of Physical Science.]
Authorised Translation, by WILLIAM C. COUPLAND, M.A.

*** *Ten Editions of the German original have been sold since its first appearance in 1868.*

"Mr. Coupland has been remarkably successful in dealing with the difficulties of Hartmann. . . . It must be owned that the book merited the honour of translation. Its collection of facts alone would be sufficient to deserve this, and the appendix in the third volume, giving a readable résumé of Wundt's psycho-physics, is a valuable addition to English psychology."—*Athenæum*.

Three Vols., post 8vo, pp. viii.—368; ix.—225; and xxvii.—327, cloth, £1, 11s. 6d.

THE GUIDE OF THE PERPLEXED OF MAIMONIDES.

Translated from the Original Text, and Annotated
by M. FRIEDLANDER, Ph.D.

Vol. I. has already been published under the auspices of the Hebrew Literature Society; but it has now been determined that the complete work, in three volumes, shall be issued in the English and Foreign Philosophical Library.

"It is with sincere satisfaction that we welcome an English translation of the well-known tractate of Maimonides, *Moreh Nebhukhim*, or, 'Guide of the Perplexed.' . . . Dr. Friedländer has performed his work in a manner to secure the hearty acknowledgment of students.'—*Saturday Review*.

"From every point of view a successful production."—*Academy*.

"Dr. Friedländer has conferred a distinct boon on the Jews of England and America."—*Jewish Chronicle*.

Post 8vo, pp. xii. and 395, cloth, with Portrait, 14s.

LIFE OF GIORDANO BRUNO, THE NOLAN.

By I. FRITH.

Revised by Professor MORIZ CARRIERE.

"The interest of the book lies in the conception of Bruno's character and in the elucidation of his philosophy. . . . His writings dropped from him wherever he went, and were published in many places. Their number is very large, and the bibliographical appendix is not the least valuable part of this volume. . . . We are tempted to multiply quotations from the pages before us, for Bruno's utterances have a rare charm through their directness, their vividness, their poetic force. Bruno stands in relation to later philosophy, to Kant or Hegel, as Giotto stands to Raphael. We feel the merit of the more complete and perfect work; but we are moved and attracted by the greater individuality which accompanies the struggle after expression in an earlier and simpler age. Students of philosophy will know at once how much labour has been bestowed upon this modest attempt to set forth Bruno's significance as a philosopher. We have contented ourselves with showing how much the general reader may gain from a study of its pages, which are never overburdened by technicalities and are never dull."—*Athenæum*.

Post 8vo, pp. xxvi. and 414, cloth, 14s.

MORAL ORDER AND PROGRESS:

AN ANALYSIS OF ETHICAL CONCEPTIONS.

By S. ALEXANDER,

Fellow of Lincoln College, Oxford.

This work is an account of the factors involved in the two central phenomena of Order or Equilibrium, and Progress, which are shown to be essential to morality. Its method is to group ethical facts under the main working conceptions of morality. It treats Ethics independently of Biology, but the result is to confirm the theory of Evolution by showing that the characteristic differences of moral action are such as should be expected if that theory were true. In particular, Book III. aims at proving that moral ideals follow, in their origin and development, the same law as natural species.

Post 8vo, pp. xx. and 314, cloth, 10s. 6d.

THE SCIENCE OF KNOWLEDGE.

By J. G. FICHTE.

Translated from the German by A. E. KROEGER.

With a New Introduction by Professor W. T. HARRIS.

Post 8vo, pp. x. and 504, cloth, 12s. 6d.

THE SCIENCE OF RIGHTS.

By J. G. FICHTE.

Translated from the German by A. E. KROEGER.

With a New Introduction by Professor W. T. HARRIS.

Fichte belongs to those great men whose lives are an everlasting possession to mankind, and whose words the world does not willingly let die. His character stands written in his life, a massive but severely simple whole. It has no parts, the depth and earnestness on which it rests speak forth alike in his thoughts, words and actions. No man of his time—few, perhaps, of any time—exercised a more powerful, spirit-stirring influence over the minds of his fellow-countrymen. The impulse which he communicated to the national thought extended far beyond the sphere of his personal influences; it has awakened, it will still awaken, high emotion and manly resolution in thousands who never heard his voice. The ceaseless effort of his life was to rouse men to a sense of the divinity of their own nature, to fix their thoughts upon a spiritual life as the only true and real life; to teach them to look upon all else as mere show and unreality; and thus to lead them to constant effort after the highest ideal of purity, virtue, independence and self-denial.

In Two Volumes, post 8vo, pp. iv.—478 and x.—518, cloth, 21s.

JOHANN GOTTLIEB FICHTE'S POPULAR WORKS.

THE NATURE OF THE SCHOLAR; THE VOCATION OF THE SCHOLAR;
THE VOCATION OF MAN; THE DOCTRINE OF RELIGION;
CHARACTERISTICS OF THE PRESENT AGE;
OUTLINES OF THE DOCTRINE OF KNOWLEDGE.

With a Memoir by WILLIAM SMITH, LL.D.

EXTRA SERIES.

Two Volumes, post 8vo, pp. xxii.—328 and xvi.—358, with Portrait, cloth, 21s.

LESSING: His Life and Writings.

By JAMES SIME, M.A.

Second Edition.

"It is to Lessing that an Englishman would turn with readiest affection. We cannot but wonder that more of this man is not known amongst us."—THOMAS CARLYLE.

"But to Mr. James Sime has been reserved the honour of presenting to the English public a full-length portrait of Lessing, in which no portion of the canvas is uncovered, and in which there is hardly a touch but tells. We can say that a clearer or more compact piece of biographic criticism has not been produced in England for many a day."—*Westminster Review.*

"An account of Lessing's life and work on the scale which he deserves is now for the first time offered to English readers. Mr. Sime has performed his task with industry, knowledge, and sympathy; qualities which must concur to make a successful biographer."—*Pall Mall Gazette.*

"This is an admirable book. It lacks no quality that a biography ought to have. Its method is excellent, its theme is profoundly interesting: its tone is the happiest mixture of sympathy and discrimination; its style is clear, masculine, free from effort or affectation, yet eloquent by its very sincerity."—*Standard.*

"He has given a life of Lessing clear, interesting, and full, while he has given a study of his writings which bears distinct marks of an intimate acquaintance with his subject, and of a solid and appreciative judgment."—*Scotsman.*

In Three Volumes, post 8vo. Vol. I. pp. xvi.—248, cloth, 7s. 6d.; Vol. II. pp. viii.—400, cloth, 10s. 6d.; Vol. III. pp. xii.—292, cloth, 9s.

AN ACCOUNT OF THE POLYNESIAN RACE:

ITS ORIGIN AND MIGRATIONS,

AND THE ANCIENT HISTORY OF THE HAWAIIAN PEOPLE TO THE TIMES OF KAMEHAMEHA I.

By ABRAHAM FORNANDER, Circuit Judge of the Island of Maui, H.I.

"Mr. Fornander has evidently enjoyed excellent opportunities for promoting the study which has produced this work. Unlike most foreign residents in Polynesia, he has acquired a good knowledge of the language spoken by the people among whom he dwelt. This has enabled him, during his thirty-four years' residence in the Hawaiian Islands, to collect material which could be obtained only by a person possessing such an advantage. It is so seldom that a private settler in the Polynesian Islands takes an intelligent interest in local ethnology and archaeology, and makes use of the advantage he possesses, that we feel especially thankful to Mr. Fornander for his labours in this comparatively little-known field of research."—*Academy.*

"Offers almost portentous evidence of the acquaintance of the author with the Polynesian customs and languages, and of his industry and erudite care in the analysis and comparison of the tongues spoken in the Pacific Archipelagoes."—*Scotsman.*

In Two Volumes, post 8vo, pp. viii.—408; viii.—402, cloth, 21s.

ORIENTAL RELIGIONS,

AND THEIR RELATION TO UNIVERSAL RELIGION.

By SAMUEL JOHNSON.

I.—INDIA.

LONDON: KEGAN PAUL, TRENCH, TRÜBNER, & CO., Lᴛᴅ

PRINTED BY BALLANTYNE, HANSON AND CO.
EDINBURGH AND LONDON.

THE
ENGLISH AND FOREIGN
PHILOSOPHICAL LIBRARY.

PHILOSOPHY

OF

THE UNCONSCIOUS.

BY

EDUARD VON HARTMANN.

SPECULATIVE RESULTS ACCORDING TO THE INDUCTIVE METHOD OF PHYSICAL SCIENCE.

Authorised Translation

BY

WILLIAM CHATTERTON COUPLAND, M.A., B.Sc.

IN THREE VOLUMES.

VOL. II.

LONDON:
KEGAN PAUL, TRENCH, TRÜBNER, & CO., Ltᴰ
1890.

The rights of translation and of reproduction are reserved.

CONTENTS OF VOL. II.

(B) THE UNCONSCIOUS IN THE HUMAN MIND
(*continued.*)

		PAGE
X.	THE UNCONSCIOUS IN HISTORY	1
XI.	THE VALUE OF THE UNCONSCIOUS AND OF CONSCIOUSNESS FOR HUMAN LIFE	28

(C) METAPHYSICS OF THE UNCONSCIOUS.

I.	THE DIFFERENTIÆ OF CONSCIOUS AND UNCONSCIOUS MENTAL ACTIVITY AND THE UNITY OF WILL AND IDEA IN THE UNCONSCIOUS	47
II.	BRAIN AND GANGLIA AS CONDITIONS OF ANIMAL CONSCIOUSNESS	62
III.	THE ORIGIN OF CONSCIOUSNESS	78
	(1.) THE BECOMING-CONSCIOUS OF THE IDEA	78
	(2.) THE BECOMING-CONSCIOUS OF PAIN AND PLEASURE	93
	(3.) THE UNCONSCIOUSNESS OF THE WILL	96
	(4.) CONSCIOUSNESS HAS NO DEGREES	104
	(5.) THE UNITY OF CONSCIOUSNESS	113

	PAGE
IV. THE UNCONSCIOUS AND CONSCIOUSNESS IN THE VEGETABLE KINGDOM	119
(1.) THE UNCONSCIOUS PSYCHICAL ACTIVITY OF PLANTS	120
(2.) CONSCIOUSNESS IN THE PLANT	138
V. MATTER AS WILL AND IDEA	154
VI. THE CONCEPTION OF INDIVIDUALITY	186
VII. THE ALL-ONENESS OF THE UNCONSCIOUS	222
VIII. THE UNCONSCIOUS AND THE GOD OF THEISM	245
IX. THE ESSENTIAL NOTION OF GENERATION FROM THE STANDPOINT OF THE UNIVERSALITY AND UNITY OF THE UNCONSCIOUS	276
X. THE ASCENDING EVOLUTION OF ORGANIC LIFE ON THE EARTH	298
XI. INDIVIDUATION	332
(1.) POSSIBILITY AND MANNER OF EFFECTING INDIVIDUATION	332
(2.) INDIVIDUAL CHARACTER	344
XII. THE SUPREME WISDOM OF THE UNCONSCIOUS AND THE PERFECTION OF THE WORLD	356

PHILOSOPHY OF THE UNCONSCIOUS.

X.

THE UNCONSCIOUS IN HISTORY.

NATURE and History, or the origin of organisms and the development of the human race, are two parallel problems. In both cases the question runs: particular contingency or universal necessity, dead causality or living conformity to an end, mere sport of atoms and individuals or a single plan and general superintendence? He who has decided the question with respect to Nature in favour of design will have no difficulty in doing the same in regard to history. The only thing likely to mislead in the latter case is the semblance of personal freedom. But I think I may confidently appeal to the general consensus of modern philosophers in respect to this matter of the freedom of the will, to the effect namely that an empirical freedom in any single act of volition in the sense of *unconditionality* is altogether out of the question, since, like every other natural phenomenon, it falls under the law of causality, and necessarily follows from the state of the man's mind at any given moment, and the motives which are acting upon him. Further, that if a claim be set up for a freedom of the will *outside* natural causality, this must *at best* be *sought* (I do not say, found) in the supersensible sphere (*mundus noumenon*), in Kant's intelligible character, but can in no case apply to the specific volitional act, since any such act is always in time, consequently belongs to the sphere of the phenomenal world, and is accordingly subject to the law of causality, *i.e.*, necessity. This, and the reasons why we are liable to the illusion of a belief in the will's freedom, may be studied in Schopenhauer's essay "On the Freedom of the Will."

But suppose we even admitted the empirical freedom of the will, if we recognise a purposive evolution in history at all, this could only be the result of the freedom of individuals if the consciousness of the step next to be taken, in its full significance and in all its consequences, were possessed by every one freely co-operating in the historic movement, before he actively intervened.

Undoubtedly since the close of the last century we have been making approaches to that ideal state where the human race *consciously* accomplishes its destiny, but, save for a few superior minds, this is still a remote condition of things, and nobody will maintain that by far the larger part of the way already traversed has been conquered in this wise. For the aims of the individual are always selfish, each one seeks only to further his own well-being, and if this conduces to the welfare of the whole, the merit is certainly not his; the exceptions to this rule are so few that they are of no account in respect of the whole. But the wonderful part of the matter is, that even the mind, which wills the bad, works the good, that the results become, by combination of many different selfish purposes, quite other than what each individual had imagined, and that in the last resort they always conduce to the welfare of the whole, although often the advantage is somewhat remote, and centuries of retrogression seem to contradict it; this contradiction, however, is only apparent, for they serve the purpose of breaking the strength of an old system, that room may be made for a new and better one, or of allowing a vegetation to grow corrupt, in order that it may manure the ground for something fresh and fairer. Even thousands of years of stagnation on one spot of earth should not mislead us, if only this phase of culture has fulfilled its appointed office, and if only at the same time the process of evolution goes forward at another place.

Just as little should we expect, as is often and unreasonably the case, that at one and the same place all the various branches or tendencies should enjoy an unchecked progress, and complain of stagnation and retrogression, if any particular branch, for which perhaps one has a personal preference, falls into decay. The evolution proceeds on the large scale, although only one or a few factors are in active progress and other fields lie fallow; for at the proper time these others will again be taken in hand, and in such a way that the elevation already attained is embraced in the new phase of the evolution (think of Raphael and Phidias, Göthe and Euripides). What is apt to blind the observer to the general development of humanity is really a too narrow limitation of the view, which keeps the eye fixed on certain painful and apparently incurable political or social diseases, or on the momentary ruin of one's favourite intellectual hopes, instead of opening it wide to embrace vast historical scenes, which would make plain not only the great civilising events of the present time, but also reveal the multiplicity of the ways of history, and the possibility and probability of an improvement of these painful conditions by a path not dreamt of, and perhaps even contemned. But in yet another sense a too narrow restriction of the historic horizon may blind to the great truth of evolution, namely, if of the long period of humanity's unfolding all too small a portion, say the last thousand years (called in the narrower sense, "historic") be selected, and the brilliant age of Pericles or of Augustus be compared with the present era. The *naïveté* accuracy and delicacy of feeling of the æsthetic culture of those times may deceive us for a moment with respect to the superiority of our own, but the delusion disappears as soon as we reflect that the age of Pericles possessed these excellences only instinctively and unconsciously, as is shown by the fact that even so deep and circumspect a thinker as Plato, with such models before him, could construct so poor a theory of æsthetics and an ideal constitution so remote from actual needs. Not the shallow common sense of the Romans, but the Germans of the last century, converted into the conscious and now inalienable possession of humanity what the Greeks only wrought out by instinct; and which we can no longer execute, because in all departments of art we have advanced in feeling from the plastic to the pictorial. The naive delicacy of taste, for which antiquity was distinguished in all directions, is naturally also far more easily destroyed by rude external influences or inner decay than the more substantial mental culture of the present day, with its rich material knowledge and self-conscious capacity, which is protected from sinking into oblivion by a thousand expedients. Other differences consist in this, that in antiquity the cultivated portion of the world was very *small* compared with that of the present day, when culture has spread more or less among all vigorous races and peoples, and new parts of the world have been taken possession of by the civilised peoples of Europe. At the same time, however, within the civilised races also education is ever extending to larger circles and strata of the population, so that for a twofold reason the cultured and mentally advanced society of the present day forms a very much larger quota of the total population of the earth than heretofore, and is growing with the greatest rapidity precisely at the present moment. But now as we have to do not with the development *of men* but *of humanity*, this increase in breadth is not less important than the growth in depth—apart from the circumstance that the imperishability of what has once been won is guaranteed by a probability advancing in geometrical progression.

It is true that the free possession of the fruits of civilisation is still hampered and embittered by the struggle with the threatening shades of the Middle Ages reaching into our own time; but we must not allow ourselves to be blinded by the struggle against these no longer justifiable existences to the historical value of the same in the past, and their abiding significance for the evolution of humanity. The utterly barbarous tribes of the Germanic migrations required during their infancy a strict schooling, in which the physiological processes of transmutation and fusion simultaneously went on, as whose result we have the nationalities of Europe of the present day. If antiquity especially developed the beautiful in *sense* and *fancy*, if the culture of the *understanding* to-day gives us the right to declare the forms of mediæval life to be relatively barbarous, it was the task of Germanism to complete the deepening of the *heart*, though naturally in a one-sided fashion, and this it could accomplish effectively by the aid of no other civilising impulse than the transcendent ideals of Christianity. It would be unjust to refuse to recognise that the working-out and development of the profoundest forces of the German mind, which will ever remain a possession to humanity after separation from that native soil, is essentially, if not exclusively, due to the imaginative inner life of the Middle Ages. Whoever has got the better of the elements hostile to civilisation inherent in the popular Christianity is for ever secured from relapsing into the elements of past periods of the development of humanity, which are hostile to civilisation, whereas the most highly cultured Greek or Roman had still *before* him the Christian phase of evolution.

Such an injustice to the Middle Ages Buckle and his school are guilty of when they set up the conscious *understanding*, which undoubtedly is *higher* than sense, fancy, and heart, and ought to govern these, as *sole* measure of advance in culture, which it by no means is, since the *harmonious* elaboration of all the mental forces appertains thereto; and since the understanding alone, without the foundation of powerfully developed sensibility, fancy, and heart, would only produce wasted shadows, but not men capable of any earnest task. The source of this error is this,—that the English, even down to the present day, are essentially at that rationalistic standpoint which we occupied in the last century; and that these historians of civilisation, instead of trying to discover the unconsciously impelling ideas of history, fancy they can explain them as a product of conscious reflection. Unconscious reason, namely, unfolds itself, as we have just seen, just as much in sensibility, fancy, and heart, as in the reflection of the conscious understanding; and it again is evidence of an all too-narrow glance, when the regulative element of *modern* life is looked upon as that which is most important for *all* time, and as a standard of culture valid for all time. In opposition to such a straitening of the history of civilisation into a "History of Rationalism" Hegel's attempts at a Philosophy of History retain their full value, since in them the discussion always and alone turns upon the (unconscious) ideas underlying the epoch.

The opposite view of Schopenhauer with repect to History rests on his conception of time as purely subjective phenomenal form, according to which all *that happens* is an exclusively subjective appearance, wherefore *history* is a subjective tissue of representations devoid of truth. He blinds himself to the manifest contradiction of this view, to the mighty organism of the historic evolution of humanity, on the one hand, by reflecting only on the indifferent and accidental framework of facts (succession of kings, battles, &c.), instead of on the content of historical culture, which is entirely neglected by him; and, on the other hand, by confounding the demand for a heightening of individual comfort with the demand for a civilised progression of humanity as a whole. *Happiness* certainly does not keep pace with human progress, but this does not militate against the truth, that this progress, both in the inner mental world and in the forms of social life, really exists, and leads to ever higher development.

If anything is calculated to prove the great progress in spiritual matters from the Greeks to the present day, it is the progress of philosophy and especially that of the German and English philosophy of the last two hundred years. Philosophy as the final summariser of the ideas which support a period of civilisation, and as the flower of the historic self-consciousness of the Unconscious Idea, may be taken as the most faithful representative of the spiritual horizon of a section of time in the narrowest and most compact frame; the progress of the development of ideas, which we perceive in the history of philosophy, shows us as through a diminishing glass the quintessence of the spiritual possessions of the corresponding ages in their various phases of development. That in the different philosophies there is really a *development* was first shown by Hegel, who constructed from the earlier detached intellectual torsos an organically connected and harmonious monumental group. Undoubtedly the individual collaborateurs had either no idea at all of this concatenation, or possessed indeed only a highly defective knowledge of a limited number of their predecessors, and just as their profoundest principles instinctively welled up from the depths of the Unconscious, so instinctively did they themselves divine the truth in regard to the place, which they had to occupy in the evolution, so that the modern historiography of philosophy must be characterised as the *bringing to consciousness* of the *unconscious* relations obtaining between different philosophies, in consequence of which they unconsciously form a great development series. But now, when we consider that at the same time each of these philosophies is only the most conscious expression of the period of civilisation which has just attained its acme, thus only the last budding branch, which has sprung from the common hidden root, whence all the achievements of this portion of time in the most diverse directions have harmoniously sprung,—then it is evident, that the epochs of civilisation taken as a whole must be as much related as phases of an ascending development series, as those common roots of the characteristic performances of each one of them (*i.e.* their unconsciously impelling ideas), or as their most conscious forms of expression (the standard philosophies). What should be regarded as the unconscious impelling Idea in any particular period, can only be determined by the Unconscious itself in reference to the phase of development which is ideally indispensable at that precise time. For the human individuals themselves, who perform the tasks answering to this phase, before they even in a small measure attain to the consciousness of the unconscious Idea, by which they are impelled, cannot possibly be the cause of this phase of the Idea, since humanity only attains a consciousness of the introduction of the same into the collective organism, and of the necessity of just these phases of development in this period of time long after the close of the period in question.

Now the means whereby a particular phase of the IDEA is actualised in a certain period are of two kinds, namely, on the one side the implanting an instinctive impulse in the masses, and on the other hand, the production of men of genius as finger-posts and pioneers. This mysterious impulse which works in the masses from time to time in the form of tribal migrations, emigrations of multitudes, crusades, religious, political and social national revolutions, and guides the same with truly demonic power to a goal of which they are unconscious, is still ever "right conscious of its *way*," if it also for the most part believes, that this way leads to quite another *goal* than is actually the fact. For in the cases, where the masses do not altogether rush headlong forward, blind with rage, and without conscious aim, but have an end in view, this conscious aim is commonly a worthless or perverse one, whereas the true purpose of history in these revolutions is only subse-

quently unveiled.—In like manner, even without exactly
inflaming the masses, history attains, by the initiative of
eminent individuals, results which were quite beside the
conscious purposes of such men. (Think in particular of the
fertile marriage of different national civilisations, how with
the national exclusiveness of earlier times they could have
been produced only by means of vast expeditions for the
sake of conquest, as, *e.g.*, those of Alexander, of Cæsar, the
Roman expeditions of the German Emperors, nay, even
the European revolutions evoked by Napoleon. Only
an unhistoric sense can make light of the fields strewed
with the corpses of these heroes duped by the Unconscious, whence have sprung harvests so fruitful and rich
in blessing.) Other ends are attained by the Unconscious
in a more peaceful way, when it calls forth the right genius
at the right time, who is enabled just to solve that problem,
whose solution his age urgently needs.[1] No more calamitous
gift for the individual than genius, for the men of genius
are, even with apparent outward good fortune, yet always
those men who most deeply and irremediably feel the
wretchedness of existence. But men of genius are not here
for their own sake, but for humanity; and for humanity
it is quite indifferent, whether in fulfilling their task they
feel miserable, or even perish in distress. The right man
has never been wanting at the right time; and the cry
sometimes heard, that men are lacking for certain urgent
tasks, only proves that the problems have been wrongly
proposed by human consciousness, that they do not at all (or
at least not now) lie in the plan of history, and that consequently even the most gifted men would vainly expend
their mental energies on *these* problems (at least at this
time). (Such an *absolutely* insoluble problem, *e.g.*, is the

---

[1] As the most natural and easiest means to this end appears the bringing together of two persons suited to produce the required individuality by a love kindled in them with the unconscious purpose of begetting this prominent human being (cf. Dr. Carl Freiherr du Prel : " The Metaphysic of Sexual Love in its relation to History,' in the " Aust. Journal for Sc. and Art.," 1872, No. 34).

regeneration and strengthening of States doomed to decay and dissolution. A *temporarily* insoluble problem, on the other hand, is the revival of original production in some special field of mental work, which, at the moment in the hands of Epigoni, must lie fallow for a season, before a new phase of development commences under the influence of a new and fertile idea.) This pre-established harmony, so to say, between historic problems and individuals with a special faculty for solving them, reaches so far, that even technical inventions (in a practically available form) are effected always, but then also always, only when the pre-conditions for their fruitful utilisation, as well as the need of such aids to culture, are given.

Now the collective *inner spiritual* evolution of humanity forms the proper content of the history of humanity; whereas State, Church, and Society, notwithstanding their organic character and their organic development, still, in respect of the inner spiritual evolution, have only the value of a scaffolding which, produced by the unconscious mental activity of individuals, now on its side again supports and furthers the elaboration of the conscious mind, by not only protecting and securing it, but also as an accessory mechanism saving one great part of the spiritual labour, and lightening another.

Like every bodily part the cerebrum also is strengthened by use and exercise, and made more capable of new allied performances; but as in every bodily part, so in the cerebrum the vigour and material perfection acquired by the parents is transmissible to the child. This transmission is not directly demonstrable in each single case; but, on the average, taking one generation with another, it is a fact, and it is likewise a fact that there is a latent transmission, which only reveals its fruits in the second or third generation (*e.g.*, when somebody inherits from his maternal grandfather a luxuriant red beard and fine bass voice). As each generation further elaborates its conscious intellect, thus also further perfects its material organ, in the course of generations these additions, imperceptibly small in a single generation, amount to clearly visible quantities. It is no mere figure of speech, that children are now born more clever, and that, less childish than formerly, they even in childhood show a tendency to become prematurely knowing. As the offspring of trained animals are more adapted for similar training than offspring captured when wild, so also the children of a human generation are the more clever in making acquisitions in the various departments of practice and theory, the greater the advance already made. I doubt, *e.g.*, whether a Greek boy could ever have become an excellent productive musician in the modern sense, because his brain was without those inherited predispositions for the wide field of musical *harmony*, which modern humanity of western Europe has only gained through an historic development of more than fifteen generations. An Archimedes or Euclid, in spite of their relative mathematical genius, would have evinced no little awkwardness as pupils of an instruction in the higher mathematics.

Thus all spiritual progress causes an enhancement of the executive capacity of the material organ of the intellect, and this becomes through inheritance (on the average) the enduring possession of humanity—a position scaled facilitating further advance. That is, the progress in the spiritual possession of humanity goes hand in hand with the anthropological development of the race, and stands in reciprocal relation with it; all progress on the one side stands the other side in good stead. There must, accordingly, be also an anthropological ennoblement of the race, which springs from other causes than that mental progress, which furthers the intellectual evolution. Of the latter kind, is, *e.g.*, the improvement of the race by sexual selection (B. Chap. ii.)—which ceaselessly exerts its unnoticed but powerful effects—or the competition of races and nations in the struggle for existence, which is waged among mankind under natural laws just as pitilessly as among animals and plants. No power on earth is able to arrest the eradication of the inferior races of mankind, which, as relics of earlier stages of development once also passed through by ourselves, have gone on vegetating down to the present day. As little as a favour is done the dog whose tail is to be cut off, when one cuts it off gradually, inch by inch, so little is there humanity in artificially prolonging the death-struggle of savages who are on the verge of extinction. The true philanthropist, if he has comprehended the natural law of anthropological evolution, cannot avoid desiring an acceleration of the last convulsions, and labouring for that end. One of the best means is the support of missions, which (according to a truly divine irony of the Unconscious) has done more to further this purpose of Nature than all the direct attempts of the white race at the annihilation of savages. The quicker this eradication of the peoples living in a state of nature incapable of competition with the white race is proceeded with, and the quicker the whole earth is exclusively occupied by races hitherto the highest, the more quickly will the struggle of different *stocks within* the highest race burst forth into immense proportions, the sooner will the spectacle of the absorption of the lower *race* by the higher be repeated among *stocks* and peoples. But the difference is, that these peoples are far more equal, thus far more capable of competition, than the lower races (except the Mongolian) have hitherto shown themselves in presence of the Caucasian race. Hence it follows that the struggle for existence between nations, because waged with more equal force, must be much more fearful, bitter, persistent, and attended with greater sacrifices, than between races, as we shall see later on (C. chap. x.), that the struggle for existence is in general the more bitter and the *more merciless*, but at the same time also the *more advantageous* for the progressive evolution of the race, the *nearer* are the species or varieties that compete with one another.

It is relatively indifferent whether this struggle for existence between peoples and races assumes the form of physical struggle with weapons, or whether it takes place in other apparently more peaceful forms of competition. It would be a great error to suppose that war is the cruelest or even only the most effective form of annihilating a competitor; it is only the most obvious, because rudest —but on that very account also the *ultima ratio* for a people which sees itself overreached by its competitor in the so-called peaceful clashing of interests. The sacrifices of even the greatest war are insignificant compared with the annihilation of millions and millions of human beings who perish when, *e.g.*, a people is drained by another of higher industrial development by means of commerce, and deprived of a part of its previous source of earning a livelihood (*comp.* Carey's "Principles of Political Economy," on the effects of the English blood-sucking system in India, Portugal and elsewhere). While by means of this struggle for existence the earth becomes more and more the exclusive possession of the most highly-developed peoples, not only does the entire population of the earth become more civilised, but also by means of the differentiations conditioned by forms of soil and climate within the people that has attained the hegemony new germs of development are always being scattered, which indeed, again, can only be unfolded by means of the cruel struggle for existence.

Awful as is the prospect of this perpetual struggle from the endæmonist point of view, equally magnificent does it appear from the teleological in respect to the goal of an extreme intellectual development. One must only accustom oneself to the thought that the Unconscious can be led astray neither more nor less by the lamentation of milliards of human individuals than by that of as many animal individuals, if only these torments further *development*, and thereby its own main design.

I said above, that the fact of an evolution of humanity

may certainly be doubted if one contemplate too limited sections of history; we may now say, that one can *only* in that case doubt evolution, but not if the total duration of humanity, from its first appearance on earth till the future perspective just hinted at, be surveyed with a single glance. The time has gone by when a Creuzer and a Schelling supposed a primitive people endowed with all wisdom, from whose decay the race of mankind had developed. To-day, comparative philology and comparative mythology, ethnology, anthropology, and archaeology, unite in their teaching that the state of culture of our forefathers was the ruder and more primitive the more remote the era to which we descend. When three to four thousand years ago the Aryans began in small detachments that national migration, whose present result is the rule of the Indo-Germanic stocks from the Indian Ocean to the Pacific, they already possessed a considerable civilisation, which can only have been the result of the antecedent ten thousands of years. Already provided with a language furnished with inflexions, with fruitful and profound philosophical nature-myths, with technical instruments for agriculture, the shaping of dwellings and clothes, they make their first appearance in history. Much as we have gained in culture since then, yet it holds good here more than anywhere that all commencement is difficult, and doubtless it was a far greater and therefore also more protracted task to work up to such an elevation from the primitive condition of speechless human animals, than, once in possession of such means of culture, especially such an incomparable language, to subjugate Nature ever more and more, and to outstrip the backward races in ever-increasing progression.

If language, mythology, and technology form the spiritual content of that pre-historic period of civilisation, the *family* expanded to the *tribe* is the form in which this content is embraced. Whilst the sexual instinct brought together man and woman to found a family, it was on the one hand the instinctive social instinct (Grotius) which hindered the atomistic sundering of blood-relations of the first and second degree; and, on the other hand, the struggle for existence, the war of all against all (Hobbes), the hostility of foreign neighbours to one another, which necessarily brought about an increase of the power of attack and defence by the closest solidarity of the family and the clan. Thus the head of the family grew into the elder of the clan or patriarch, and—with increasing expansion of the clan into the tribe—into the chief of the tribe, or patriarchial king. In this condition do we find the Aryans, when they conquered Hindostan; the Greeks, at the time of the Trojan war; the Germans, in their tribal migrations. It is true that animals also found families, also wage war with one another; but they immediately relapse into the inorganic mass of the *herd*, as soon as more than the family in the narrow sense remain together, whereas the clan is organically parted into families, and therefore really exhibits the higher unity of the latter. Wherefore the union of the three instincts (sexual impulse, social impulse, and instinct of enmity of all to all) is, in fact, in man something new and higher than in the animal, and makes him the ζῶον πολιτικὸν of Aristotle.

The higher unconscious content of those instincts in the case of man is shown in this, that its proximate products, the family, the clan, and the tribe, must be regarded as the germinal vesicle and embryo of all later political, ecclesiastical, and social forms. The head of the family is first *king* (leader in battle, exclusive representative of the family to the outer world, and judge, with power of life and death); secondly, *priest* (in the then exclusive family worship); and thirdly, *teacher and taskmaster* of his own people. These three departments are here still united in inseparable unity; or, more correctly, they have not yet at all worked themselves out of their state of indifference. This emergence does not take place suddenly but gradually; each of the three spheres has the tendency to develop into a *formal organism*, which dominates according to possibilities the other life-spheres. That one of the three spheres now, on whose elaboration in an historical period most popular energy is expended, in fact rules during this period. But since the departments can only be worked at one after another, it lies in the nature of the case that the sides which first emerge must implicitly contain in themselves those which are not yet unfolded, so far as the latter do not still remain in the primitive bosom of the family.

The development of the *State* is everywhere the first and most urgent requirement; but the ecclesiastical and social functions, so far as they have emerged from the family circle, must be supplied at the same time (thus, *e.g.*, in the Græco-Roman constitution, where the kingly high-priests, and also in the republican phase the ecclesiastical institutions were integral parts of the State). In Hindostan, a few centuries after the conquest by the Aryans, there took place that powerful revolution, whereby the military nobility was almost exterminated, and the rule of the priesthood was permanently established down to the present day. In the West this revolution (which in India stifled all germs of progress) happily took place after a complete cycle of the political development of antiquity; a circumstance which, after the expiration of the mediæval-ecclesiastical phase of development, made possible the re-birth of German life, even in political and mental respects, by means of the renascence of antiquity.

As the *Church* only appeared as the second element, it could not absorb the already existing State in the same way as in antiquity the State the yet-undeveloped Church; but it could push it back into the second rank, and itself occupy the first place. Whilst in the last century secular life again gained the upper hand over the spiritual, it was only in appearance the State as such that gained the victory over the Church. In truth it is the *social* interests which have repressed the ecclesiastical, and only because society as such is still occupied in fashioning an organ of its own has it been provisionally the State that has outstripped the Church in the perception and advocacy of certain social and especially economic interests, and so in general has obtained precedence of her; whilst, on the other hand, the hitherto-existing Church likewise derives its best power of persistence from certain social functions which she still vicariously champions. This phase is, therefore, particularly interesting, because it offers something really new under the sun.

The commencement of the evolution of *society* as such into an independent organism *beside* Church and State is something so new, that there are only a few who notice it at all. Most people think, because the organism of the State must at present vicariously perform social functions (*e.g.*, instruction of youth, care of the poor, guaranteeing of interest for industrial undertakings), that these things are really State-functions, and then perhaps commit the error, like Lassalle, of expecting from it the establishment of associations for purposes of production, instead of rather co-operating in the organisation of society, and transferring to the latter social functions hitherto performed by the State. But where exceptionally the ideal separation of State and Society, and the necessity of gradually procuring a real separation is recognised, there perhaps we hear talk of a necessary and irreconcilable strife between them, instead of the harmony of political and social interests (Gneist). Negatively expressed, Society embraces the wide sphere of life-relations and forms of intercourse, that are not given in the conceptions State and Church; positively expressed, it is the *organisation of labour* in the widest sense. The organisation of labour especially signifies the ordering and regulating of the division of labour between the sexes and individuals; but, in addition also, the preparation of youth for their life-work, and the care of those who have become incapable of work. The notion of the division of labour of course includes the highest as the lowest, unqualified manual labour as well as the mental labour of the investigator and artist, and not less the labour of education and of social self-government. It is evident that "Society," in this sense, in fact embraces all forms of civilised life except State and Church; a meaning in which it has hitherto been understood only by Lorenz Stein. The tendency of this working-out of a social organism (Socialism) is to *limit* the freedom of competition, which has been the means of emancipating labour from its former shackles, in favour of a systematic division of labour, and to prevent the gain of one (as in free competition) being only too often purchased at the disproportionate loss of another. But, as said, this phase is still so much in its very commencement, that the How of such organisations as will infallibly arise in the future is thus far quite indeterminable.

We will now bestow one more hasty glance on the development of the forms of the State, the Church, and (if only as yet implicit) Society.

I shall first try to describe with a few strokes the outline of the development of the *Idea of the State*, as it appears to me. History exhibits three main contrasts in the life of the State, large state and small state, republic and monarchy, indirect and direct government. The problem is, to unite large state and republic as the preferable forms, the means to that end indirect government. The patriarchal chieftainships and royalties show us the union of small state and monarchy, the Asiatic despotisms that of the large state and monarchy. Here only one man has civil liberty, all others are bond-slaves or thralls of the ruler. The Greek town and district republics are the first specimens of the Republic. Favoured by the natural divisions of their small country, the Greeks could, even in their petty states, exhibit the republican form of government as an aristocracy of free citizens, ruling over twice as many slaves. The Roman Empire combines the Greek town-republic with the Asiatic despotism of the Great State; in place of the despot appears the Roman citizenship, and all subjugated lands contain only slaves. When therefore the republican power of the Roman citizens waned, it likewise relapsed into the Monarchy of the Great State.—Germany brings a new principle into the idea of the State by its system of feudalism, that of indirect government or the pyramidal graduated system of rule, whereas antiquity only knew direct government. The ancients had only free-men and slaves, but now appears a gradation of freedom from the king down to the thrall, in that each man is lord of his own vassals. I might therefore call the State of the Middle Ages the monarchical pyramid.—Lastly, the modern world utters the decisive word with its postulate of universal human freedom; it aims at large states having their natural limits in nationalities, it revives the Greek town-republic in the self-government of the towns and communes, and finds in the principle of representation by chosen deputies a means of rearing a republican pyramid, of which up to this time the best, but by no means perfect, example exists in North America, but which must and will at some time or other, with the universal spread of civilisation, embrace all the countries of the earth, since the sovereignty of the *national* states is just as much a moment to be sublated as that of the *territorial* states.—The constitutional hybrid of monarchy and republic is nothing but a prodigious palpable lie, and has an historical authorisation only as a transitional form and the political school of nations. In the Federal Republic, which certainly will come to pass when the individual states have become republics, the state of nature in which communities at first exist will pass into the state of right, and self-protection by war into legal protection by the federal republic, as the natural condition and self-protection of the individual passes into the legal condition and legal protection on the formation of the State. (Here is opened the possibility of a termination of the struggle for existence alluded to on page 25, namely when tolerably uniform climates are occupied by *the same* people organised in the universal State, and competition between the peoples inhabiting different climates is excluded by the limits of their capacity of climatic accommodation, which assigns them different geographical areas of diffusion.)

The *second* of the forms to be noticed, the *Church*, has a more limited and more one-sided function than State and Society; for whilst the latter simultaneously subserve many interests, and satisfy many needs, the Church subserves exclusively the need of the religious sentiment, and indeed not of *any* religious sentiment, but only of that, which either requires for its full satisfaction a *common* cultus, or feels itself far too weak to rely on the consciousness and feeling of the individual self, and now seeks, by means of the external institution of the visible Church, a palpable external support in lieu of the internal. As a natural consequence, with the growth of the solidity of the inner spiritual substance of mankind the visible Church must lose in importance. Nevertheless at the present standpoint of civilised nations the Church is still a factor of the highest importance, and will still long remain so, even when it takes the third place (after Society and State).

As already mentioned, the State is the first of the three forms to unfold itself, and the Church is bound up with it. Even there, where exceptionally (as in Judaism) the State is from the commencement an ecclesiastical State or theocracy, it does not advance beyond the national limitation of theocracy. The idea of a cosmopolitan Church or theocracy can always be only the result of a religious revolution. Thus in India, Buddhism; on the shores of the Mediterranean, Christianity, broke up the earlier national narrowness of ecclesiastical institutions, and thereby inaugurated an oriental and an occidental Middle Age. This cosmopolitism of the Mediæval Church is of the greatest significance, and most important in results both politically and socially, for it gives for the first time a solidarity of consciousness to the members of different peoples and States, thereby extends both extensively and intensively the peaceful intercourse of different peoples with one another, and prepares the cosmopolitan consciousness of modern times, which is based on the social principle of Humanity, and surmounts the barriers of *ecclesiastical* antitheses, just as the cosmopolitism of the Mediæval Church had burst the barriers of the constitutional antagonisms which it embraced. Thus the Church naturally leads us to the *third* form, *Society*.

Social development exhibits four leading phases, of which the first three are to be looked upon as stages preparatory to the fourth, in which for the first time Society is unfolded as an *independent*, co-ordinate form.

The first phase is the *free state of nature*, where every one only works for himself and his family, as, *e.g.*, among the Indian hunting-tribes. From this condition an ascent to greater comfort, and thereby to greater civilisation, is impossible, because in the atomistic freedom of individuals there is no motive to bring about the *division* of labour, through which alone that *economy* of labour is possible, which is indispensable for a production in excess of the momentary needs of life, *i.e.*, of an elevation of national well-being through the accumulation of capital.

The second phase is that of *personal rule*, where the lord is the proprietor of the persons or the working-powers of his slaves or thralls. Here the lord soon finds it to his interest to introduce a division of labour among his slaves, whose work now produces an excess beyond their and his requirements, which is applied to establish a stock-in-trade (capital). Thus national wealth grows through accumulation of capital, to the advantage, however, certainly only of the master, not of the serf. The Roman Empire and the Middle Ages afford an example of this stage.

The third phase, which is only rendered possible by the

prolonged agency of the second, is that of the *rule of capital*. In this period the fixed capital, hitherto alone of importance, is surpassed by free capital, and driven more and more to become mobile if it is not to lose disproportionately in value. This process goes on simultaneously and in reciprocation with the greatest mitigation and abolition of bond-service, whereby the power of labour becomes a free commodity, and falls under the general laws of price (which is determined by supply and demand). As capital can organise the division of labour on a far grander scale, a far larger quota of the total labour will also now become superfluous for present needs and available for the future, *i.e.*, for productive investment; thus also the increase of capital and the growth of national comfort must proceed far more rapidly than in the foregoing phase. But here too this increase of national wealth is essentially to the advantage of the possessors of capital alone, since that part of it which falls to the working classes is immediately followed by a *numerical* increase of the labouring classes, which in the redistribution always keeps the share falling to each individual at the level of the usual indispensable minimum for maintaining life. Experience at least confirms this for the industrial forces of labour accessible to the market of the world.—But free capital also is an Idea, which unfolds and attains maturity, only to perish after its task has been fulfilled, and to make place for other structures. Its historical task also is transitional, and only consists in preparing the ground for the next stage, just as the function of slavery consisted in preparing and making possible the rule of capital.

The fourth and last phase is that of *free association*. If, namely, the value of slavery and rule of capital was only to be measured by the degree in which they made possible, and introduced a division of labour, and thereby economy of labour, these always still highly imperfect coercive measures of history, which bring in their train accompanying unutterable misery, must become superfluous as soon as the character and understanding of the workman are developed to the degree of civilisation, in order by free conscious agreement to undertake an appropriate part of the work in the universal division of labour. As before the difficulty was, to educate the freed slave to voluntary labour, so now the difficulty is to educate the labourer, in order that when set free from the yoke of this rule of capital, he may adequately fill in the association the place *assigned him*. To conduct this education (by means of Schultze-Delitzsch Unions, better school-teaching, labourers' educational unions, &c.), is the most important social problem of the present day. Free association the future will of itself bring forth, if one cannot yet exactly say, with what means and ways, whether by some kind of peaceful development, or by catastrophes which will exceed in awfulness all that has hitherto happened in history.—In this last phase the actual payment of money (except coins) will be made just as superfluous by the general introduction of *banking*, as in the foregoing stage *barter* was superseded by the *use of money*.

If the rule of capital has already done much more for the division of labour than slavery, free association will far exceed the former in an incomparably higher degree (think of an indivisible organisation of production and sale on the whole earth analogous to the indivisible political organisation of the whole earth). In correspondence herewith the growth of material wealth will take place much more rapidly than at present, supposing that it be not neutralised or outstripped by the increase of the number of the population, which to be sure has its limits assigned it by the maximum of nutritive plants produced on the whole earth and of fishes yielded by the waters; or, if one takes into account the inorganic conditions of the means of subsistence, by the limited habitable space of the earth's surface.

The goal of this social evolution would be, that every one, with a period of work which allowed him sufficient leisure for his intellectual culture, should lead a comfortable existence, or, as one is wont to say with a more sonorous expression, an existence conformable to the dignity of man. Thus, as the final political state would secure to man the *external and formal*, the final social condition would afford him the *material* possibility of ultimately fulfilling his positive and proper task, for the fulfilment of which the *internal* conditions must necessarily be sought in the before-noticed mental or *intellectual* development.

If in this entire development we cannot miss a single plan, a clearly-prescribed aim, towards which all stages of development are tending; if, on the other hand, we must allow that the several actions which prepared or led up to these stages had by no means this conscious goal, but that the human being almost always aimed at something else, effected something else, we must also acknowledge that something else than the conscious intention of the individuals, or the accidental combination of the several actions, is occultly operative in history, that "far-reaching glance, which already discovers from afar, where this lawlessly roaming freedom is conducted in the bond of necessity, and the selfish aims of the individual unconsciously tend to the perfection of the whole" (Schiller, vol. vii. pp. 29, 30). Schelling expresses this in the System of Transcendental Idealism (Works, i. 3, p. 594): "In freedom there shall be necessity, means then as much as: Through freedom itself, and in that I think to act freely, there shall unconsciously, *i.e.*, without my assistance, come to pass what I did not intend. Otherwise expressed: to the conscious, that is, that freely determining activity which we have before deduced, there shall be opposed an unconscious one, whereby, in spite of the unlimited expression of freedom, something arises quite involuntarily, and perhaps even against the will of the actor, which he himself could have never realised by means of his own volition. This proposition, however paradoxical it may appear, is indeed nothing else but the transcendental expression of the generally accepted and presupposed relation of freedom to a concealed necessity, which is called now fate, now providence, without anything being clearly thought by the one or the other; that relation, in virtue of which human beings, through their free action itself, and indeed against their will, are compelled to be causes of something which they never willed, or conversely in virtue of which something must fail and go wrong, which they have willed with freedom and with the exertion of all their energies" (*Ibid.* p. 598). "But this necessity itself can only be conceived by means of an absolute synthesis of all actions, from which everything that happens, thus also all history, is developed, and in which, because it is absolute, everything is so weighed and calculated beforehand, that all that may happen, however contradictory and inharmonious it may appear, yet has and finds in it its point of union. This absolute synthesis itself, however, must be placed in the Absolute, which is the intuitive and eternally and universally objective in all free action." Whoever has well understood this passage, of which it may be said that it represents the view of all philosophers since Kant, and the substance of which has been reproduced in detail by Hegel in the introduction to his "Lectures on the Philosophy of History," for such an one I have nothing to add.—To any one who prefers to stop at the conceptions Fate or Providence, one can only object that he can therewith frame no clear idea how *my* act, whether it is the work of my freedom, or the product of my character and the efficient motives, how this *my* deed is to actualise another than *my* will, say of a God enthroned in heaven. There is only one way in which this demand is capable of fulfilment, if this God descends into my bosom, and *my* will is to me in an unconscious way at the same time God's will, *i.e.*, if I unconsciously will something quite different to what my consciousness exclusively thinks to will; if, further, consciousness *errs* in the choice of the means to its end, but the unconscious will appropriately chooses this same means for its purpose. Otherwise is this psychical process not at all thinkable, and as much as this is said in the first half of the passage from Schelling.—But now, if we cannot do without an unconscious will in addition to the conscious will; if, on the other hand, we add the long known clairvoyance of unconscious representation, why bring a transcendent God in addition into the affair, when the individual is sufficient of himself with the faculties familiar to us? What then is this fate or providence but the rule of the Unconscious, the historic instinct in the actions of mankind, as long as just their conscious understanding is not yet mature enough to make the aims of history their own? What is the impulse to form a State but an instinct of the masses like the linguistic instinct, or the gregarious impulse of insects, only mixed with more infusions of the conscious understanding?

If, in the animal, as we have seen, instinct always appears just when a need is not to be satisfied in any other way, what wonder if also in all branches of the historical evolution the right man is always born at the right time, whose inspired genius perceives and satisfies the unconscious needs of his time? Here the proverb holds good: When the need is most, the help is nearest.

Why should we trouble a god who stands without and pushes and guides from the outside in the case of the historical instinct of man, when we have not found it necessary in the case of all the other instincts? *Only then*, if in the progress of the inquiry it should appear, that the unconscious in the individual has *nothing individual* in it except the reference of this its activity to this definite individual, then will Schelling be right also in the second part of the quoted passage, that the Absolute is the percipient (clairvoyant) in all such action, and its absolute synthesis (inweaving), or as Kant once expresses it (Works, vii. 367), that "Instinct is the voice of God," but now of the God in one's own breast, the *immanent* God.

If we have found the stopping short at the idea of a fate or a providence to be inadmissible, it is not to be understood, that these ways of looking at the matter, just as that of the exclusive self-activity of individuals in history, are in themselves illegitimate, but only, that they are one-sided. The Greeks, Romans, and Mohammedans are quite right in their idea of εἱμαρμένη or fate, so far as this signifies the absolute necessity of all that happens in the thread of causality, so that every link of the series is determined, predetermined by the foregoing, thus the whole series by the commencing link.

Christianity is right in its idea of *Providence*, for all that happens happens with absolute wisdom, with absolute fitness, *i.e.*, as means to the *fore-seen* end, by the never-erring Unconscious, which is itself the absolutely logical. At any moment only one thing can be logical, and therefore always only one thing can, and this the one logically demanded, must happen, just as fitly as necessarily (comp. further on C. Chap. xv. 3). Lastly, the modern rationalistic empirical conception is right, that history is the exclusive result of the *self-activity* of the individuals determining themselves according to psychological laws without any miracle of an incursion of higher powers. But the supporters of the first two views are wrong, in denying the spontaneity, those of the latter, in denying fate and providence, for only the union of all three points of view is the truth. But this very union was self-contradictory, as long as one assumed merely conscious self-activity of the individual. It is the cognition of the Unconscious which at once makes this possible and evident, by bringing into scientific clearness the hitherto only mystically postulated identity of the individual with the Absolute, yet without effacing their difference, which is a no less one than that of metaphysical essence and phenomenal existence (comp. C. Chap. vi.–viii. and xi.)

XI.

THE VALUE OF THE UNCONSCIOUS AND OF CONSCIOUSNESS FOR HUMAN LIFE.

I HAVE hitherto made sufficiently conspicuous the value of the Unconscious, so that it might appear that I was desirous of exalting the Unconscious in comparison with consciousness. To repel such a charge, to recall the value of conscious thinking, and to compare the worth of the conscious and unconscious and their respective offices, is the object of the present chapter.

Let us first consider the worth of the Conscious, of conscious reflection, therefore, and of the application of acquired conscious knowledge for mankind.

The fundamental question would be this: "Can reflection and knowledge determine action and character, and in what manner?" The affirmative answer, with which common sense would not be backward, might be placed in doubt through the consideration, firstly, that the specific will, from which action proceeds, springs from a reaction of the character on motive, a process which remains for ever closed to consciousness; and secondly, that volition and ideation are incommensurable things, because they belong to quite different spheres of mental activity. Their heterogeneity and incommensurability are however limited by this circumstance, that an idea forms the content of the will, and an idea its motive or exciting cause, and the eternal unconsciousness of the process engendering the will would only make any knowledge of the connection of motive and desire entirely impossible, if either character were in itself quickly alterable, or there were no necessary uniformity in the process of motivation, but a freedom of the will in the sense of the Indeterminists. As neither condition obtains, the possibility is open to every one, like the physician with those drugs, whose physiological effect is incomprehensible to him, to collect an empirical knowledge of what desire is called forth by what motive and in what degree. So far as human characters resemble each other in general, this cognition will be general empirical psychology, but so far as characters are different, it will be special knowledge of self and man (Science of Character). If we combine with this the knowledge of those psychological laws according to which the excitability of the different kinds of desires is temporarily changed, as, *e.g.*, the laws of our moods, of passion, of habit, &c., and if we secure ourselves in the manner shortly to be considered from the illusions of the intellect, that are produced by passions, then if all these conditions are ideally satisfied, we shall be able to predict any moment the kind and degree of the resulting desire in respect of any motive, and the errors regarding the issue of the unconscious will-producing process mentioned in Chapters III. and IV. will disappear of themselves.

Now as every motive can only take the form of the idea, and the revival of ideas is subject to the influence of the conscious will, by voluntarily calling up an idea known as motive of a certain desire, there follows from what has been said the possibility of indirectly arousing this desire. Further, as the will is nothing but the resultant of all contemporaneous desires, and as the union of all the components into the one resultant has the simple form of an algebraic sum, because indeed all the components in respect of a future action can have only two directions, positive or negative, there follows further the possibility of influencing the resultant by arousing one or more new desires through a voluntary representation of the appropriate motives, or by strengthening those already present. The same means is also available for suppressing such desires as would certainly not so soon attain to manifestation in action on external grounds, but which act prejudicially through disturbance of the mind, confusion of the intellect, production of useless feelings of pain, &c. But conscious reflection can never influence a present desire directly, but only mediately, by arousing an opposite one.—That this stated mode of influencing the will through the intellect is in fact the only possible one, and that which always occurs in practice, will readily be granted by everybody who makes this department of psychology a little the subject of his reflection. This, as well as the circumstance that the subject is somewhat wide of our proper theme, deters me from further discussing it. I will merely further add, that only from this point of view can a change of character through conscious reflection be explained. We have, namely, seen the possibility of determining the issue in every single case otherwise than by merely leaving it to the action of the motives spontaneously presenting themselves, and thereby the possibility of successfully making head against the emotions which are most easily excited in consequence of the now formed character, and therefore most frequently arise. If now this suppression regularly occurs on every occasion for a longer time, according to the law of habit, by the persistent inactivity and non-satisfaction of the particular impulse, its liability to stimulation will be enfeebled; while, on the other hand, the frequently and strongly excited tendencies will be strengthened, *i.e.*, the character will be changed. In the same manner the possibility of a change of character by means of conscious reflection, certainly only with the help of long habit, becomes intelligible (comp. Phil. Monatshefte, vol. iv. Hft. 5, on Bahnsen's Ethology).

The above fundamental question is herewith answered in the affirmative in both its parts, and we can now take a brief survey of what conscious reflection and knowledge have to offer to man as regards practice.

1. *Prevention of illusions of knowledge due to influence of emotions.*—We have already seen how the emergence of ideas is essentially dependent on a momentary interest. Hence it happens that, with a predominant one-sided interest, *e.g.*, emotions, probable reasons for the case in accordance with the interest always preferentially enter into consciousness, and fewer contrary reasons; that seeming reasons *pro* are too readily assumed to be perceived to be faulty; but that seeming reasons *contra*, if they at all crop up, are immediately unmasked, and even good reasons *contra* depreciated or refuted by seeming reasons, and thus error arises. No wonder, therefore, that terror, anger, sensuous desire can so deprive us of our wits that we no longer know what we say or do, that hate causes us to see only faults in our enemies; love, merely excellences in our loved ones; that fear paints in gloomy, hope in rosy hues; that the former allows us often no longer to perceive obvious resources, the latter makes the most improbable probable, if it only corresponds to our wishes, that we mostly err to our own advantage, rarely to our disadvantage, and only too frequently hold that to be fit and just which is to our own advantage.

Interest even insinuates itself into pure science, for a favourite hypothesis sharpens the glance for everything confirmative, and causes us to overlook the plainest counter-evidence, or to let go out at one ear what comes in at the other.

There are two remedies for this: the first is, that one form once for all an empirical coefficient of reduction dependent on the degree of the passion or interest, and multiply this in any single case by the acquired coefficient of probability of the judgment; the second, that one allows no passion to attain the degree where it begins to perceptibly affect the judgment. The latter means will alone stand the test, but is not a general favourite, because inconvenient, and only attainable by long practice in self-command; the former entirely fails in the case of strong emotions and passions, when all the mental powers are concentrated on a single point; moreover the magnitude of the coefficient of reduction is often difficult to fix, the actual estimate of the degree of personal passion still more difficult.—The value of intellectual clearness ($\sigma\omega\phi\rho o\sigma\acute{v}\nu\eta$) is pretty obvious in a verbal dispute, where the one allows himself to be carried away by passion, and not the other. Among women almost every real dispute passes into a personal one, whether clothed in the most delicate irony or in the choicest Billingsgate. Still more conspicuous is the value of sobriety and restraint of emotions in cases of peril.

2. *Prevention of thoughtlessness and irresolution.*—The largest part of all the remorse in the world arises from inconsiderate action, in which the possible consequences of the deed in all its bearings were not considered, the result being painful surprise on their appearance. If the evil consequences fall back upon the doer himself, inconsiderateness becomes levity. All this remorse would accordingly be spared by more deliberation in action. Irresolution on the other hand proceeds partly from want of courage, partly from want of confidence in one's own reflective powers. The characteristic of courage may, however, be supplied by conscious reason, since courage is risking one evil to avoid another, or to gain an advantage, on the supposition that the chances are favourable to the attempt, whether in consequence of the relative magnitude of the two evils or the probabilities of their occurrence. Want of confidence in one's own reflective powers is likewise corrected by reflection itself, when we say to ourselves that no one can do more than is in his power; that therefore if he have done the utmost, he may calmly await the result of the action, but that too long reflection as a rule not merely helps no more than a brief reflection, but by delaying action, does more harm than any possible improvement of the result can bring advantage.

3. *Appropriate selection of means to end.*—If an aim is

irrational, it is itself an inappropriate means to the main aim of every being, the greatest possible sum of happiness in life, which, if not clearly conscious to every one, yet as faintly sounding organ-point is heard in all the chords of life. But even where the ends are rational, or their choice and estimation does not devolve upon the individual, but only the choice of the means is entirely or partially left to him, by irrational selection of the means unspeakable evil is wrought, which can never be made good again. In important cases this is sufficiently striking; but far greater is the influence in the thousand petty cares, drudgeries, comforts and discomforts, pleasantnesses and unpleasantnesses of the day, in the intercourse of business, office, vocation, society, family life, the relationship of master and servant. It is especially in these cases, where the immediate ends are partly frustrated by improper means, partly attained at a disproportionate expense, and where accordingly people make the life of themselves and others far more difficult and bitter than it already is, by all kinds of distress, torment, trouble, vexation, and spite. And far more of all this comes from the limited insight of the average man and his unsuitable choice of means to the end in view, than from evil will, so that one is often tempted to exclaim, "Would that people were more wicked, if they were only less stupid!"

4. *The determination of the will not according to the passion of the moment, but according to the principle of the greatest possible personal happiness.*—The brute, with the few exceptions of the higher animals trained by man, is essentially dependent on the momentary sensuous and instinctively aroused emotion. Where instinct does not involve a reference to the future, the consciousness of the animal also does not easily concern itself therewith, and only too often must it suffer from the consequences of its absolute levity. Man, through his more highly-developed consciousness, enjoys the privilege of being able to oppose to the passions of the sensuous

moment desires, which are voluntarily produced by representations of the future, and has therein a means of securing for the Ego of the future an ideal equality with the Ego of the present. But now, owing to the less vivid character of voluntary ideas, the strength of the opposing desires is considerably circumscribed, and they are no longer able to offer a successful resistance to a tolerably strong emotion begotten by the sensuous present. Such an emotion rather hurries the man back to the stage of animality, and if he re-emerge from it with moderate loss and repentance, he may thank his lucky stars. If, then, the claim of the future Ego, and the principle of the greatest possible personal happiness, is to be preserved, there is nothing for it but to prevent the growth of the passions to so overpowering a degree, *i.e.*, to suppress them earlier, most surely and most easily in their origin. Here we have found the second reason for suppressing the emotions. An important office of reflection further is, to decide which of the many simultaneous aims of life that run athwart one another at any moment deserves to be supported, in order at any moment to contribute as much as possible to the total happiness; for the continually changing circumstances also require that we continually change, sometimes entirely let go, sometimes resume at a more favourable time, the aims for whose attainment one happens to be labouring.

5. *Value of conscious reason for morality.*—Most immoral actions are completely prevented by a prudent egoism, which proceeds according to the principle of the greatest possible personal happiness, especially in a State with an orderly system of law, and a society which punishes with its contempt such immoralities as the State cannot punish. That not many cases remain in which the ordinances of morality cannot be established in an egoistic manner is sufficiently proved by this, that so many ethical systems are openly or disguisedly based on egoism and the principle of the greatest possible personal

happiness, *c.g.*, the Epicurean, the Stoic, the Spinozistic. For all such cases one sees that the exercise of reason hitherto spoken of must suffice for morality, and in point of fact, along with custom brought about by compulsion, this reference to egoism is almost the only successful way to teach and to improve morality. What is not attained by it is hardly at all attainable from the point of view of individual ethics.

If one, however, disregards the practically vital effect of a rule of conduct, and contemplates the theoretical value of the ethical *systems*, there will hardly be any doubt that, whatever theoretical foundations of ethics be assumed, they can only be such as consist of principles of conscious reason, if they possess any scientific ground whatsoever, and are to be capable of supporting a system. I shall not, however, say more on this point now, in order not to wander too far from our theme.

6. *Correct choice of a calling, occupation of leisure, intercourse, and friends.*—" Whoever is born with a talent, finds therein his fairest existence " (Göthe), therefore it is very important, on the one hand, to recognise one's talent, which may be very considerable and yet be entirely missed; and, on the other hand, in youthful enthusiasm for an object, not to imagine a talent which one does not possess. Were both cases not frequent, so many men would not miss their vocation, the choice of which, in spite of all limitations, affords the individual tolerably wide scope. Still more difficult is it to detect the chief among several talents; more easy, on the other hand, to make the equally important choice of the dilettante occupation of leisure, because so much does not depend on alternation, and time is thereby gained for experimenting. As the choice of a calling requires a large self-knowledge, so the choice of intercourse and of friends requires a large knowledge of the world and of men. This is a human need; and one has not to choose whether, but with whom one will associate. The importance of the matter may be imagined when we

consider how the possession of a single, entirely congenial and true friend is able to afford consolation in the greatest misfortunes, but what bitter disappointments may be prepared by the choice of unsuitable friends. Nevertheless one often sees friendships concluded and persisted in for a long time, which are so little harmonious that one would think the people must be smitten with blindness. In fact, however, did not human beings, in their heart of hearts, actually regard themselves as as unreasonable as they are, it would not be possible for reconciliations so commonly to take place after occurrences which, referred to faults of character, could never be forgiven, and are only to be excused by unreason, wherefore men are fond of designating their mad pranks aberrations.—The imprudent choice of a friend is most bitterly avenged in marriage, because here the loosening of the relations is supremely difficult; and yet this is a case where regard is paid to almost anything else (beauty, money, family) than to harmony of character. Were people not afterwards so intellectually indifferent about fitting well or ill, when they see that they have been mistaken in each other, there would be many more bad marriages in the world than there are.

7. *Suppression of useless feelings of pain.*—Pleasure and pain consist in satisfaction and non-satisfaction of desire, which are produced by converse with the outer world, and which man can only influence by reacting on the external circumstances, which is the end of all action. If his power does not extend so far as to procure the satisfaction of his desires, he must just bear the pain, and can then only diminish or annihilate it by diminishing or annihilating the desire, in the non-satisfaction of which the pain consists. If one consistently carries this out in the case of every pain, the exciting capacity of the desires is blunted in accordance with the law of habit, consequently the future feelings of pleasure are as much diminished as the future feelings of pain. Whoever is of my opinion,

that on the average in human life the sum of the painful feelings far outweighs the sum of the pleasurable feelings, must perforce admit this general principle of hebetation as logical consequence of this view. But whoever does not at all or only in a qualified sense assent to this opinion, I refer to the not inconsiderable number of those painful feelings which are opposed to no feeling of pleasure at all, *i.e.*, in which the satisfaction of the underlying desire lies outside the domain of possibility, as *e.g.*, in pain for past events which cannot happen over again, vexation, impatience, envy, spite, remorse, which can bring no moral profit, further excessive sensibility, groundless jealousy, immoderate anxiety and care for the future, too lofty expectations of life, &c. Only consider how much the life of humanity would gain if one could eradicate every one of these foes of the mind's peace—the advantage would be incalculable; and yet it is open to every one to purify his life from these disturbers of his freedom by the application of conscious reason, if only he does not at once lose heart for the struggle through a few unsuccessful attempts. Thus we have found here a third ground for the suppression of the passions.

8. *The highest and most enduring human enjoyment afforded by the search for truth.*—The more concentrated and vehement is an enjoyment, the shorter time can it last, before reaction sets in, and the longer one must wait for its repetition; think of the delights of the table and of the amatory impulse in particular. The calmer, clearer, and purer an enjoyment is, the longer it can endure, the fewer pauses it needs for recreation; compare the musical, poetical and scientific pleasures. Thus it happens, that the strongest enjoyments, on account of the brevity of their duration and their necessary rarity, are not the greatest in amount, that rather the most spiritual, above all the scientific, afford a far larger total of pleasure in the same time by reason of their duration. The other reasons why the enjoyment which lies in striving after truth is

the highest, are so well known, that I will spare my readers an enumeration of them. Moreover, no one will doubt that we owe the mass of our science, especially the abundance and elaboration of its material, to conscious reason.

9. *The support of artistic production by conscious labour and criticism.*—I can here appeal in the main to what has been said in Chap. V., B. Although the Unconscious has to furnish the invention, yet in the first place criticism must step in to prevent feeble execution and to purify what is good from excess of phantasy; and secondly, conscious work must fill up the pauses, when the inspirations of the Unconscious are silent, and the conscious concentration of the will must carry the work to completion with iron industry, if enthusiasm for the same is not to perish of ennui on the road.—

What has been hitherto said with regard to the value of conscious reason and knowledge could, having regard to our main object, only consist of hasty hints, which may have been all too trite; the opportunities for interesting psychological remarks could not but be passed over unused, and the living clothing of the dry abstraction be left to the reader, and yet such a comparison could not be omitted, in order to offer a counterpoise to the value of the Unconscious, which was made prominent in all the earlier chapters.

I may perhaps be permitted to state these points quite succinctly once again.

1. The Unconscious forms and preserves the organism, repairs its inner and outer injuries, appropriately guides its movements, and mediates its employment by the conscious will.

2. The Unconscious supplies every being in its instinct with what it needs for self-preservation, and for which its conscious thought does not suffice, *e.g.*, man the instincts for comprehending sense-perception, for the formation of language and political constitutions, and many other things.

3. The Unconscious preserves the species through sexual and maternal love, ennobles it through selection in sexual love, and conducts the human race historically steadily to the goal of its greatest possible perfection.

4. The Unconscious often guides men in their actions by hints and feelings, where they could not help themselves by conscious thought.

5. The Unconscious furthers the conscious process of thought by its inspirations in small as in great matters, and in mysticism guides mankind to the presentiment of higher, supersensible unities.

6. It makes men happy through the feeling for the beautiful and artistic production.—

If now we institute a comparison between the Conscious and Unconscious, it is first of all obvious that there is a sphere which is always reserved to the Unconscious, because it remains for ever inaccessible to consciousness. Secondly, we find a sphere which in certain beings only belongs to the Unconscious, but in others is also accessible to consciousness. Both the scale of organisms as well as the course of the world's history may teach us that all progress consists in magnifying and deepening the sphere open to consciousness; that therefore in *a certain* sense consciousness must be the higher of the two. Further, if in man we consider the sphere belonging both to the Unconscious and also to consciousness, this much is certain, that everything which any consciousness has power to accomplish can be executed equally well by the Unconscious, and that too always far more strikingly, and therewith more quickly and more conveniently for the individual, since the conscious performance must be striven for, whereas the Unconscious comes of itself and without effort. This convenience of abandoning oneself to the Unconscious, its feelings and inspirations, is tolerably familiar, and hence the conscious use of reason is so decried in all and every one by the indolent. That the Unconscious can really outdo all the performances of conscious reason, is what we should not only *à priori* expect of the clairvoyance of the Unconscious, but we see it also realised in those fortunate natures which possess everything that others must acquire with toil, who never have a struggle of conscience, because they always spontaneously act correctly and morally in accordance with feeling, can never comport themselves otherwise than with tact, learn everything easily, complete everything which they begin with a happy knack, and live in eternal harmony with themselves, without ever reflecting much what they do, or even experiencing difficulty and toil. In respect to action and behaviour, the fairest specimens of these instinctive natures are only seen in women, who then surpass all imagination in their bewitching womanliness.—

But now what disadvantage lies in this self-surrender to the Unconscious? This, that one never knows where one is or what one has; that one gropes in the dark, while one has got the lantern of consciousness in one's pocket; that it is left to accident, whether the inspiration of the Unconscious will come when one wants it; that one has no criterion but success, what is an inspiration of the Unconscious, and what a wrong-headed flash of whimsical fancy, on what feeling one may rely, and on what not; finally, that one does not practise conscious judgment and reflection, which can never be entirely dispensed with, and that then in any case which occurs one must put up with wretched analogies instead of rational inferences and all-sided survey. Only the Conscious one *knows* as one's own, the Unconscious confronts us as something incomprehensible, foreign, on whose favour we are dependent; the Conscious is possessed as ever-ready servant, whose obedience may be always compelled; the Unconscious protects us like a fairy, and has always something uncomfortably demonic about it. I may be proud of the work of consciousness, as *my own* deed, the fruit of my own hard labour; the fruit of the Unconscious is as it were a gift of the gods, and man only its favoured messenger; it can therefore only teach him humility. The Unconscious is, as soon as it is there, complete from top to toe, has no judgment on itself, and must therefore be taken just as it is,—the Conscious is its own measure, it judges itself, and improves itself, and is to be changed any moment, as soon as a newly-gained cognition or changed circumstances require it. I know what in my consciously obtained result is good, and what it lacks for perfection, therefore it gives me the feeling of security, because I know what I have; but also that of modesty, because I know that it is still imperfect. The Unconscious leaves no room for improvement. A man can never acquire greater perfection in the works of the Unconscious, because his first as his last appear as involuntary inspirations,—consciousness contains in itself the infinite perfectibility of the individual and of the race, and therefore fills man with the infinite striving after the perfection which blesses. The Unconscious is independent of the conscious will at any moment, but its functioning is altogether dependent on the unconscious will, the fundamental emotions, passions, and main interests of mankind, —the Conscious is subject to the conscious will at every moment, and can entirely emancipate itself from interest and the emotions and passions. Action in conformity with the inspirations of the Unconscious consequently exclusively depends on the innate and acquired character, and is good or bad accordingly,—action from consciousness may be regulated according to principles which reason dictates.

After this comparison there will be no hesitation in admitting consciousness to be *for us* the more important, and herewith confirming our previous conclusion from the organic series and the progress of history. Wherever consciousness is able to replace the Unconscious, it *ought* to replace it, just because it is to the individual the higher, and such objections to it as that the constant application of conscious reason renders pedantic, costs too much time, &c., are mistaken, for pedantry only arises from *imperfect* use of the reason, when in applying general rules one does not take account of the *particular differences,* and reflection costs too much time only with deficient material of knowledge and unsatisfactory theoretical preparation for practice, or with irresolution, which can only be obviated by the use of reason itself. One ought, therefore, to try to expand the sphere of conscious reason as much as possible, for therein consists all the progress of the world-process, all the salvation of the future. That this sphere is not positively transgressed, for that provision is made by its impossibility; but another danger certainly lurks in such an attempt, and this is the place for warning on that head. Conscious reason, namely, is only denying, criticising, contrasting, correcting, measuring, comparing, combining, classifying, inducing the general from the particular, ordering the particular case according to the general rule; but it is never creatively productive, never inventive. Here man is entirely dependent on the Unconscious, as we have seen before, and if he loses the faculty of hearing the inspirations of the Unconscious, he loses the spring of his life, without which he would drag on his existence monotonously in the dry schematism of the general and particular. The Unconscious is, therefore, *indispensable* for him, and woe to the age which violently suppresses its voice, because in one-sided over-estimate of the conscious-rational it will only give heed to the latter. Then it falls irrecoverably into a vapid, shallow rationalism, which struts about in childish senescent knowingness, without being able to do anything positive for its posterity, as the time of the Wolff-Mendelssohn-Nicolai mock-enlightenment at which we now smile. Not with rude fist should one crush the tender germs of the unconscious inspirations, when they shall come again, but watch for them with childlike devotion, and tenderly touch and cherish them. And this is the danger to which every one is exposed who one-sidedly tries to make his existence entirely dependent on conscious reason, when he desires to transfer it to art and feeling and everything, and tries to renounce the rule of the Unconscious wherever it seems to him possible. Wherefore occupation with the arts is so necessary a counterpoise to the rationalistic education of our time, as that in which the Unconscious finds its most immediate expression, certainly not such a technical art-exercise as is carried on at the present day from fashion and vanity, but initiation into the feeling for the beautiful, into the comprehensive and the true spirit of art. Equally important is it to make youth more acquainted with animal life as the unadulterated spring of pure Nature, in order that it may learn to understand in it its own essence in simplified form, and may quicken and refresh itself therein as a relief from the unnaturalness and distortion of our social states. Further, one ought to be quite particularly on one's guard against making the female sex too rational, for where the Unconscious must first be reduced to silence, success is only attained at the cost of repulsive caricatures; but where the unconscious tendency harmonises with the demands of consciousness, it is a useless and in general injurious task. Woman namely is related to man, as instinctive or unconscious to rational or conscious action; therefore the genuine woman is a piece of Nature, on whose bosom the man estranged from the Unconscious may refresh and recruit himself, and can again acquire respect for the deepest and purest spring of all life. And to preserve this treasure of the eternal womanly, the woman also should be as far as possible shielded by the man from all contact with the rough struggle of life, where it is needful to display conscious force, and should be restrained in the sweet natural bonds of the family. Undoubtedly also the high worth of woman for man is found only in the period of transition, when the division between Conscious and Unconscious has already taken place, but the reconciliation of the two has not yet been completed. This transitional stage in which at the present day all civilised nations still are, will also not be spared the individual in his period of development for the whole future, and therefore the eternal womanly will remain for all time an indispensable, complementary, and educating moment for the youth of the male sex. It is not saying too much that for a young man noble female intercourse is far more helpful than male, and in a greater degree the more philosophical the man's bent; for female intercourse is related to the male, as the survey obtained in actual life to the survey in books. Lack of male intercourse may be compensated by books, of female never.—Lastly, we ought constantly to keep before our own and others' eyes all that we owe to the Unconscious, as a counterpoise to the advantages of conscious reason, in order that the already half-exhausted spring of everything true and good may not completely dry up, and humanity enter upon a premature old age; and to direct attention to this need was one powerful impulse more, determining me to reduce to writing the thoughts presented in this work.

C.

METAPHYSIC OF THE UNCONSCIOUS.

"Come to Physics, and see the Eternal!"—SCHELLING.

I.

THE *DIFFERENTIAE* OF CONSCIOUS AND UNCONSCIOUS MENTAL ACTIVITY AND THE UNITY OF WILL AND IDEA IN THE UNCONSCIOUS.

1. *The Unconscious does not fall ill,* but conscious mental activity can sicken if its material organs suffer disturbances, whether from bodily causes, or through violent shocks, arising from violent mental emotions. This point, so far as we are able to enter upon it, has been already touched upon in the chapter on the *Vis Mediatrix* (vol i. 161–168).

2. *The Unconscious does not grow weary,* but all conscious mental activity becomes fatigued, because its material organs become temporarily unserviceable, in consequence of a quicker consumption of material than nutrition can repair in the same time. Undoubtedly, fatigue may be avoided by occupying a different sense, or by changing the object of thought or of sense-perception, because then other organs and parts of the brain are brought into requisition, or at least the same organs are constrained to a different kind of activity; but the general fatigue of the central organ of consciousness is not to be prevented, even by the change of objects, and with every new object takes place the sooner, the longer attention has already been absorbed with other objects, until at last complete exhaustion ensues, which is only to be compensated by fresh absorption of oxygen during sleep. The more we approach the sphere of the Unconscious the less is fatigue observable, as, for example, in the department of the feelings, and the less defined they are in

consciousness, for so much the more does their proper essence belong to the Unconscious. Whilst a thought is probably not to be retained in consciousness without interruption for more than two seconds, and thinking grows weary in a few hours, one and the same feeling remains, with fluctuating intensity it is true, but uninterruptedly, often for days and nights, nay, for months, and if it at last becomes blunted, yet, in contrast to thinking, the receptivity for other feelings does not appear to be impaired, and these then do not grow weary earlier than they would otherwise have done. The latter assertion only so far needs limitation, as the frame of mind is to be taken notice of at the same time.—Before falling asleep, when the intellect becomes weary, the feelings which oppress us emerge the more powerfully because they are not impeded by thoughts, so strongly indeed that they often prevent sleep. Even in dream vivid feelings are often much more frequent than clear thoughts, and very many dream-images manifestly owe their origin to present feelings. Further, let any one remember the restless night before an important event; the waking of the mother at the slightest cry of her child, accompanied with total insensibility to other stronger noises; the awaking at a fixed hour, if a decided volition has been exerted to that end, and the like. All this proves the unwearied persistence of the feelings, the interest and the will in the Unconscious, or even with quite weak affection of consciousness, whereas the wearied intellect rests, or at the most idly gazes on the juggle of dreams. Where we have to do with that condition which, of all those that are at all accessible to our observation, lies most deeply in the Unconscious and least emerges into consciousness, the ecstasy of the mystics, there, agreeably to the nature of the case, the fatigue is also reduced to a minimum, for "a hundred years are as one hour," and even bodily fatigue, as in the winter sleep of animals, becomes almost obliterated by the incredible slackening of all organic functions;—think of the ever-praying pillar-saints, or the Indian penitents and their distorted postures.

3. *All conscious Ideation has the form of Sensibility; unconscious Thought can only be of a non-sensuous kind.*—We think either in images, when we directly receive the sense-impressions and their transformations and combinations from memory, or we think in abstractions. These abstractions are, however, also merely abstracted from sense-impressions, and however much is allowed to *drop out* in abstracting, so long as *anything* is retained *at all*, it can only be something that *already inhered* in the whole *from* which abstraction was first made, *i.e.*, even the abstract ideas are for us only *remnants of sense-impressions*, and have consequently the *form of sensibility*.—That the sense-impressions which we receive from things have no resemblance to these is already sufficiently known by natural science. Further, every sense-perception is *co ipso* united with consciousness, *i.e.*, it always *excites* the latter, whenever it does not light on an already existing sphere of consciousness and is apperceived by this. The Unconscious, accordingly, if it willed to represent things in the form of sensibility, would not only represent them inadequately, but it would always, in this mode of perception, step out of the sphere of unconscious into that of conscious mental activity, as it does in fact do in the individual consciousness of organisms. If we then inquire into the nature of the *unconscious* spiritual activity of the Unconscious, it follows from what has been said that it can *not* take on the form of *sensibility*. But now as *consciousness* on its part, as we have seen above, can represent nothing at all unless in the form of sensibility, it follows that now and never can consciousness *frame a direct conception* of the mode and manner in which the unconscious idea is presented; it can only know *negatively* that the former is represented in *no way of which* it can form any idea. One can, at the most, form the very probable supposition that things are repre-

sented in the unconscious idea as they are in themselves, since it would be far from intelligible why things should *appear* to the Unconscious *otherwise* than they *are;* rather things *are what* they are just because they *are represented* by the Unconscious thus, and not otherwise. Certainly this explanation throws no light on the nature of the idea itself, and we do not become wiser in respect to the mode and manner of unconscious representation.

4. *The Unconscious does not vacillate and doubt;* it needs *no time* for reflection, *but instantaneously grasps the result* at the same moment in which it thinks the whole logical process that produces the result, all at once, and not *successively*, which is the same thing as not thinking it at all, but discerning the result immediately in intellectual intuition with the infinite penetration of the purely logical. This point also we have already often mentioned, and have everywhere found so thoroughly confirmed, that we might employ it as an infallible criterion, in order to decide, in any particular case, whether we had to do with the action of the Unconscious or with a conscious performance. Wherefore the conviction of this proposition must be essentially gained from the sum of our previous considerations.—Here I shall only add the following:—The ideal philosophy demands an intelligible world without space and time, which is opposed to the phenomenal world, with its forms valid for conscious thought and being, space and time. How *Space* is *posited* only *in* and *with* Nature we shall see later on; here we are concerned with *Time*. Now, if we may assume that the Unconscious compresses every process of thought, along with its results, into a *moment*, *i.e.*, into *no time*, the thinking of the Unconscious is *timeless*, although still *in time*, because the moment in which there is thought has its temporal place in the remaining series of temporal phenomena. If we, however, reflect that this moment in which there is thought is only perceived in the coming-to-manifestation of its

result, and the thought of the Unconscious in each special case only acquires existence for a definite entrance into the phenomenal world (for it does not need reflections and resolutions), the conclusion is obvious that the thought of the Unconscious is only so far *in time* as the entering into manifestation of this thought is in time, but that the thought of the Unconscious, *apart* from the phenomenal world and from entrance into it, would in fact be not only *timeless*, but also *non-temporal*, *i.e.*, *out of all time*. Then, too, we should cease to speak of ideational *activity* of the Unconscious in the strict sense; but the world of possible representations would, as ideal existence, be enclosed in the bosom of the Unconscious, and the activity, as being something temporal, at least time-*positing*, in its very notion, would only begin in the moment that from this quiescent ideal world the one or other of all possible presentations enters into real manifestation, which comes to pass precisely through this, that it is laid hold of by the will as its content, as we shall subsequently see at the end of the present section. We should have hereby comprehended the realm of the Unconscious as the metaphysically tenable side of Kant's intelligible world.—It is in thorough agreement with this that *duration* only enters into conscious thought through the *material organ* of consciousness; that conscious thought only requires time because the cerebral vibrations on which it rests require time, as I have briefly shown in Sect. B., chap. viii. (vol. i. pp. 346, 347).

5. *The Unconscious does not err.*—The proof of this proposition must be confined to establishing that that which, on a superficial view, might be taken for errors of the Unconscious, on nearer inspection could not be so regarded. Thus, *e.g.*, the supposed errors of instinct may be reduced to the four following cases:—

(*a.*) Where no special instinct exists, but merely an organisation, which, owing to the exceptional strength of certain muscles, preferentially contracts these muscles. Thus, *e.g.*, the aimless butting of young cattle as yet destitute of horns, or when the secretary-bird (serpent-eater) crushes all its food with its strong legs before devouring it, although this has only a purpose in the case of living snakes. In these cases the organisation is there to render superfluous, and to supply the place of, a special instinct which would be suitable in certain cases; the organisation, however, urges to the same movements that are appropriate in certain cases, in other cases, also, where they are superfluous and useless. But as the Unconscious does the work once for all through the machinery of the organisation which it otherwise would have to do in each single case, one would still have to recognise this arrangement itself as suitable on account of the saving of energy to the Unconscious, if in certain cases this organisation acted not only superfluously but even inappropriately and injuriously, and if only the number of the cases where it is suitable considerably preponderates. But of this no single example is known to me.

(*b.*) Where instinct is killed by unnatural habits, a case which frequently occurs in man and the domestic animals, *e.g.*, when the latter devour on the pastures poisonous weeds and plants which they avoid in a state of nature, or when man artificially accustoms many animals to a food contrary to their nature.

(*c.*) Where instinct, for accidental reasons, is not functional; thus the inspiration of the Unconscious is entirely wanting, or occurs in so feeble a degree that other opposing impulses overcome it, *e.g.*, when an animal does not shun its natural enemy, and thereby falls a sacrifice to one whom other animals of its kind are wont instinctively to flee, or when maternal affection is so slight in a pig that the desire for food leads it to devour its offspring.

(*d.*) Where instinct, indeed, performs its functions correctly on the occurrence of a conscious idea, but this conscious idea contains an error. If, *e.g.*, a hen broods on a piece of chalk rounded like an egg that has been placed under it, or the spider carefully nourishes a bundle of cotton substituted for its ovisac, in both cases it is the conscious idea that errs in consequence of defective sense-perception, which takes the chalk for an egg, the ball of cotton for an ovisac. Instinct, however, does not err, for it quite rightly makes its appearance on the presentation. It would be unreasonable to require that the clairvoyance of instinct should be here manifested to correct the error of conscious representation; for the clairvoyance of instinct always is only concerned with just those points which conscious perception is in general not able to attain, but not with those for which the mechanism of sense-knowledge suffices in all ordinary cases. But even if this claim were set up, one could never say that the Unconscious erred, but only that it did not come into play with its clairvoyance when it should have come into play.

To these four cases everything might easily be referred which one might be tempted to regard as apparent errors of instinct. What in the human mind might be taken for false and bad inspirations of the Unconscious might be still more easily refuted. When one hears of mistaken clairvoyance, one may be as sure one is dealing with intentional or unintentional deception, as in dreams which do not prove true, that they are not suggestions of the Unconscious. In the same way, one may take it for granted beforehand that all the morbid and worthless excrescences of mysticism or in artistic conceptions do not spring from the Unconscious, but from consciousness, namely, from morbid excesses of the fancy, or from perverted education and formation of principles, judgment, and taste. Lastly, one must distinguish how far, and to what degree, the influence of the Unconscious has reached in any particular case. For I may, *e.g.*, brood over some invention, and have already made a start in a particular direction; when, now, I am cracking my brain over a certain point which seems to me to be alone wanting to complete the whole, I shall certainly have to thank the Unconscious if this suddenly occurs to me. But now the invention need by no means be herewith finished in a serviceable fashion, for I may possibly have erred in my belief that only this one point was wanting to complete the whole, or the whole may be completed but be worth nothing at all; and yet one cannot assert that the suggestion of the Unconscious was mistaken or bad, for it was decidedly good and right as regards the point which I was in search of, only the point sought was not the right one. If another time a suggestion of the Unconscious instantly shows the invention complete in all its outlines, this latter inspiration has only gone further; but correct and apt for the purpose, so far as they go, they are both, as are all influences of the Unconscious.

6. *Consciousness only acquires its value by means of memory, i.e.*, through the property of the cerebral vibrations to leave behind abiding impressions or molecular changes of such a kind, that in future the same vibrations are more easily excited than heretofore, in that the brain now responds more easily, as it were, to the same stimulus. This makes possible the comparison of present perceptions with former ones, without which all formation of conceptions would be almost impossible; in general terms, it renders possible the collection of *experiences*. Conscious thought increases in perfection according to the abundance of the materials of memory, the store of conceptions and judgments, and the exercise of thought. *To the Unconscious, on the other hand, we can ascribe no memory*, since we can comprehend the latter only with the help of the impressions persisting in the brain; and memory may, in whole or in part, be temporarily or for ever lost by injuries of the brain. The Unconscious also thinks everything which it needs for a special case implicitly in an instant; it *therefore needs to institute no comparisons;* just as little does it need *experiences*, since, in virtue of its clairvoyance, it knows or

can know everything as soon only as the will requires it with sufficient urgency. The Unconscious is therefore always perfect, so far as it can be in conformity with its nature, and a further perfection in this direction is unthinkable. If advance is to be made beyond that, it must take place through a change of the direction itself, *i.e.*, through the transition from the Unconscious into consciousness.

7. *In the Unconscious, Will and Representation are united in inseparable unity;* nothing can be willed which is not presented, and *nothing can be presented which is not willed.* In consciousness, on the contrary, undoubtedly also nothing can be willed which is not presented, but something may be presented without its being willed. *Consciousness is the possibility of the emancipation of the intellect from the will.*—The impossibility of a volition without presentation has been already discussed in Sect. A., chap. iv.; here we are concerned with the impossibility of an unconscious idea without the conscious will to its realisation, *i.e.*, without this unconscious idea being at the same time content or object of an unconscious will. This relation is clearest in instinct and the unconscious presentations which have reference to bodily processes. Here every single unconscious idea is accompanied by an unconscious will, which stands to the general will of self-preservation and preservation of the species in the relation of willing the means to the willing of the end. For that all instincts, with few exceptions, follow the two main purposes in nature—preservation of self and of the race—can hardly be doubted, whether we look to the origin of reflex movements, the healing actions of nature, organic formative processes and animal instincts, or to the instincts concerned with the understanding of sensuous perception, the formation of abstractions and indispensable ideas of relation, the formation of language, or to the instincts of shame, disgust, selection in sexual love, &c. It would

be a bad look-out for men and animals if even only one of these were wanting to them, *e.g.*, language or the formation of ideas of relation, both alike important for animals and man. All instincts that do not appertain to the preservation of self or the species have reference to the third chief end in the world—perfection and *ennoblement* of the species—a something that especially makes its appearance in the human race. Under the general willing of this end falls the willing of all special cases as means, where the Unconscious furthers historical progress, be it in thoughts (mystical acquisition of truths) or deeds, whether in the individual (as in heroes of history), or in masses of the people (as in the constituting of states, migrations of nations, crusades, revolutions of a political, ecclesiastical, or social kind, &c.) There still remains the action of the Unconscious in the sphere of the beautiful and in that of conscious thought. In both cases we have already been obliged to confess that the incursion of the Unconscious is, indeed, independent of the conscious will of the moment, but rather altogether dependent on the interior interest in the object, on the deep needs of the mind and heart for attaining this particular goal; that it is, it is true, tolerably independent of the circumstance whether one is consciously occupied just at the moment with the subject, but that it very much depends on a lasting and urgent occupation with the same. If, now, the profound spiritual interest and need of the heart is already itself a will essentially unconscious, only in slight degree entering into consciousness, or at least, like the earnest occupation with a subject, is highly adapted to arouse and to excite the unconscious will; if, further, the suggestion ensues the more easily, the more profound is the interest, and the more it has withdrawn from the clear heights of consciousness into the dark abysses of the heart, *i.e.*, into the Unconscious, we shall certainly be authorised in assuming in these cases likewise an unconscious will. In the mere apprehension of the beautiful, however, we shall certainly be obliged to acknowledge an instinct which belongs to the third main purpose, the perfection of the race, for one has only to think what the human race would be, what, in the most fortunate case, it could attain to at the end of history, and how much more wretched this wretched human life would become, if nobody knew the feeling of the beautiful.

There only remains yet one more point, which perhaps will present no difficulty to most readers; I mean clairvoyance in dreams which come true, visions, spontaneous and artificial somnambulism. But whoever accepts these phenomena will be soon convinced that the unconscious will is always co-operative. When clairvoyance refers to the prescribing of remedies to one's self, this is at once evident, and a clairvoyant prescription of remedies for other persons I should be strongly inclined to doubt, unless they were intimates, whose welfare was almost as much a matter of concern to the clairvoyants as their own. Prophetic dreams, forebodings, visions, or flashes of thought, which have other objects, refer either to important points of one's own future, warning against danger, consolation for sorrow (Goethe's vision of his double), and the like, or they make disclosures concerning beloved persons, wife and child, announce, *e.g.*, the death of the absent, or imminent misfortune; or, lastly, they relate to events of awful magnitude and extent, which touch every human heart, *e.g.*, the conflagration of large cities (Swedenborg), especially of one's native town, &c. In all these cases one sees how closely the suggestion of the Unconscious is bound up with the inmost volitional interest of mankind; in all these cases one is also, therefore, entitled to assume an unconscious will, which stands for *the universal interest made specific for this particular case yet unknown to consciousness.* Never will the clairvoyance of a human being light of itself on things which are not most intimately interwoven with the core of his own being; but as for the answers of artificial somnambulists to indifferent questions, I may be permitted to doubt their derivation from the Unconscious, as much as I feel bound to contemn those magnetisers as vain braggarts or deceitful charlatans, who do not scruple to put other questions to somnambules than such as have reference to personal well-being. Although the somnambulistic state is more receptive for the suggestions of the Unconscious than any other, yet only a very small part of what occurs to a somnambulist is the suggestion of the Unconscious, and experienced magnetisers know well enough how much one has to take care lest the fancies and dissimulation peculiar to women deceive even in the somnambulist state, without the somnambulist herself having the conscious intention to deceive.

We may assume, as result of this inquiry, that we know no unconscious idea which may not be united with unconscious will, and that, too, when we consider that the unconscious idea is something quite other than that which appears in consciousness as conception or inspiration of the Unconscious; the former and the latter are rather related as essence and phenomenon, but at the same time also as cause and effect. We shall thus find it very instructive that the unconscious will directly united with the unconscious presentation, *which represents the application of the general interest to the particular case*, consists in nothing else than *in the willing of the realisation of its unconscious representation*, if by realisation we understand manifestation in the natural world, and, moreover, immediately *in consciousness as representation in the form of sensibility by excitation of the appropriate cerebral vibrations*. This is, however, the *true unity of will and idea*, that the will wills absolutely nothing but the realisation of its own content, *i.e.*, the representation united with it. On the other hand, if we consider consciousness and the grand apparatus brought into play for its production, and remember from the last chapter of the foregoing section what we shall more exactly prove in chapter xiii. of the present section, that all progress in the scale of beings and in history consists in the expansion of the sphere where consciousness prevails, but that this extension of rule can only be conquered by liberation of consciousness from the sway of passion and interest, in a word—the will—and by sole subjection to conscious reason, the conclusion is obvious that the progressive *emancipation* of the intellect from the will is the proper motive and main purpose of the creation of consciousness. This would be, however, absurd if the Unconscious as such already contained the possibility of this emancipation, for the whole vast apparatus for introducing consciousness would then, with this intention, be superfluous. From this, and from the phenomenon that we are nowhere acquainted with an unconscious idea without unconscious will, I conclude that will and idea can only exist in inseparable unity in the Unconscious; for it would be, to say the least, very wonderful if unconscious representation separately existed and we nowhere observed it.—To this may be added the following confirmatory consideration.—

Thought or ideation, as such, is perfectly self-contained, has no volition at all, no endeavour, or anything like it; it has also, as such, no pain or pleasure; is therefore also quite unconcerned. All this does not attach to ideation, but to volition. Consequently, ideation can never find in itself a moment impelling to change; it will comport itself absolutely *indifferently*, not only with respect to its being thus or thus, but also with respect to its being or not-being, since all this is quite indifferent to it, because it is in fact altogether unconcerned. It follows from this that ideation, since it has neither an *interest* in its own existence, nor any *endeavour* after the same, can also find in itself no ground at all for passing from non-being into being, or, if one prefers, from *potential* being into *actual* being, *i.e.*, that it requires for the existence of every *actual* representation a basis outside ideation itself. This basis is, for conscious ideation, matter in the form of sense-impressions or cerebral vibrations; for unconscious ideation it cannot be this, otherwise it too would attain to consciousness, as will be shown in the third chapter; consequently for this material substratum there only remains the unconscious will. This perfectly accords with our experience, for everywhere it is the interest, the definite will, which, directed to the particular case, compels the idea into being. The particular will, however, besides the power of volition, shows also a definite (ideational) content, and this *content* it is which determines the quality or essence of the unconscious idea of the next moment, which it, however, could not determine if its existence were not demanded by the *willing* of the foregoing moment, and made possible by the persistence of the form of volition even up to this moment.—I will here once more add the remark, that since the act immediately follows the will, there can be no spiritual activity in the Unconscious save at the moment of the commencing act. Even when the will is too weak for the realisation of its content and for overcoming the present resistance, this holds good; for either the deed consists in the abortive *attempt*, or the Unconscious immediately thinks the appropriate preparatory means *instead of* the end. But, possibly repeated impulses on the part of the Unconscious may be requisite, namely, when the mechanical progress of the act stumbles upon obstacles which must be overpowered by *modified* action.

An objection might here be raised, namely, that the Unconscious *wills* only the final results, but must think the whole thought-process leading to these results; but whoever has attentively read No. 4 of this chapter will have already found there the answer to this objection. Unconscious thought embraces all the terms of a process, reason and consequent, cause and effect, means and end, &c., in a single moment, and thinks them, not before, beside, or beyond, but *in* the result itself; it never thinks them except *through* the *result*. Therefore, this thinking cannot be regarded as a *special* thinking outside the result; it is rather implicitly contained in the thinking of the result, without ever being explicated; consequently the result is that which is alone thought in our ordinary sense, and the proposition holds that only that can be unconsciously thought which is willed.—Moreover, even in the ordinary category of unconscious thought, in means and end, one may say that the end implicitly thought in the idea of the willed means is also implicitly willed.

According to the foregoing, the sole *activity* of the Unconscious consists in willing, and the unconscious representation filling the will is only a non-temporal content, merely dragged along with it, as it were, into time. *Volition* and *activity* are accordingly identical or reciprocal notions. Only through them is Time posited; only through them is the idea hurled from *potential* into *actual* being, from being in the essence into being in the phenomenon, and therewith into time. Quite otherwise is it with the conscious idea, which is a product of different factors, of which one, the cerebral vibrations, is from the first subject to duration.

II.

BRAIN AND GANGLIA AS CONDITIONS OF ANIMAL CONSCIOUSNESS.

ALMOST all naturalists, physiologists, and physicians are materialists, and the more the knowledge and method of physics and physiology is diffused among the educated public, the more does the materialistic view of the world gain ground. What is the cause of this? The simplicity and impressive evidentness of the facts on which the materialistic conception of the animal and human soul, the only spiritual being known to us, is supported. Only those unacquainted with these facts, as the unscientific multitude, or the learned world without physical and physiological knowledge, or those who approach these facts with the preconceived opinions of religious or philosophic systems, can alone remain outside their influence; they must absolutely convince every unprejudiced thinking man, because they need only to be taken just as they are; they declare their meaning with such naive plainness that it is not at all necessary to look for it. And this naive clearness and directness, this forcible self-evidence, which can only be denied with violence, this it is which secures for the materialistic conception of the mind so great a superiority over the difficult and subtle deductions and probabilities, over the arbitrary assumptions and often distorted consequences, of the spiritualistic psychology, which induces all clear heads averse to mysti-philosophic speculation to enrol themselves under the banner of Materialism, which is simple as the Nature that teaches it, and clear and precise in all its correct consequences as this its august mother. That Materialism thereby offends the religious systems can in our time only gain it the more adherents; but that it contradicts speculative philosophy, that does not trouble it at all; for how few men have a speculative need; how far fewer still philosophical culture? Accordingly Materialism has neither the need nor the capacity to investigate the not-understood abstractions, such as force, matter, &c., of which its system consists, and it comports itself to the higher questions of philosophy partly sceptically, in that it denies that their solution lies on this side the limits of the human understanding, partly it denies the title of these questions altogether. Thus it feels quite comfortable in its skin in all directions, and is perfectly contented with the daily progressive discoveries of the natural sciences, in the good faith that everything which man calls experience must be derived from the pursuit of the special sciences. It is, accordingly, no wonder that Materialism gains whereas Philosophy loses ground; for only a philosophy *which takes full account of all the results of the natural sciences*, and accepts without reservation the perfectly legitimate point of departure of Materialism, only such a philosophy can hope to make a stand against Materialism, if at the same time it fulfils the condition of being universally intelligible, which the philosophy of Identity and absolute Idealism unfortunately is not.

The first attempt to receive Materialism into Philosophy in an intelligible fashion was made by Schopenhauer, and not the least part both of his merit and of his growing popularity is due to this attempt. But his compromise was unsatisfactory; it allowed Materialism the intellect, and reserved to speculation the will. This violent dismembering is his weak point; for if once conscious ideation and thought is handed over to Materialism, it has full right to claim also conscious feeling, and therewith conscious desire and volition, since the physiological phenomena have the same expression for all conscious activities of mind. It is entirely inconsequent of Schopenhauer to refer the stores of memory, together with the intellectual foundations, talents, and aptitudes of the individual, to the constitution of the brain, and to exclude from the same and to hypostatise as an individual metaphysical essence, in defiance of his fundamental monistic principle, the character of the individual, which just as easily, if not more easily, is capable of such an explanation. In fact, there are no means of overturning the first fundamental proposition of Materialism, "All conscious mental activity can only come to pass by normal function of the brain," but by the ignoring or subtle explaining away of facts. But now, as long as any one knows or will know no other than conscious mental activity, this proposition asserts, "*All* mental activity can only come to pass through brain function." The conclusion is obvious: "Either all mental activity is pure function of the brain, or a product of brain function and something else, which is inherently incapable of expression, but is purely potential, and only attains expression in and by the normal brain function, which now appears as mental activity." It is evident that a decision between these alternatives, all others being laid aside as useless, meaningless ballast, is hardly to be evaded. Quite otherwise does the matter appear as soon as one already recognises unconscious mental action as the original and primary form, without whose assistance conscious mental activity would be paralysed. Then the proposition only says, "*Conscious* mental activity can only take place through the function of the brain." With respect to unconscious mental activity, on the other hand, it says nothing at all; it remains, therefore, since all the phenomena demonstrate their independence of brain functions, as something self-dependent, and only the form of consciousness appears conditioned by matter.

We pass on now briefly to present the facts, the theoretical expression for which is the above proposition.

1. The brain is in formal and material respects the highest product of organic formative activity.

"We find in the brain mountains and valleys, bridges and aqueducts, beams and arches, vices and hoes, claws and Ammon's horns, trees and sheaves, harps and sounding staves, &c., &c. Nobody has perceived the significance of these strange forms" (Huschke in "Skull, Brain, and Soul of Man").

There is no animal organ which has tenderer, more wonderful, more varied forms, finer and more peculiar structure. The ganglionic cells of the brain send off primitive fibres, and are in part mutually connected and in part surrounded by the same. These primitive fibres, hollow tubes filled with an oily, coagulable content, about $\frac{1}{1000}$th line in thickness, again intertwine and cross one another in the strangest fashion. Unfortunately the difficult anatomy of the brain is still as backward as its chemical investigation; but even from the latter we already know this much, that the chemical composition of the brain is by no means as simple as was formerly believed; that it is exceedingly different at different places; that the peculiar cerebral fats with their phosphorus content play a great part in it, and find other matters there which occur in no other tissue in the same way, *e.g.*, cerebrin and lecithin. For the rest, how backward our chemistry still is in regard to such investigations, one may infer from the fact that it cannot distinguish blood or pus which is infected with contagious matter from healthy blood; that the differences between isomeric substances (of the same composition, but of unlike qualities owing to different atomic position, as is shown by the different refraction of light and rotation) frequently vanish on analysis, so that it is only now beginning to discover a number of finely distributed metals by means of spectrum analysis, minute quantities of which in organic substances may be of the greatest importance. All these things acquire the more importance the higher the organic tissues with which one is concerned.

2. In the brain the change of material is more rapid

than in any other part of the body, wherefore also the flow of blood is disproportionately much stronger. This points to a concentration of vital activity in the brain, such as takes place in no other part of the body.

3. The brain (by which in this section the cerebrum is always alone to be understood) has no direct importance for the organic functions of bodily life. This is proved by the experiments of Flourens, who showed that animals from which the brain had been removed can live and thrive for months and years. Care must certainly be taken that the operation itself and the accompanying loss of blood be not too violent, and does not reduce too much the force of the animal; wherefore the experiment can only perfectly succeed in those animals from which the brain may be removed without too much difficulty, *e.g.*, fowls. From these first three points it may be concluded that the brain, the flower of the organism and the seat of the most vital activity, must have a *mental* destination, since it has *no corporeal* one.

4. With increasing perfection of the brain or of the ganglia representing it increases the mental capacity in the animal kingdom, whereas the corporeal functions of all animals, clever or stupid, may, as a rule, be performed equally well. As low down as the Insects it is strikingly manifest how the size of the cephalic ganglia is proportional to the intelligence of the orders and species. The Hymenoptera have in general larger ganglia than the stupid beetles, and they are particularly large in the clever ants. In the case of the vertebrates, one must make the inner space within the skull the ground of comparison, as this includes the central organs of motion, which of course must correspond in size to the mass of nerve and muscle of the animal, in order to be able to expend the requisite energy on its motor impulses. If we now merely consider the cerebrum proper, there appears in animals of not too different size a clear parallelism between quantity of brain and intelligence. So far, however, as in animals of very different

size (*e.g.*, very small and very large dogs, canary birds and ostrich), this parallelism appears disturbed, a qualitative compensation of the cerebrum is distinctly perceptible, especially by abundant and deep convolutions and furrows.

5. The mental tendencies and executive capacity of mankind are in proportion to quantity of brain, so far as the quality of the same does not give rise to exceptions. "According to the exact measurements of Peacock, the weight of the human brain gradually and very rapidly increases up to the twenty-fifth year, remains at this normal weight up to the fiftieth, and thenceforward gradually diminishes. According to Sims, the brain, which increases in bulk till the thirtieth or fortieth year, only attains the maximum of its volume between the fortieth and fiftieth year. The brain of old people becomes atrophied, *i.e.*, smaller; it shrivels, and there arise hollow spaces between the several convolutions, which before were firmly attached to one another. By this the substance of the brain becomes tougher, the colour greyer, the blood-content less, the convolutions narrower, and the chemical constitution of the brain of the old man, according to Schlossberger, again approaches that of the earliest life-period" (Büchner, Force and Matter, 5th edit., p. 109). The average weight of the brain, according to Peacock, amounts in the man to fifty, in the woman to forty-four ounces; according to Hoffmann, the difference amounts only to two ounces. Lauret drew from the measurements of two thousand heads the result, that both the circumference as well as the diameter, measured at different places, is always less in women than in men. Whilst the normal weight amounts to three to three and a half pounds, the brain of Cuvier weighed over four pounds. Inherited mental imbecility always shows a surprisingly small brain; conversely abnormal smallness of brain is always combined with imbecility. Panhappe proves from 782 cases the gradual diminution of the brain's weight in correspondence with the decrease of intelligence

in madness or with the depth of mental disturbance. In all cretins brain and skull are surprisingly small, the latter exhibiting assymmetry and deformity; the hemispheres in particular are wasted. The brain of the negro is much smaller than that of the European, the forehead retreating, the skull less in circumference, generally more animal; the natives of New Holland lack the higher parts of the brain in a surprising degree. Also the structure of the European skull has made no slight advance in historic times. Especially with the progress of civilisation the anterior region of the head becomes prominent at the expense of the posterior, as is proved by excavations relating to widely different times. The same relation also occurs in general between the rude and cultured classes of the present day, as, among other things, the experiences of hatmakers confirm. That here not isolated cases, but only average numbers are decisive, is matter of course; individual exceptions, *e.g.*, of clever people having a small, stupid people a large skull, must be referred partly to the thickness of the skull, partly to the difference of plan and finish, partly to the form of the convolutions and the quality of the brain.

What we know of the influence of quality is but little, but still something; *e.g.*, the child's brain is more pulpy, richer in water, poorer in fat than that of the adult; the differences between grey and white matter, the microscopic peculiarities, are only gradually formed; the so-called fibrillation of the brain, very distinct in the adult, is imperceptible in the child's brain; the plainer this fibrillation becomes, the more decided appears also the mental activity; the brain of the foetus has very little fat, consequently little phosphorus, but the fatty matter increases until birth, and after birth tolerably rapidly. In animals also the brain has, on the average, more fat the higher they are in the scale, and the smaller the brain in proportion to the intelligence of the animal, *e.g.*, in the horse. This fat seems to be very important, for in animals caused to starve the brain does not, like other organs, lose a part of its fatty matter.—On the number, depth, and form of the actions of the brain depends, with equal volume, the size of its surface,—a highly important factor, which may neutralise a less weight. On the average, the convolutions and furrows are the more numerous, deeper, and more complicated the higher the species of animals or race of man.

It would now be comprehensible if an exception were formed to the law of the proportion of brain mass and mental endowment by some few animals, the largest of the present day, exceeding the human brain in bulk. Nevertheless, even this apparent deviation only depends on a preponderance of those parts of the brain which serve the nervous system of the body as central organs of voluntary motion and sensation, and which, partly on account of the larger number and thickness of the nervous strands concurring in them, partly on account of the greater mechanical development of energy needful for the motion of a greater mass, cannot but show a larger volume. On the other hand, the anterior parts of the brain, which especially preside over the functions of thought, in no animal attain, *even in respect of quantity*, the same perfection as in man.

6. Conscious thinking strengthens the brain, as all activity its organs, and the manifested energy of thought is always accompanied by consumption of material. As any muscle, if it is considerably exercised, becomes stronger and increases in bulk (*e.g.*, the calves of dancers), so, too, the brain becomes more capable of thinking through exercise of thought, and increases in quality and quantity.

Albers in Bonn relates that he dissected the brains of several persons who had been exceeding mentally active for several years; in all he found the brain substance very firm, the grey matter and the convolutions strikingly developed. The increase in bulk is proved partly by the difference in the cultivated and lower ranks, partly by the increment due to the progressive civilisation of Europe, both of which certainly only reaching an amount capable of measurement in virtue of hereditary transmission.

That all thought is connected with the consumption of the materials of the brain follows from the simple phenomenon of the fatigue of thought, which without it would be incomprehensible. Mental just as much as bodily labour not only increases the desire for food in order to replace the waste of tissue, but according to Davy's measurements even animal heat also, as is announced by accelerated breathing, which takes place in order to again decarbonise the blood, whose carbonisation is more freely induced by the quicker interchange of material.

Further, it is well known that sedentary manual occupations without bodily effort, as tailoring, cobbling, light manufacturing, are those which produce most dreamers, religious and political fanatics; whereas severe bodily manual labour leaves the brain no force for thinking; for the body, like every machine, has only a certain stock of vital force at its disposal, and if this is converted into muscular energy, there remains nothing over for the play of the cerebral molecules for thinking. Any one can see this in his own case. No one will be able during a considerable leap to carry further a train of thought once set a-going, or simultaneously to run a race and to meditate profoundly; even in slow walking one involuntarily stops when thoughts are concentrated, and not seldom the outward man falls into complete rigidity in the profoundest meditation. All this points to a consumption of vital force in thinking, or what is the same thing, a chemical consumption of material, for this produces living force.

7. Every disturbance of the integrity of the brain produces a disturbance of conscious mental activity, unless the function of one hemisphere is carried on by the corresponding part of the other hemisphere; for as every human being chiefly sees, hears, and smells with one eye,

ear, and nostril, and after one side of the sense-organs has been rendered useless sense-perception still continues by means of the other side, so every human being chiefly thinks with one half of the brain, as often the physiognomy, especially the forehead, allows us to see; and likewise after one half of the brain has been rendered partially useless, the other half can undertake the whole function of thought, as one half of the lungs the whole function of breathing. This substitution is always with the brain the rarer case, and only occurs when, in the first place, the morbid or injured part does not impair the functions of the rest of the brain, which, however, mostly takes place in one way or another, *e.g.*, through propagation of pressure, and when, secondly, the injury is of such a kind that it entirely abolishes the functions of the particular part, and does not simply render them abnormal; for then there is developed just the disturbed mental activity, which renders valueless the results of the sound functions of the other parts. If now such disturbed functions of morbid parts all at once cease, or relieve the rest of the brain of the pressure which it has hitherto experienced, the normal function of the other part of the brain again appears as clear mental activity,—a case which not seldom takes place, especially in progressive destruction of morbid parts shortly before death, and then presents the phenomenon, surprising to the layman, of a last spiritual transfiguration after long mental aberration.

In the above-mentioned experiments of Flourens on fowls with extirpated brains, the animals remained as in deep sleep, sitting on any spot where they were placed; all capability of receiving sense-impressions was completely extinguished, and they had, therefore, to be supported by artificial feeding; on the other hand, the reflex movements proceeding from the spinal cord, *e.g.*, swallowing, flying, running, were preserved. "If one removes the two hemispheres of a mammal by slices, the mental activity sinks the lower the farther the loss of substance has proceeded.

When the ventricles of the brain are reached, complete unconsciousness is wont to occur" (Valentin). "What stronger proof of the necessary connection of mind and brain will any one require than that which is afforded by the knife of the anatomist when he cuts away the soul piece by piece?" (Büchner).

Inflammation of the brain causes delusion and madness; an effusion of blood on the brain, stupefaction and perfect loss of consciousness; a lasting pressure on the brain (*e.g.*, hydrocephalus, children's dropsy), weakness of understanding and idiocy; a surcharging, *e.g.*, in the drowning and the intoxicated, or evacuation of the blood-vessels of the brain, produces swoons and loss of consciousness; the quicker blood-circulation of a simple fever produces the delirium of fever, which indeed is also a temporary insanity; pressure of blood in intoxication by alcohol introduces the mental disturbance well known as the state of drunkenness; opium, haschisch, and other narcotics, severally another state of intoxication peculiar to it, each of which is identical with certain states of frenzy.

Parry was able to suppress attacks of madness by a compression of the cervical artery, and according to Flemming's experiments the same procedure produces in the healthy sleep and flitting dreams. Short-necked men and animals are, on the average, more sanguine than long-necked, because, in consequence of less remoteness from the heart, a more vivid blood-circulation takes place in their brain. The so-called after-diseases of the brain, in consequence of more serious injuries or even internal diseases, also many apoplexies, affect quite specially the memory, either destroy it entirely or weaken it in general, or abolish memory for certain categories of knowledge, *e.g.*, merely for language, without any paralysis of the organ of language, the understanding being otherwise clear (aphasia), or exclusively for all proper names, or the language of a particular country, or the events of certain years, or notions of time (especially with destruction or rendering inactive of particular parts of the brain). Many extremely striking examples of the foregoing, and of the recovery of the lost knowledge after easing the part of the brain in question, are to be read in Jessen's "Psychology."—Stronger proofs that memory depends on permanent changes of certain parts of the brain, which on certain stimulations contribute to the easier reproduction of former vibrations, can scarcely be desired, than that certain sets of ideas, with the becoming unserviceable of certain parts of the brain lose, and with their return to the normal state regain, the capability of re-emerging into consciousness.

The well-known experience that no class of diseases depends to so great an extent on transmission as that of mental diseases, points tolerably clearly by itself to the circumstance that all mental disturbances depend upon (direct or indirect) disturbances of brain function; for we can well conceive anomalies of the central organs of the nervous system to be inherited by way of material generation (just as tuberculosis, scrofula, cancer, and other diseases), but never immaterial psychical anomalies, of the possibility of which we can frame no conception at all (comp. vol. i. pp. 164, 165).

8. *There is no conscious mental activity outside or behind the cerebral function;* for if, in conformity with the foregoing, we may assume it proved that every disturbance of the normal functions of the brain disturbs the activity of consciousness, we may well assume it as certain that, with the complete abolition of the cerebral function, the activity of consciousness is likewise actually abolished, and not merely its manifestation prevented.

Were there not this progressive derangement of consciousness running parallel to the degree of disturbance of brain function, and passing quite gradually through all stages of idiocy into the loss of all consciousness (except that which manifests itself in the reflex instincts of the spinal cord), the supposition would, of course, be possible that a withdrawal of consciousness upon itself might take place, in which merely every *manifestation* of the same is suppressed; but, as the case stands, this possibility, to which one can only have recourse at all as a desperate attempt to save one's prepossessions in favour of a preconceived system, has too low a probability for it to deserve the notice of an unprejudiced inquirer. In addition to the parallelism above mentioned, and the circumstance that the entire apparatus of nature would be superfluous for the setting up of consciousness, if consciousness could exist without it, the want of memory tells against it; for if consciousness during the inactivity of the brain withdrew upon itself, yet a memory thereof should remain behind. Others think to evade this circumstance when they assume a double individual consciousness (thus also double personality [!] in everybody), namely, one free from the body and a brain-consciousness, whereby the former is to be unconscious for the latter. Whatever cogency there is in the argument for this double-sidedness of the mind refers entirely to the spiritual background of the brain-consciousness distinguished by us as the Unconcious, which certainly those who only know conscious mental activity must hold to be a second consciousness; what, however, is adduced expressly for the duality of *consciousness* is very unfortunately chosen. First of all, the consciousness of the magnetic sleep is claimed as non-embodied consciousness, which, however, is only differentiated from the consciousness of dreams in the ordinary sleep by this, that the communication with the external senses is somewhat less impeded, and the functioning part of the brain is found in a state of artificial hyperæsthesia (over-irritation, over-sensibility), which has for its consequence that, firstly, the influence of the Unconscious can more easily find an entrance into consciousness, and that, secondly, the amplitude of the cerebral vibrations with equal vividness of the presentation is less than at other times, and consequently leaves behind fewer impressions of memory, which in most ordinary dreams undoubtedly remain after the disappearance of the hyperæsthesia of the brain, but are too weak to return into conscious memory upon the usual stimuli.

Accordingly it is no wonder that the dream-consciousness can just as well include the memories of the waking state as its own, but not conversely. In general, the somnambulistic is so closely allied to the ordinary dream through the movements of sleep and the different stages of night-walking and spontaneous somnambulism, that it is quite impossible to see in it an unembodied consciousness. And then also one does not get far with the *consciousness* of these states; they are rather to be called a dreamy semi-consciousness than an enhanced consciousness. So the heightened mental performances which are sometimes observed, always only resembling brief flashes of light, are to be reckoned partly to the facilitated suggestion of the Unconscious, partly to cerebral hyperæsthesia, which has for consequence an easier revival of ideas, as then in such states memories from early times of apparently long-forgotten things make their appearance, which were so weak that in the normal state of the brain no stimuli of sufficient intensity to arouse them had made their appearance. Thus all is naturally explained by familiar laws, without that ambiguous hypothesis being anywhere useful.

A still more unfortunate instance for the disembodied consciousness is the already mentioned recurrence of consciousness which sometimes occurs before death. Here again, too, an inner hyperæsthesia of the brain co-operates with outward anæsthesia, which sometimes produces that transfiguration of the spirit which has its prophecies and sharpness of memory in common with the somnambulistic state, its joyful rest and calm painless cheerfulness in common with the same nervous state (analgesia) in the highest degree of torture and certain narcotic intoxications. The external anæsthesia is there only the natural counterpoise to the inner hyperæsthesia; we find the same likewise in the ecstasy of mystic ascetics, in somnambulists, after slight administrations of chloroform, and many other narcotics, *e.g.*, haschisch; also in several states of frenzy it is sometimes exhibited. Thus this feeling of freedom from the body by no means proves a diminution, but rather a heightening of the irritability of the brain, and anything but the disembodiment of consciousness. States entirely similar induce similar phenomena just before drowning. Lastly, if the criterion of the disembodied consciousness is maintained to be the abolition of time in the sequence of thought, this would be equivalent to the intuitive, timeless, momentary, implicit thinking, which contradicts all discursive consciousness, as a something requiring the comparing of explicit ideas. But in the examples only the *more rapid* course of thought is specified, as it occurs in states of the highest cerebral irritation, in narcotic poisonings, before drowning, and the like, and has always been familiar as "flight of ideas" in certain forms of frenzy. What wonder that in an over-stimulated brain the ideas follow one another much more rapidly than usual? Altogether, so long as the ideas follow one another *in time*, they prove the action of matter, through the vibrations of which time first comes into thought; so far, however, as thought is disembodied, it is timeless, and therewith unconscious.

What we have proved in this chapter of the human consciousness, as the highest known to us, in which one might soonest suppose an independence from the body, holds of course also of the ganglia of the lower animals, which are the equivalents of the brain of the Vertebrata; and it holds just as much of the special consciousness of every independent ganglion in man and the higher and lower animals; and it holds, finally, also of the substances which, in the lower animals, form the central nervous system; and likewise, if a consciousness should be made out in the plants or inorganic substances, it holds also for this.

As conclusion to this chapter, a passage of Schelling

may find a fitting place (Werke, i. 3, 497), which sums up the contents of the same in a few words, although the assertion in Schelling's mouth has a somewhat different turn owing to the background of transcendental idealism: "Not the presentation *itself*, but rather the *consciousness* thereof is conditioned by the affection of the organism; and if empirism limits its assertion to the latter, nothing can be alleged against it."

III.

THE ORIGIN OF CONSCIOUSNESS.

1. *The Becoming-Conscious of the Idea.*—Consciousness is not a quiescent state, but a process—a continual becoming-conscious. That this mental process, to which consciousness owes its origin, cannot be immediately apprehended by the consciousness of the observer, is a matter of course; for that which first produces consciousness must of course lie behind consciousness, and be inaccessible to conscious introspection. We can thus only hope to attain to our goal by an indirect path.

The first condition is that we define the notion of consciousness more sharply than was hitherto necessary.—In the first place, it must be distinguished from self-consciousness. My self-consciousness is the consciousness of myself, *i.e.*, the consciousness of the subject of my mental activity. By subject of my mental activity, however, I understand that part of the whole cause of my mental activity which is not external, and accordingly the inner cause of the same. Self-consciousness is thus only a special case of the application of consciousness to a definite object, namely, to the supposed inner cause of mental activity which is denoted by the name Subject. It is not the active subject *itself* which becomes in the act of self-consciousness the content of consciousness or object of consciousness, but it is only the *idea* of the subject, regressively inferred by means of the category of causality from the activity of the subject, that becomes the object of consciousness. The active subject itself remains just as inaccessible to consciousness as the external thing in itself, to which it corresponds as internal thing. All belief in an *immediate* self-apprehension of the Ego in the act of self-consciousness depends on the same self-delusion as the naive realistic belief in the immediate conscious apprehension of the thing in itself that exists independently of consciousness. Consciousness as such is, consequently, according to its own notion, free from conscious reference to the subject, in that in and for itself it refers only to the *object* (*i.e.*, not to the external correlate of the object of ideation or the thing in itself, but merely to the represented object which results from the ideational process, and presents itself as content of consciousness), and only becomes self-consciousness by the *idea of the subject* becoming accidentally *object* to it. It follows from this that no self-consciousness can be conceived without consciousness, but undoubtedly consciousness without self-consciousness. Only for conscious reflection as it takes place in the brain of the philosopher, who stands in thought outside the process and objectively regards it, but not for the subject of the process itself, must object and subject be simultaneously given, and in the same degree. For it lies in the conceptions themselves that subject and object require each other as correlatives; but this correlation is patent only to the consciousness of the philosopher, not to the unreflecting feeling of the natural man, and therefore to the latter in the intuitive apprehension of the concrete object the relation of the concept of the object to the concept of the subject, and especially the latter remains unconscious. (See more particularly below, pp. 56–58.) — Still less than with self-consciousness has consciousness to do with the notion of *personality*, or the identity of all the subjects of very different mental activities—a notion which is for the most part comprehended in the word self-consciousness, a practice which we shall also in future follow for the sake of simplicity.

But now, what is consciousness? Does it merely consist in the form of sensibility, so that the two conceptions are identical? No; for the Unconscious also must have conceived the form of sensibility, otherwise it could not so aptly have furnished the same. We could, however, also conceive a consciousness as possible with quite other forms, if a world were otherwise fashioned, or if, besides and beyond our space-time world, yet other worlds exist in other forms of being and consciousness, which contains no inherent contradiction, since these worlds, however numerous, could not at all disturb or affect one another, and the One Unconscious, free of all these forms, would be the same for all. The form of sensibility can thus only be regarded as something added to consciousness, accidental, not as something necessary, essential.—Or shall we say that consciousness consists in memory? Memory is certainly no bad criterion of consciousness, for the more vivid consciousness is, the stronger must the cerebral vibrations be, and the stronger these are, the stronger must be the permanent impression they leave behind in the brain, *i.e.*, the easier, and with equal stimulus the stronger, memory becomes. One easily overlooks, however, the circumstance that memory is only an indirect consequence of the essence of consciousness; it cannot possibly, therefore, form its essence itself. Just as little can the nature of consciousness consist in the possibility of the comparison of ideas, for this again is only a consequence of the form of sensibility, especially of time; and, moreover, consciousness may be present in the greatest intensity if only a single idea fill the mind without any object of comparison.

According to all this, we have only one certain support which must guide us on the right way, namely, the result of the preceding chapter—the cerebral vibrations, more generally material movement, as *conditio sine qua non* of consciousness. Also, if we posit as many worlds as we please with other forms than space and time, yet, if the parallelism of being and thought is to be retained, something must exist in them corresponding to matter, and an activity of the same answering to motion must then likewise be condition of consciousness.—Accordingly, if we suppose the essence of consciousness to be founded in its material origin, and at the same time remember that the unconscious mental activity must of necessity be looked upon as something immaterial, on closer consideration two cases present themselves: *either* we adhere to "Will and Idea" as that which is common to unconscious and conscious representation, and posit the form of the Unconscious as the original, but that of consciousness as a product of the unconscious mind and the material action on the same; *or* we divide the whole system of mental activity between Materialism and Spiritualism in such a way that the conscious spirit belongs to the former, the unconscious to the latter, *i.e.*, we assume that the unconscious mind indeed has a self-dependent existence independent of matter, but that the conscious mind is an exclusive product of material processes without any co-operation of unconscious mind. The alternative, after our previous inquiries on the co-operation of the Unconscious in the genesis of all and every conscious mental process, is not difficult to decide. The essential similarity of conscious and unconscious mental action alone causes a fundamentally different origin for both to appear unthinkable; at least, this cutting up of the spiritual system and the distribution of its separate parts to different fundamental conceptions would appear more arbitrary than that of Schopenhauer in respect to Will and Intellect. Add to this, that we shall, in Chapter v., resolve matter itself into Will and Idea, and thus prove the *essential likeness of Mind and Matter;* that thus Materialism could offer us no final resting-place. We must, therefore, make our own the former of the two assumptions.

But now it is at once evident that we again have not yet grasped the essence of consciousness, for we only know its factors—on the one side, mind in its original unconscious state; on the other side, the movement of the matter which acts upon it. In any case, the origin of consciousness can only be given in the *mode and manner in which* ideation comes to its object. Of matter consciousness knows nothing; thus the process producing consciousness must lie in the mind itself, if also matter gives the first impulse to it. Material movement determines the content of representation, but the nature of consciousness does not lie in this *content*, for the same content can indeed, the form of sensibility being abstracted, be also conceived as unconscious. But now, if consciousness can lie neither in the content, nor also, as we have seen before, in the sensuous form of the idea, it *cannot at all lie in the idea* as such, but must be an accident, which comes to the idea from elsewhere.

This is the first important result of our investigation, which certainly, at the first glance, may seem to conflict with the ordinary views, but on closer inspection must soon display its correctness to every observer, and shall immediately receive fuller elucidation. The common error is therefore to be ascribed to this, that we, for the most part, think of consciousness as something inhering *only* in the Idea, in that we forget the apperception of Pleasure and Pain; hence it is taken, without investigation, on trust and credit, as something immanent in the idea, especially as long as the unconscious idea is not more precisely known; and accordingly the question is never raised, To what then does the idea owe the accident of consciousness? who assigns it this predicate, as it were? when one would soon observe that it cannot itself give it to itself. But if the consciousness-producing process, in spite of its material occasion, must necessarily be of a spiritual nature, there remains nothing but the Will.

We have seen in Chapter i. of the present section how Will and Idea are united in the Unconscious in an inseparable unity, and shall further see in the final chapters how the salvation of the world depends on the emancipation of the intellect from the will, the possibility of which is given in consciousness, and how the whole world-process is tending solely towards this goal. Consciousness on the one hand, and the *emancipation of the idea from the will* on the other, we have thus already recognised as standing in the closest connection; we only need to go one step further and to declare their identity, and we have found the answer to the riddle in harmony with the results just obtained. The essence of the consciousness of the idea is the extrication of the same from its native soil, the realising will,[1] and the opposition of the will to this emancipation. We had previously found that consciousness must be a predicate which the will imparts to the idea; we can now also assign the content of this predicate; it is the stupefaction of the will at the *existence* of the idea *not willed and yet sensibly felt by it.* The idea, namely, as we have seen, has in itself no interest in its own existence, no endeavour after being; therefore, as long as there is no consciousness, it is always only called forth by the will. Thus the mind before the rise of consciousness can have according to its own nature no other ideas than those which, called into being by the will, form the content of the will. Then organised matter suddenly breaks in upon this self-contained peace of the Unconscious, and in the reaction of sensation occurring according to necessary law thrusts upon the aston-

---

[1] This emancipation must not, however, be understood as if the conscious idea hovered, as it were, in the pure ether of the ideal out of all relation to the will. This is already sufficiently refuted by the previous expositions of the present book, and will be directly still more evident, if it turns out that the predication of consciousness issuing from the will itself is, at the same time, non-satisfaction of the will, *i.e.*, feeling of pain; that the conscious idea consists of sensuous elementary sensations, and every such sensuous elementary sensation is, at the same time, non-satisfaction of a definite volition. This only is meant by the emancipation of the idea from the will, that the conscious idea, unlike the unconscious idea, alone possible as content of a will realising it (comp. above, p. 58), can and does exist without its being directly evoked by a will which possesses it as a content to be realised; that it is idea pre-eminently free from every effort at self-realisation, but without prejudice to all other possible relations to the will, nay, even without prejudice to the possibility of *afterwards* becoming itself again content of will.

ished individual spirit an idea which falls upon it as from the skies, for it finds in itself no will to this idea. For the first time "the matter of intuition is given to it from without." The great revolution has come to pass, the first step to the world's redemption taken; the idea has been rent from the will, to confront it in future as an independent power, in order to bring under subjection to itself its former lord. This amazement of the will at the rebellion against its previously acknowledged sway, this sensation which the interloping idea produces in the Unconscious, this *is Consciousness*.

To speak less figuratively, I conceive the process in the following way:—There arises the idea impregnated from without. The unconscious individual mind is amazed at the unwonted circumstance that an idea exists without being willed. This amazement cannot proceed from the will alone, for the will is indeed the absolutely irrational, thus also too blind for wonderment and surprise; but it can also not proceed from the representation alone, for the idea impregnated from without is as it is, and has no reason to be surprised at itself; all the rest of the ideal sphere, however, except this one, is, as we know, fast bound in the Unconscious in inseparable unity with the will. Consequently, in the first place, the startling can only be effected by both sides of the unconscious will and idea in union, *i.e.*, by an in-formed will, or a willed idea; and secondly, that which in the startling is idea can only exist through a will whose content it forms. Accordingly, the matter is only to be conceived in this way, that the idea impregnated from without acts on the will as *motive*, and, moreover, evokes *such* a will as has for its *content* to *negate* it; for should the now excited will be related affirmatively to it, there would again be *no opposition* and no consciousness. The excited will must thus be related negatively to it, and the startling is the moment of origin of this negating will, the sudden, momentary occurrence of the opposition of the will. But the word "startle" also signifies nothing further in ordinary language, only that the process in our human experience is an opposition suddenly occurring between *conscious* moments, but here takes place between *unconscious* moments.

Lastly, it should be mentioned that the opposing will is *too weak*, with respect to the idea impregnated from without, to carry through its negating intention; it is thus an impotent will to which satisfaction is refused, which, consequently, is linked with pain. Thus every process of the becoming conscious is, *eo ipso*, united with a certain displeasure. This is, as it were, the vexation of the unconscious individual mind at the interloping idea which it must endure and cannot get rid of. It is the bitter medicine without which there is no healing—a medicine, to be sure, which at every moment is swallowed in such very small doses that its bitterness escapes self-perception.—

The peculiar difficulty of this exposition appears to be, how it is possible that matter in the form of the vibrating molecule should be able to plunge into the peace of the unconscious will itself, and that, too, in the double sense; how it has power, as *matter*, to affect the *mind*; and how the mind is at all able to enter into communication with *anything* external? This difficulty thus essentially concerns the old problem of the reciprocal influence of body and mind, which we are here neither able to evade, like Kant and Fichte, by converting the body into a subjective appearance of the mind, nor, as Materialism, by converting the mind into an external appearance resulting from objective material processes, but which we must boldly face, since the (unconscious) mind and matter both pass for real. Already, at the beginning of A. Chap. vii., this problem met us in reference to the medium whereby the will realises itself in the body, especially in the muscular movements; here it is the reverse of the question at which we have arrived, namely, how the mental idea can be conditioned by the organism. There the question reduced itself to this: how the will can influence the movements of the central nerve-molecule, here to this, how the movements of the central nerve-molecule can influence the idea? There we were obliged to assume the realisation of the unconscious *will* to be effected by an unconscious one (A. Chap. ii.); here we must contemplate the origin of the conscious *idea* as brought about by unconscious mental reactions. There the (unconscious) will, directly influencing the molecule, was to be conceived united with unconscious *representation;* here we must suppose, for the sake of coming to pass of the sensation, an unconscious *will* conceived as essential factor. The *direct* reciprocation thus in both cases exists between the forms of movement of central nerve-molecules on the one hand, and *unconscious* mental functions on the other, in which, as we quite generally know from A. Chap. iv., an union of unconscious will and unconscious idea always takes place.

If, now, matter and unconscious mind were really heterogeneous departments of existence, as the dualistic view prevailing since Descartes in the consciousness of European culture assumes, it would in fact not be apparent how the *influxus physicus* presupposed in these processes could be possible. Fortunately, however, it will turn out in C. Chap. v. that matter itself is in its essence nothing else whatever but unconscious mind, whose representations are only limited to spatial attraction and repulsion of uniformly varying intensity, and whose volitional manifestations consist in the realising of this limited ideational province. If we at this place anticipate this identity of being subsequently to be demonstrated, it is immediately comprehensible that the reciprocal action of body and soul can no longer, as before, be frustrated by the incapability of bridging the gulf between heterogeneous substances. The psychical will can just as well include in itself in the ideas, which form its content, spatial relations and change of existing spatial relations, as can the atomic will of a cerebral atom. Both can accordingly just as easily collide with one another and conclude their collision by a compromise as two opposing atomic wills. In both cases the weaker will must in the compromise yield the more the weaker it is than its opponent. When, *e.g.*, there exists the will to a special bodily movement, it will, for the most part, considerably surpass in intensity the single cerebral atomic wills, which would *per se* follow only their own mechanical laws, and therefore usually sufficiently carry its point. When, on the other hand, such a special will is not aroused and concentrated, there the cerebral atomic wills excited by the propagated stimulus of the sense-organs produce a relatively considerable effect on the psychical will directed to the organism, *i.e.*, in the compromise resulting from this conflict of will it will now also, on its part, have a relatively considerable share in concession and accommodation, only that this share, on its side, is not, as on the side of matter, presented spatially as objective phenomenon (which merely arises from the difference to be hereafter mentioned in C. Chap. xi., that the directions of the will in the atomic wills exclusively intersect at a single point when prolonged backwards, and thereby produce the appearance of a localisation of the seat of force).

As *matter, as objective real phenomenon* (*i.e.*, independent of every intelligence intuiting it), could not at all come to be without two or more atomic wills intersecting and falling into conflict with one another in their volitional manifestations, so also the primitive conscious representation of *sensation as subjective ideal phenomenon* only becomes possible through precisely the same conflict. An atomic will existing isolated and alone in the world would have no objective existence at all, because the possibility would be wanting to it of self-objectivation, *i.e.*, of bringing its essence to external manifestation. An isolated and sole-existing incorporeal individual mind (assumed *per impossibile*) would, even if it should display ever so much unconscious will and idea, yet never attain to the subjective manifestation of consciousness. An *ad libitum* number of atomic wills and of individual minds, which were, however, isolated from one another, and incapable of thrusting against one another and clashing with their wills, would be altogether in the same position as one existing solitary and alone. Only when the radiating will meets with a resistance by which it is checked or broken can it lead to objective manifestation of *existence*, to the subjective phenomenon of *consciousness.* Such a resistance it can, however, only find in its like, in another will with which it has a certain *common* sphere of action, whilst the tendency and goal of the latter is, in a certain sense, *opposed* to its own. The common sphere of action makes *contact* possible; the opposite tendency and goal condition the *collision* in encounter, which finds its *solution* in the *compromise* determined by the content of both. The yielding of each of the colliding wills is now, however, no longer willed by it, but forced, pressed upon it by the other will, which is for it mainly only resistance, and the compromise as result does not correspond to the goal of volition on either side, so that a contrast between the willed and attained arises, just as between the centrifugal function, as it were, of the volition itself and the centripetal rebound on collision. Now, the breaking of the will on the resistance of a foreign will crossing it, or the centripetal rebound, is *sensation*, and, moreover, as non-satisfaction of the will, *pain*-sensation. As non-satisfaction of a definite will, *i.e.*, one filled with a definite ideational content, sensation is also *qualitatively determined*, *i.e.*, sensation characterised by a (here unconscious) ideational content. (Comp. B. Chap. iii.) As qualitatively definite sensation, however, it is *element of the conscious idea*, and in so far it may even be described as *elementary* conscious representation. The predicate of consciousness enters into the sensation just through the exhibited contrast, and this contradiction between volition and impression of the resistance answers to what I have above named by an expression transferred from the conscious mental life to the unconscious, the *startling* of the will at the *intruding* idea not willed by itself. Perhaps the more general mode of treatment here entered upon may contribute to the comprehension of the matter, and allow it to be more clearly perceived that the figures there employed were, in fact, only employed as figures.

The difficulty which occasioned this digression is, however, not yet exhausted by the foregoing. In spite of the admitted essential identity of mind and matter, the second question always remains open—how the psychical individual will can at all come in contact with any other will than, in fact, with the atomic will of the brain, since, *e.g.*, it is indeed not able decidedly to touch and to collide with other psychical individual wills? We must here, too, anticipate and acknowledge the future course of the inquiry—that the possibility of such a contact and collision would not be visible if the individual mind on the one hand and the atoms of matter on the other were discrete substances. It only becomes comprehensible on the assumption that they are merely different functions of one and the same essence, and, moreover, of an unconscious essence; for were it conscious, there would be the common consciousness in all functions, and through the conflict anticipated by the common consciousness, and brought to conclusion in it, as it were, it could no more attain to special consciousness, whereas in the root of one unconscious essence the separated functions have just only the necessary common bond for reciprocal influence, but yet still room enough for the establishment of separated consciousnesses, as it were, on their broken points or jolted peripheral endings. Now it is true a reciprocal influence in general is made possible through the common metaphysical root of the substance, but the latter does not of itself suffice to introduce this coincidence of certain functions at their separated peripheral ends. For that there is also necessary, as a second condition, that the ideational contents of these wills should contain in themselves the common sphere of their contact, just as well as the opposite tendency; and this second condition is simply not fulfilled between the different individual minds, but doubtless between the atomic wills, which, in their ideal content, contain also the spatiality of their relations (creating in its realisation the one objective space). This is the metaphysical reason why minds only communicate through their bodies. The bodies move and act in the one objective space as in their common sphere in which they may collide; minds, however, have neither a direct relation to this general space of matter (for the subjective consciousness-space is, for every mind, a different one, unapproachably self-enclosed), nor do they possess another analogous sphere of direct spiritual encounter, as the bodies (or rather their atoms) possess them in space.

The conditions of a mutual sphere for the contact of different wills are, however, also given between the mind and the body connected with it. In C. Chap. ix., namely, we shall see that the individual mind or the soul of a body is nothing more than the sum of the functions of the All-one Unconscious directed to this corporeal organism. This organism, *i.e.*, this then and there ordered aggregate of atoms, is thus the goal expressly included in the unconscious ideal content of the total will-functions of this individual mind. There cannot be in this individual mind a single function which does not unconsciously refer to this organism, and which does not include even quite definite parts of this organism or quite definite spatial changes of position of such parts in its ideal content (say, *e.g.*, the excitation of certain cerebral vibrations of a metaphysical thought). Each individual mind accordingly possesses the possibility of colliding with the atomic wills of its organism, but only with those of its own, not with those of any other, because its organism alone is included, conformably to its spatial relations, in the (unconscious) content of representation of its functions, but not any other. Every function of the All-one Unconscious, namely, which is related to another organism, truly belongs to the sum of the functions directed to this other organism, *i.e.*, to *its* soul or individual mind.[1]—We hardly need remind the reader that the possibility of a collision of wills for both kinds of reciprocation between body and mind holds good not merely for that where the mind is the preponderating *determining* part of the compromise, but also where it is the prevailingly yielding or *receptive* part, *i.e.*, not merely for the influence of the will on the body, but also for the arousing of ideas by means of impressions of sense and brain. If the function of the individual mind rightly affects the atomic wills of the brain, conversely also, as a matter of course, must the atomic wills of the brain just as correctly affect this same individual mind.

Through these elucidations, in part forestalling the contents of subsequent chapters, our exposition of the origin of consciousness may have received illumination, and this may serve as an excuse for the digression from the regular course of the inquiry. Hints, intelligible to a certain degree, of such an origin of consciousness from an opposition of different moments in the Unconscious, I have only found in Jacob Böhme and Schelling. The former says (of the divine contemplation, c. i. 8): "Nothing can become manifest to itself without repugnance; for if it has nothing to oppose it, it is ever going out of itself, and does not return to itself; but as it does not return to itself, as to that whence it originally proceeded, it knows nothing of its primitive state." —— Similarly Schelling says (Werke, i. 3, p. 576): "If, however, the Absolute is to appear to itself, it must on its objective side be dependent on something else, on something foreign. But this dependence does *not* belong to the *Absolute itself*, but merely to its *appearance*." ——

The contrast between Will and Idea is still more height-

---

[1] Through this consequence of the doctrine of the Unconscious, Spinoza's proposition, that the soul is the idea or representation of the body, receives for the first time a comprehensible signification.

ened by the idea not being directly given through material movement, but only through the *uniform reaction of the unconscious psychical on this action.* It accordingly follows, that the unconscious individual mind must answer with an *activity* (of sensation) which is, as it were, peripherally *thrust* upon it through the impression produced on its volition by a foreign manifestation of will. In this manner chiefly arise the simple qualities of sense-impressions, as sound, colour, taste, &c., from whose mutual relations all sensuous perception is built up, from which again, by reproduction of the cerebral vibrations, memories, and by partial dropping out of the content of the latter abstract conceptions arise. In all cases of conscious thought we have to do with *cerebral vibrations,* which affect the individual mind and compel to uniform reaction; in all cases the *sensible qualities* are the results of this reaction, and of these elements the total conscious presented world is composed. If, now, these *elements* always excite the process which produces consciousness, and thereby become conscious, it will not surprise us that also the *combinations* of these elements takes part in consciousness, although the *kind of combination* is often produced by the will itself.

Hereby the apparent contradiction is explained that ideas which are evoked by the will, consequently not opposed to this will, may yet become conscious because they just consist of elements which have become ideas through extorted reactions of the Unconscious. The will, namely, can only evoke a conscious idea through the particular memory being aroused, *i.e.,* by former cerebral vibrations being reproduced. Before the conscious idea is there, it must be contained as content in the unconscious will, certainly in non-sensuous form, otherwise the will indeed would not be able to excite *this* idea. Further, as means to this end, the point of attack in the brain must be unconsciously represented, whence the particular vibrations of memory may be excited and the stimulation of the same be willed. Further, however, even the unconscious will does not go, for it can only produce the idea in the sensuous form as reaction on these vibrations; now occur the vibrations and the reaction of the Unconscious happens, compelled, as ever, by a lawful reaction, and therewith the consciousness of the representation is also given. The like holds good also of the co-operation of the Unconscious in the coming to pass of sensuous perception, as before taken note of. It also holds good when the conscious representation becomes content of a will, which is then termed conscious will; for the conscious representation must previously be present in conscious form before the will can grasp it in this form and make it its content. But if the idea once possesses the conscious form, it does not lose the same again, on account of the will combining with it, because its elements, which, as long as it exists, must reproduce themselves ever and ever anew, always do this in conscious form.

2. *The Becoming Conscious of Pain and Pleasure.*—If we have always hitherto spoken of the becoming conscious of the *Idea*, it was not thereby meant that the idea is the sole object of consciousness. The exclusive reason for this limitation was rather the endeavour not to make more difficult the penetration into this difficult province by prematurely increasing the objects and complexity of the points of view. This is the sole reason why we have, instead of speaking of the general "object of the becoming conscious," treated the problem from its especially characteristic side. But now, if the principle thus gained of the origin of consciousness is to be held correct, it must be adapted to every possible content of the becoming conscious. There must be logically deducible from it what elements can enter into consciousness, what not, in that they are brought one after another within the formula. This we will now do with Pain, Pleasure, and Will, which remain along with the Idea as possible objects of consciousness. What we thus *a priori* derive as consequences of

our principle must prove to be correct *a posteriori* in the face of experience. In this *a posteriori* confirmation we have, then, the controlling test of the principle that everything which experience offers us as a something to be explained also actually flows from it, whilst we gained the principle itself originally *a priori* by elimination of the incorrect assumptions from all possible ones, when finally only one remained to us.

If, after the principle is thus justified *a priori* and *a posteriori*, it may possibly be desired that I should show *how and in what way* there results from the process indicated just that which we know in inner experience as consciousness, this demand would be just as improper as one made upon the physicist to show *how* from the aerial waves and the arrangement of our ear that results which in inner experience we know as sound. The physicist only shows us, and can only show, *that* that which is subjectively felt as sound consists, objectively regarded, in a process which is compounded of such and such vibrations. In the same way I can only show *that* that which we know in subjective apprehension as consciousness, objectively regarded is a process, which is built up in such and such a way out of such and such terms and factors. To experience more I hold to be impossible, and therefore to ask for more improper; for in order to understand the How of the transmutation of the objective process into subjective sensation, one would be obliged to adopt a third point of view, which is neither subjective nor objective, or, what is the same thing, is both at once. This standpoint, however, the Unconscious alone possesses, whereas consciousness is just the division into subject and object.

Feeling can be pleasure or pain, satisfaction or non-satisfaction of the will; all else, as shown in B. Chap. iii., are more precise determinations, which belong to the department of ideation. The non-satisfaction of the will must always become conscious, for the will can never will its own non-satisfaction; consequently non-satisfaction must be thrust on it from without; consequently the condition of the origin of consciousness is fulfilled in the startling of the will at something *not issuing from itself*, and yet really existing and making itself felt, the partial compulsion to yield on the collision with another will, and the contrast of this rebound with the goal striven after; and experience corresponds to it entirely, in that nothing speaks more emphatically to consciousness than pain— pain conceived also as freed from the nearer determinations belonging to the idea.

The feeling of *pleasure* or the satisfaction of the will cannot be conscious in and for itself, for while the will realises its content, and thereby brings on its own satisfaction, nothing takes place which could come into opposition with the will; and since all compulsion from without is wanting, and the will only gives place to its own consequences, it can arrive at no consciousness. Otherwise does the matter appear when a consciousness has already established itself, which collects and *compares* observations and *experiences*. This soon learns from the many non-satisfactions to know the resistances which oppose every will in the external world, as well as the *external conditions* which are necessary if the realisation of the will is to *succeed*. As soon as it is compelled to acknowledge these external conditions of success, and therewith satisfaction as something partially or wholly conditioned from without, consciousness appertains to pleasure also.—All this is thoroughly confirmed by experience.

One sees especially in infants that they give very expressive signs of pain for weeks before the slightest trace of pleasure is legible in their countenances and gestures. Clear confirmation is afforded by the case of pampered children, who are wont always to get their way, and who accordingly do not know what to make of it when for once their wish is not complied with. These children have, in fact, as good as no enjoyment at all from the satisfaction of their desires; however, the latter remain, for the most part, unconscious. About the only enjoyment they have is from satisfaction of the senses (eating of sweetmeats), because the solicitude of the environment cannot here save them disagreeable comparisons. How much, however, our assertion fits even the case of adults, doubtless every observer of his race will admit; for any kind of satisfaction which permanently recurs without interruption by non-satisfaction ceases to be a conscious satisfaction, *i.e.*, a conscious enjoyment, as soon as one begins to think: it must be so indeed, and cannot be at all otherwise. On the other hand, even a slight satisfaction enters into consciousness as pleasure, the more vividly the more distinctly it is seen that we owe it to external circumstances, because, in spite of its being always willed, one has rarely been able to procure it.

3. *The Unconsciousness of the Will.*—Now as concerns the *Will* itself, we have hitherto called it conscious when it has a conscious, unconscious, when it has an unconscious idea for its content. It is, however, easy to see that this is only a figurative expression, since it only refers to the content of the will; but the will itself can *never* become conscious, because it can never contradict itself. There may very well be several desires at variance with one another, but volition at any moment is in truth only the resultant of *all* the simultaneous desires, consequently can always be only conformable to itself. If now consciousness is an accident which the will bestows upon that of which it is compelled to recognise not itself, but something foreign as its cause, in short, what enters into opposition with it, the will can never impart consciousness to itself, because here the thing to be compared and the standard of comparison are one and the same; they can never be different or at all at variance with one another. The will also never gets so far as to recognise something else as its cause; rather the appearance of its spontaneity is indestructible, since it is the primal actuality, and all that lies behind it potential, that is, unreal. Whilst dis-

pleasure, then, *must always* become conscious, and pleasure *can* become so under certain circumstances, the will is said *never* to be able to become conscious. This latter result perhaps appears unexpected, yet experience fully confirms it.

We have seen in A. Chap. vii. that only a conscious idea is able to excite the unconscious will to any movement or action, even without a motive proper being contained in the idea. But if the idea contains a motive at all, a proper ground of excitement, the excitation of the unconscious desire must certainly follow. If, now, the man has the conscious idea of a movement, and thereupon sees himself execute this movement with the certainty of not being necessitated from outside, he instinctively concludes that the cause of the movement lies in himself, and this inner unknown cause of movement he calls will. That the conception thus attained only rests on causality just as little detracts from the instinctive apprehension of its reality, as it detracts from that of the external objects, that we possess them only as *unknown external causes* of our sense-impressions, and as it detracts from the subject of ideation or the intellectual ego that we know it only as *unknown internal cause* of ideation. The one as the other we fancy we directly apprehend because we do not attain it by conscious reflection, but through unconscious processes, and philosophic contemplation must first teach us that all these notions are for us intangible essences, whose only hold on our thought lies in their causality, without this knowledge being detrimental to the immediate instinctive certainty of their direct possession. In the same way a writer thinks he has the feeling directly in the point of the pen itself, whilst the simplest consideration teaches him that he has it only in his fingers, and unconsciously applies the principle of causality without being able to avoid the unconscious illusion of his tactile sense, only that here the correction succeeds much sooner than in those deeply rooted psychological illusions.

When a man has once in the way indicated grasped the conception of will (albeit by a process of unconscious thinking), he very soon observes that ordinary ideas rarely draw after them phenomena of motion, but always such as contain the feeling of a pleasure or displeasure, and that, too, according as actions are persistent and in themselves attractive, or repellent. From this he becomes acquainted empirically with the law of motivation, according to which each representation of pleasure excites positive desire, each idea of displeasure negative or repellent desire. This law is exceptionless, and all instances to the contrary rest on an error; *e.g.*, when a past enjoyment is represented, and yet not again desired or wished over again, it follows from that that it would now no more be enjoyment. If other opposed desires, which simultaneously arise, suppress the emergence of this desire, so much force is consumed in the suppression as the desire would have had had it arisen. When, now, the man has perceived this law of motivation to be exceptionless, he knows that every time a desire is united with the representation of a feeling of pleasure or displeasure, and supposing other desires or external circumstances not to hinder the execution of the corresponding movement, he sees the latter ensue. This process, again, goes on unconsciously, and whereas the man before only possessed the notion of volition as cause of an effect, he has it now as effect of a cause. With that, however, he has the possibility of perceiving it also then in himself, if its effect, the execution, is prevented by other desires or external circumstances.

Further, the man sees a gradual proportion between the sensuous vividness of the presentation and the magnitude of the presented pleasure and displeasure, on the one hand, and the violence of the movements, the energy of the action, the duration of the attempts at action, on the other, and concludes therefrom that also the link intermediate between the two ends of the causal chain must stand in a proportional relation to each of them; hereby he obtains a measure of the *intensity* of the will.—The points mentioned would certainly suffice for mediate knowledge and the appearance of a direct cognition of the will; however, they are still somewhat of an external nature, and the illusion becomes still much greater through other accompanying circumstances. It is, namely, only in the very rarest cases that the desire can obtain satisfaction at the very moment of its arising; there always elapses a shorter or longer time before realisation takes place, and so long lasts a *feeling of non-satisfaction, of unpleasant expectation and deprivation* (tension, impatience, longing, yearning), certainly for the most part *sweetened by hope*, which either is prolonged until the gradual disappearance of the desire, or induces by a perception of impossibility and destruction of hope the full non-satisfaction and displeasure (with an undiminished persisting violent desire despair), or finally passes into satisfaction and pleasure. These feelings are the constant attendants or successors of desire, and can only arise through it. They also enter into consciousness, and are here the proper and most immediate representatives of the desire, which it is true one can again only properly apprehend as cause of the same, but which one thinks to grasp immediately through the above-mentioned illusion. Just as desire in general is perceived in the feelings spoken of, so every special kind of desire is perceived through the special and peculiar kind of the feelings accompanying it. The constant connection of the two hereby becomes visible, that the special kind of desire is indeed already determined for consciousness by the kind of motive and the kind of ensuing actions. Yet the possibility of error still remains open, especially in the cases where the accompanying feelings (longing and hope in general) are the *sole* signs of the presence of the will. Then the mistake easily occurs of seeking the desire giving rise to these feelings in other well-known desires, whereas the same are entirely guiltless thereof.

This case, for example, occurs in the instincts, most

distinctly in love, where the willing of the metaphysical end is unknown to the lover, who, on this account, erroneously lays the extravagant longing and hope merely to the account of the willed means (intercourse with this particular individual), and accordingly imagines a quite special enjoyment in intercourse with such individual, and is then so disagreeably smitten with disillusion. This is not contradicted by the fact that there may notwithstanding be consummate bliss, because the unconscious clairvoyance of the metaphysical goal begets an extravagant longing, which again awakens an extravagant hope of an extravagant enjoyment, whose essence, however, consciousness is unable to express, and which is never realised. Here, too, the saying holds: "Hope was thy allotted portion."

Those concomitant feelings of desires are generally of a highly peculiar and characteristic nature, conditioned at the same time, for the most part, by bodily feelings which are reflectorially called forth in adjoining parts of the body by the respective cerebral affections. Think of anger and its rush of blood; of fear and terror, with their arrest of the circulation, difficulty of breathing, and trembling; the suppressed sob, vexation, and grief, with their life-corroding influences; impotent rage, with its choking and bursting sensations; affection, with its tears and its relaxed breast and stomach; longing, with its consuming woe; sensuous love, with its gushing glow; vanity, with its heart-leapings; effort at thought and strained reflection or considering, with its peculiar reflex feelings of tension at different parts of the scalp, according to the part of the brain subjected to strain; defiance, inflexible obstinacy, and fixed resolution, with their peculiar muscular contractions; disgust, with its anti-peristaltic movements of the fauces and stomach, &c., &c.

How much the character of these feelings is dependent on such bodily admixtures will be easily granted by every one. How much it is simultaneously conditioned by accompanying unconscious representation has been discussed at the end of Chap. iii. B.—If, now, the man thinks to apprehend the will directly in consciousness in three ways (1) from its cause, the motive; (2) from its accompanying and succeeding feelings; and (3) from its effect, the act; and all the time (4) has the content or object of the will as representation actually in consciousness,—it is no wonder that the illusion of being immediately conscious of the will itself is very tenacious and firmly fixed by long habit, so that it allows the scientific view of the eternal unconsciousness of the will itself only with difficulty to make way and to obtain a firm footing in the mind. But let any one only once carefully test himself with several instances, and my assertion will be found confirmed. If any one at first believes himself conscious of the will itself, he soon observes, on closer examination, that he is only conscious of the *conceptual representation "I will,"* and at the same time of the idea which forms the content of the will; and if he pursues the investigation, he finds that the ideal presentation "I will" has always simultaneously arisen in one of the stated three ways or in several, and *nothing* more is found in consciousness, even after the most searching examination. One thing, however, is still very remarkable, viz., if (as happens to everybody) we are vexed that our previous opinion has to be abandoned, and one says to oneself, "Still I can will what and when I will, and know that I can will, and now, *e.g.*, I do will," yet that which is taken for direct perception of the will is nothing else but reflex *bodily feelings* vaguely localised, and, indeed, feelings of defiance, obstinacy, or even merely of decided firm resolve. Here, then, arises the semblance of consciousness of the will itself in the second mode, from accompanying feelings. This, too, will be found verified certainly only when one gives oneself the trouble to make trial of it.

Finally, however, I have to mention yet one last decisive reason for the unconsciousness of all will, which quite directly decides the question. Every man *knows what he wills only so far* as he possesses the *knowledge* of his own *character* and of the psychological *laws*, the sequence of motive and desire, feeling and desire, and the strength of different desires, and can from these calculate beforehand the *result* of their struggle, or their resultant, the will. Entirely to fulfil this requirement is the ideal of wisdom, for only the ideally wise man always knows what he wills; all other men, however, know the less what they will the less they are accustomed to study themselves and the psychological laws, to keep their judgment always free from disturbance by passion, and, in a word, to make conscious reason (as suggested in Chap. xi. B.) the motive of their life. Therefore a man knows the less what he wills the more he abandons himself to the Unconscious, the inspiration of feeling. Children and women rarely know it, and only in the simplest cases; animals probably still more rarely. Were knowledge of the will not an indirect constructive calculation, but a direct conscious apprehension, as in pleasure, displeasure, and representation, it would be absolutely incomprehensible how it should so frequently come to pass that we firmly believe we have willed one thing but are taught by the act that we have willed another. (Comp. vol. i. pp. 252 and 262.) In the case of something directly entering into consciousness, *e.g.*, pain, there can be no room for error; that of which we have immediate self-apprehension truly exists, for we apprehend it immediately in its own nature.

Since the will in and of itself is under all circumstances unconscious, it is now also comprehensible that, for the becoming conscious of pleasure or displeasure, the will itself is precisely similarly circumstanced, whether it is united with a conscious or an unconscious representation. For the becoming conscious of displeasure, which indeed is already in opposition with will in such and such a manner, it is obviously indifferent whether the idea which forms the content of will is conscious or unconscious; at the most, it might appear of importance for the becoming conscious of pleasure. If the content of the will is a conscious representation, the possibility of the becoming conscious of its satisfaction is clear without more ado ; perhaps also, if it is an unconscious idea, this possibility exists with the help of accompanying feelings and perceptions. If, namely, in n cases these accompanying feelings and perceptions have had for their consequence m times a displeasure and $n-m$ times none, one *instinctively* concludes that these feelings and perceptions may be the work of an unconscious will which was not satisfied m times, *i.e.*, produced pain, whence it immediately follows that it must be satisfied $n-m$ times. Thus this satisfaction may, in consequence of the contrast, also attain to consciousness with a will whose content always remains unconscious, if it is only accompanied by regularly recurring marks, which, in place of the idea which forms its content, can figure as representative of the inherently eternally unconscious will. This must be added as supplementary to Chap. iii. B., where these points could not be weighed.

The insight thus obtained of the unconsciousness of the will in itself throws an interesting light on ever-recurring endeavours in the history of philosophy to resolve will into idea; I merely name the most prominent—Spinoza, and in recent times Herbart and his school with the most detailed attempt in this respect. This endeavour, which in less degree is manifested also by Hegel, would be utterly inexplicable in the case of such great thinkers, if the will, which in its essence is entirely heterogeneous to the idea, were something immediately given in consciousness; they become, however, through the circumstance that one never finds in consciousness the *will itself*, but always only the *idea of the will*, not only explicable, but *authorised and demanded* for the *exclusively conscious* standpoint, since the will has actual existence only in the sphere of the Unconscious. It is, therefore, also characteristic that just the most dilettante of all considerable philosophers, Schopenhauer, disregarding this requirement of strict thought, claims to have found the will as core of his own being directly in consciousness. As the philosophising of common sense thinks to grasps things immediately in external perception, just as dogmatically did Schopenhauer imagine himself to have apprehended the will immediately in inner experience. Criticism annihilates the one as the other dogmatic semblance of instinct, but science gives again to cognition, as conscious mediate possession, what it has destroyed of blind, immediate instinctive faith.

4. *Consciousness has no degrees.*—Our principle has yet to stand one final test. If, namely, our assumption is correct, that consciousness is a phenomenon the essence of which consists in the opposition of the will to something not proceeding from it and yet sensibly present, that thus only those elements of ideation or feeling can become conscious which light upon a will found in opposition with them, *i.e.*, on a will which does not will or negates them, it follows from this that consciousness can as little as naught or negation have differences of degrees. The question is one of a pure alternative: "Becoming conscious or remaining unconscious?" If the will comports itself affirmatively, the latter occurs; if it is negatively related, the former. There is no stronger or weaker in negation, for negation is a positive, not a comparative conception. There may, indeed, be a partial and complete negation, but this is not difference in the negation, but in the negated object, and can, therefore, establish no difference of degree in negation itself. A partial negation must in our case have for its consequence the becoming conscious of the one and the remaining unconscious of the other part, but in no case could there emerge a difference of degree in consciousness as such.

What becomes conscious, the object or the content of consciousness, may then show a more or less; but consciousness itself can only be or not be, never be more or less. Undoubtedly the will also, which by its negating of the object posits the becoming conscious of the same, may exhibit difference of degrees, be stronger or weaker; but the strength of this will, presupposing that it at all lies above the threshold, has no influence at all on the alternative, "becoming conscious or not," only whether its *content* be affirmatively or negatively related to the object of the becoming conscious affords ground for a decision. Hence no difference in the degree of consciousness can be derived from the strength of the opposing will; either something becomes conscious or does not become conscious; in no case can it become more or less conscious. I will try to make this state of the case still clearer by an example in the matter of willing.

If I will to give something to a beggar, I certainly will more if I give him a half-crown than if I give him a penny; this is the more or less of content, which does not at all touch the question of the intensity of will as such, for the will itself may, in both cases, be equally strong, whether I intend to present him with half-a-crown or a penny. On the other hand, with the same content the will may have very different strength; *e.g.*, if of two men each wills to give the beggar a penny, the one may possibly be dissuaded from so doing by a very slight cause, whereas the will of the other overcomes strong counter-motives. This is the degree of difference of the will as such. The degree of difference of the content we have in consciousness also; the graduated difference of consciousness as such must, on the other hand, be wanting according to the *a priori* derivation from our principle; should this *a priori* consequence of the same not be confirmed by experience, this would be an indirect attack on the principle itself.

What especially stands in the way of the empirical recognition of that proposition is the confusion of the notion consciousness with two other allied notions, first attention, secondly self-consciousness.—*Attention* we have already repeatedly (vol. i. pp. 131-132, 174-175, also 275, 276) seen to be a nerve-current, produced both reflectorially as well as voluntarily, which runs its course in sensory nerve-fibres from centre to periphery, and serves the purpose of heightening the conductivity of nerves, especially for weak stimuli and weak differences of stimuli. Attention accordingly consists of material nervous vibrations. Inasmuch as these run from centre to periphery, it is inevitable that they should, even without giving rise to perception, be reflected from periphery to centre. Moreover, through attention a number of muscles are contracted for every sensory sphere, in order to facilitate the reception of the perception by the organ; and lastly, certain other muscles, especially muscles of the scalp, are reflexively contracted. These three movements agree in this, in bringing sensations to the organ of consciousness by means of material vibrations, *i.e., attention as such is an object of perception, and consequently of consciousness.* One may be easily convinced of this if in the dead of night one has occasion to listen attentively for a signal, or to look towards the horizon to see whether a rocket will be sent up. If for pure ideation certainly also muscular tension of the sense-organ is absent, yet the reflex tension of the muscle of the scalp remains (whence the word "cracking one's brain"), and the effect of the nervous vibrations as such. Wherefore also that attention is distinctly felt which is not directed to an external sense, but merely to the inner ideational life of the brain, as any one may easily observe in himself when he is searching for a word that has escaped him.

Attention enhances the irritability of the parts which it affects, and thereby facilitates both the revival of former ideas and also the perception of weak stimuli and differential stimuli. We cannot definitely assert that it magnifies the amplitude of the vibrations, because the intensity of a sensation (*e.g.*, intensity of sound) is not perceptibly increased by enhancement of attention. Yet this also, as I hold to be extremely probable, may be merely apparent, in that the increase of intensity has already begun unconsciously to abate, just as the magnifying of an object by nearer approach is not easily perceived, and the comparison of two circular openings equidistant from the eye is not essentially easier than that of two unequal ones at a greater distance.—Be that, however, as it may, this much is certain, that we have a double estimate in every sensation, both of the strength of the sensation, so far as it depends on the stimulus, and also of the degree of the applied attention; that thus an element is added to perception through the cerebral vibrations of attention, which makes the total perception richer and more comprehensive (quite apart from the circumstance that all sensations cannot at all reach the brain and its consciousness without a certain degree of reflex attention). The like holds good, however, for mere cerebral ideas, and in still greater degree.

An idea emerging from memory is also enriched and heightened by attention. It is certainly not changed in its general contents, but whereas in an idea for which one is inattentive everything is misty and dissolving, pale and colourless, indiscernible as if at a great distance, the outlines, colours, and details become the more defined, vivid, and closer the higher the degree of attention. The reason of this is, that all our ideas rest on sense-impressions, and only in these do the pale, spectral notions become clothed with flesh and blood, but that the sensuous representations become so much the more plastic and vivid, the larger is the part of the special nerve of sense and organ of sense which is drawn into sympathy, the wider the representation is peripherally projected outside. In sense-perception there thus occurs by the increase of attention an enrichment of content only so far as, by means of the enhanced conductivity, also slighter concomitant details reach the cerebral consciousness, and the perception of the vibrations of attention themselves becomes more intense. In the idea of memory, however, beside these moments there is also added the enhancement of sensuous vividness and definition.

To this must in all cases be added the hitherto unmentioned prevention of disturbance by other perceptions, which is of the highest importance. Usually, namely, there exists in the waking state a certain sense of attention in the whole sensitive nervous system, which naturally is feeble for any single point of the same, and is only enhanced reflexively in this direction by a more strongly acting stimulus. Accordingly there usually arises a great division and distraction of attention, so that consciousness finds in itself an infinitely mixed content of merely weak perceptions. But if now there takes place a severe strain of attention in a particular direction, thus, *e.g.*, on a sense or the brain only, this, with the limited sum of energy of the organism, can only happen at the expense of attention in all other directions, and therefore all partial enhanced attention is a *concentration* of the same, which forms a contrast to the distraction. Instead of the infinitely numerous weak perceptions, consciousness now finds as its content one energetic idea, whilst the sum of all other perceptions is reduced to a minimum. One sees that the content has essentially changed so much that it perfectly suffices for the explanation of the changed state; there is nothing present which pointed to a gradual change of consciousness in itself. It is, however, on the other hand, obvious how easily a defective discrimination of attention and consciousness may lead to the opinion that consciousness, just as much as attention, has degrees; and it will often be found that consciousness is spoken of where attention is meant. Attention may have degrees, because it consists of nervous vibrations, and in all nervous vibrations the magnitude of the vibrations of amplitude conditions the intensity of the sensation; consciousness, however, can have no degrees, because it is an immaterial reaction, which either does or does not occur, but, if it occurs, always takes place in the same way.

The distinction between consciousness and *self-conscious-*

ness has been already indicated at the beginning of this chapter. Self-consciousness can, of course, not be conceived without consciousness; how far a complete absence of self-consciousness can be in fact established must still remain doubtful, since, indeed, self-consciousness also is in the first instance instinctively born as so-called slight self-feeling. Thus much is certain, that a very clear consciousness occurs pretty often with the minimum of self-consciousness; nay, even the more clear becomes the objective consciousness in the same individual, the more self-consciousness disappears. Nobody is in a position really to enjoy a work of art unless he really forgets himself. In the same way self-consciousness almost entirely ceases when one is steeped in some scientific book; but when one is productive and absorbed in deep reflection, then one is so absent not merely from the surroundings, but even from oneself, that no thought remains for one's own most important interests; nay, even, on being suddenly addressed, one has first to recollect one's own name. And yet in these moments consciousness is clearest of all, just because it is wholly merged in the subject, *i.e.*, attention has reached the highest degree of concentration. This absorption in a subject is, however, necessary wherever the ideational process is called upon to do something considerable, except in practical questions of personal interest, because here all the aims of the whole life are to be regarded in their importance with respect to one another; thus the identity of the Egos of different times, the personality, plays a leading part. For the same reason, however, exclusively practical natures also, who can never forget themselves and their aims and interests, are regularly devoid of every higher scientific and artistic faculty.

One sees, then, that consciousness and self-consciousness are very different things; nevertheless the confusion of the two is something quite common. For example, one says of a somnambulist that in that state he is without consciousness, whilst his performances (poems, written compositions) attest a very clear consciousness; but he is certainly without full self-consciousness, since his attention, steeped in a one-sided object, is wanting to all other perceptions that do not cohere with this particular object, and therefore also no remembrance of the other aims and interests arises in him which do not touch this object.

So far as complete self-consciousness includes the memory of all ends and interests which previous Egos have ever had, we often talk of *recollection;* and where one may correctly say a man was at such and such moment, in such and such an action, without his senses or without self-consciousness, one often says incorrectly he was without consciousness. On the other hand, one often says, when somebody loses or has lost consciousness (*e.g.*, in swoon, stupefaction), he is or is becoming senseless, or is losing self-consciousness; in this case the confusion of the words says too little, as in others too much. Now, however, it is clear that self-consciousness has degrees, for it is most perfect when it merely embraces the Ego of present mental activity, and is the more perfect, *i.e.*, its degree is the higher, the more Egos of past or future action it embraces. For self-consciousness is not indeed, like consciousness, bare, empty form, but it is consciousness *of a quite definite content*, the self; and as this definite content already belongs to its *notion,* the degree of self-consciousness must also rise and fall with the degree of this *content.* Consciousness, on the other hand, leaves its content quite undetermined; it only requires a content at all, if it is to come to manifestation, to reality; in its essence, however, it is *pure form*, and therefore its notion cannot admit of differences of degree in consequence of the varying nature of the perfectly indifferent content. But if this difference between consciousness and self-consciousness is not yet, or at least not in this respect, cleared up, it is no wonder that, through the frequent confusion of the two notions, one becomes imperceptibly accustomed to believe also in gradual differences in consciousness itself. Still more pardonable becomes the illusion when attention and self-consciousness mingle; when, *e.g.*, I listen to a signal with fullest self-consciousness, knowing that my whole life-happiness is dependent thereon, and the sound of a distant shot finally reaches the ear, I can also fall into the error that the consciousness with which I have now heard the sound is degrees higher than that with which I should have casually heard it as a passer-by. But if one conscientiously deducts the several elements: first the thought that the whole Ego of the future depends on the sense-perception of the next moment, then the thought that it is I myself who am intentionally straining my attention, then the muscular tension and the perception of the attention as such; finally, the strengthening of the sensuous perception, its greater definiteness, &c., one will be obliged to grant that the residue remaining to consciousness as such is the same in both cases, and that the differences only affect partly the content presented to consciousness by the brain, partly self-consciousness.

After the common illusions of human introspection have been thus laid bare, the assertion will have lost its paradoxical air that the so-called highest and lowest consciousness, that of man and the lowest animals, are as consciousness quite alike, and are only distinguished by the content presented to them. We saw that the simple sensuous qualities, of which all sense-perception is compounded, are reactions of the Unconscious on the material vibrations of the central organ (brain, ganglia, animal and vegetable protoplasm); it is matter of course that the reactions take place according to the kind of the vibrations, turn out the stronger and more vivid the stronger are the vibrations, and are more definitely compounded and more clearly discriminated from other similar sensations, the more definite and varied are the vibrations, and the fewer differences of external stimuli they bring to manifestation in the central organ.

It is accordingly obvious that the eye of the snail,

which, according to exact observations, must literally compensate all the five senses without its being able to distinguish therewith more than bright and dark in general, that this eye causes vibrations in the central organ, which, neither in respect of vision, smell, taste, hearing, and touch, exhibit such great differences as in animals with distinct sense-organs, nor are capable even of considerable variety within each of these special provinces of sensation. But that which gives the power of distinguishing one perception from another confers also *definiteness*, and therefore perceptions are the more indefinite the lower we descend in the animal kingdom. This indefiniteness is only to be conceived in such a way that in the perception the detail is wanting which in higher organisations determines differences. If we eliminate this detail from perception, it will, however, become *poorer in content*, for there only remains over *the universal*, which is ever *the same in the midst of difference*. All indefiniteness of perception thus depends on poverty, whereas richness in content is the ground of definiteness and distinguishability. We can now say wherein the distinction of an apparently lower consciousness consists: *in the slight intensity and the poverty of the content presented to it; in the material scantiness both of the individual perception and idea, and of the whole accessible mass of ideas.* When I look at a single point of light on a dark night, I see it sharply defined as a point with a definite degree of brightness and the background in a definite degree of darkness. I also see both in quite definite colours: this is the wealth which lies in this single perception. The snail, however, does not see this point at all, or, if it is very bright, it sees a weak shimmer of light before it, and of all else it sees nothing: that is the poverty of its perception.

But, moreover, the snail sees with much less intensity, because with less attention. The enfeeblement of attention in all other directions, coincident with concentration in a single one, proves the limited total amount of the same for a definitely constituted being, which manifestly is related to its total nervous energy. Nothing is more obvious than that the total quantity of attention varies in the animal series with the development of the whole nervous system. Thus a snail with the utmost possible strain of attention at a point of light will hardly be able to apply as much attention as I, when I do not in the least think about that point of light at all; for the central organ of the snail stands in any case lower than my *corpora quadrigemina* which receive the visual impressions, and beyond which they do not reach when the brain is occupied with other matters. We have now a tolerable picture of the consciousness of the lower animals with a single perception; and yet consciousness is always the same, only the matter presented to it is so much weaker and scantier.

The disproportion is still more increased when we take into account the whole thought-material which underlies comparison, abstraction, and combination; then we soon see that the indefiniteness and obscurity of the single idea is still more exceeded by the poverty of the whole sum of experiences which are at the command of such an animal and by the incapacity of a central organ to retain sufficiently in memory the experiences once had, or at all to work them up into more manageable partial ideas (concepts). This hardly needs further development. The result of it all is the confirmation of the proposition derived from our principle, that consciousness as such, *i.e.*, in its form, is everywhere the same, and is only differentiated by the matter presented to it; for nowhere did we have occasion to ascribe to consciousness itself differences of degree, as we are obliged to do, *e.g.*, in the will, even apart from its content; the principle has thus stood even this final test.

5. *The Unity of Consciousness.*—At the close of this chapter the question forces itself upon us, "*What is unity of consciousness?*" We can, of course, agreeably to our principles, only regard the question here from the empirical

side. Thus we cannot refer, for example, to the unity of the underlying individual psychical essence, because we do not yet know anything at all of this psychical existence, its individuality, and its unity, but, on the contrary, can only learn something of it by answering this question. Moreover, the advocates of indivisible individual souls must allow that even the unity of consciousness may be resolved into a multiplicity of strictly separated and perfectly incoherent consciousnesses, whereas they must acknowledge the unity of the mind underlying these different consciousnesses. I allude only to such examples as Jessen cites in his "Psychology," of a girl who, after an intense lethargy, had lost *all* her memory without enfeeblement of her mental faculties and capacity for instruction. She had to begin again to learn her alphabet. The attacks were repeated, and after each the memory of the immediately preceding portion of her life had disappeared, whilst that of the one before the last reappeared in its place unweakened, so that she always resumed her studies as if she had left them off before the last attack but one. This example only presents phenomena in a more striking and complete form, which in a weaker degree and more partial way may be observed everywhere. We can only recognise a unity of consciousness between a *past and present* moment where in the present there is the memory of this past moment, or where there is at least a possibility of this memory. In strictness one can speak of a real or actual unity of consciousness only in the case of actual memory, whereas with merely possible memory the unity of consciousness is merely possible or potential.

If we further see what we have in actual memory, what is added to a representation when I know it as a *well-known* idea or *memory*, it is, according to B. Chap. vii. vol. i. pp. 305, 306, an instinctive feeling, which, analysed into its discursive moments, has the following meaning:—I have in addition to the main idea a very much weaker contiguous idea excited by the former, which I know to be in causal relation with a former similar idea. Place and time of this former idea may likewise be fixed by means of the accompanying circumstances of the same surging up in memory.

It is thus nothing but the *comparison* of a present and a past representation, that determines the unity of consciousness between temporally separated moments. The possibility of this comparison is attained by this: that of two *present* ideas the one represents the present, the other the past; and the latter again becomes possible by this: that I know the present idea to be in causal connection with a former one similar to it. While, now, of the two ideas, the one represents the past, consciousness comprehends in this indivisible act of comparison the representations of the present and past consciousness into one, and therewith becomes conscious of the unity of consciousness for that past and the present representation. To wit, if I have two conscious representations, there exists a consciousness of the one and a consciousness of the other idea; and I should never have the right of maintaining a unity of these two consciousnesses if I could not prove it. But now, when I bring together two ideas for comparison, I merge both consciousnesses in the third consciousness of the comparison, and in this way have brought their unity to immediate intuition. The comparison is thus the moment which first of all makes possible the thought of a unity of consciousness, and with the possibility of comparison the possibility of the unity of consciousness also ceases.

As we have here seen the act of comparison to be the judge of the unity of consciousness of a past and a present, *i.e.*, temporally separate representations, so does it also decide in respect of spatially separated ideas, *i.e.*, such as are excited by different material parts. A human brain has a certain magnitude, and the representations which arise at one end of it are many inches removed from those arising at the other end; nevertheless we do not doubt the unity of the cerebral consciousness. The reason is simply this: that in the healthy waking state every idea arising anywhere in the brain may be *compared* with any one arising anywhere else. On the other hand, the ideas of the spinal cord and the ganglia, as they must of necessity exist in reflex movements, &c., in injuries of the viscera and the like, have in general no unity of consciousness along with the cerebral representation; they have rather each their *separate* conscious existence, since they cannot be taken up into a common conscious act of comparison. Only a few strong sensations of the lower nerve-centres are comparable, and a unity of consciousness possible so far as it is exhibited in common feeling. Whilst for the different nerve-centres of an organism this unity of consciousness is established with stronger stimulation of the one or the other, it is in no way to be established for the nerve-centres of different individuals, unless with partial coalescence of two organisms by abortion, or between mother and foetus, where echoes of such unity of consciousness are found for strong stimulations.

The cause of these phenomena is obvious. In the brain, beside the special commissures, innumerable nerve-fibres traverse the whole mass and establish a manifold intimate union of every particle with the rest; the spinal cord has already a much more imperfect union with the brain; the sympathetic nervous system is only connected with it by the single *nervus vagus*. In individuals which have grown together only more or less casual concrescence of subordinate nerve-strands can take place; in the case of separate individuals all union is wanting. The more perfect is the *path* between the functional part of the central nerves, the less stimulus it needs to propagate the stimulus of the one to the other unenfeebled and undisturbed; the more imperfect and longer the paths of conduction, the greater the resistances, the stronger must be the stimuli, if they are to be propagated to the other central spot, and the more obscure and more effaced are they on arrival.

For him who is accustomed to the endless intermingling of the phenomena of physical vibrations without any mutual disturbance, this mode of viewing the nervous processes, according to which each thought at one spot of the brain is simultaneously telegraphed to all other spots, will not appear strange; it is impossible to interpret the anatomical construction of the brain with its numerous connecting fibres in any other manner. The *capability of conduction* it is then, in fact, which physically conditions *the unity* of consciousness, and with which this is *proportional*. We lay down, then, as a principle: *Separate material parts give separate consciousness*, a proposition which is as much recommended *à priori* as the distinct individuals confirm it empirically. As long as the Australian ant is an animal, its fore and after body acts with undivided consciousness; as soon as one has cut it in pieces, the unity of consciousness is abolished, and both parts turn against one another.—We further assume: the comparison of two ideas produced at different places only becomes possible by the vibrations of the one place being carried over to the other unenfeebled and undisturbed; only by the comparison of the two representations is the abolition of their two consciousnesses in the indivisible consciousness of the act of comparison possible; with it, however, we may add, it is also *eo ipso given*. (The *metaphysical* condition of the identity of the psychical unconscious substance, which will be discussed in Sect. C. Chap. vii., is here, of course, tacitly assumed. Without it the physical condition of nerve-conduction would be just as vague as the former without the latter.) The Siamese twins refused to play draughts with one another, thinking that this would be as if the right hand should play with the left. The negresses coadjunct at the lower part of the back, who allowed themselves to be exhibited at the beginning of 1873 in Berlin, under the name of the two-headed nightingale, are said to have sympathetic feelings of their mutual sensations in the lower extremities., *i.e.*, possess a unity of consciousness with respect to a certain sensitive area in spite of the duality of their persons. But if one imagined the union of the *brains* of two men possible by a bridge as capable of conduction as is that between the two hemispheres of the same brain, a mutual and indivisible consciousness, including the thoughts of both brains, would immediately embrace the hitherto separate consciousnesses of both persons; each would no longer be able to distinguish his own thoughts from those of the other; *i.e.*, they would no longer know themselves as two Egoes, but only as one Ego, as my two cerebral hemispheres also only know themselves as one Ego.

IV.

THE UNCONSCIOUS AND CONSCIOUSNESS IN THE VEGETABLE KINGDOM.

THE question of the animation of the vegetable kingdom is an old one; outside Judaism and Christianity it has been almost everywhere affirmed. Our time, which has been nourished by the theories of these two systems of belief, and has not yet by a long way bridged over the gulf between spirit and sense, rent asunder by Christianity, has with difficulty admitted the kinship of men and *animals;* no wonder that it has not yet been able to elevate itself to the admission of the *vegetable* soul, since its physiology is accustomed to regard, even in the animal, the organic functions and reflex actions as merely material mechanisms. The subject has been best treated by Fechner in his memoir, "Nanna; or, The Psychical Life of Plants" (Leipzig, 1848), if also with an infusion of much of the fantastical; comp. further Schopenhauer, "On Will in Nature," chap. "Vegetable Physiology," and Autenrieth, "Views on Nature and Psychical Life." I shall content myself with giving a short exposition of the doctrine, and with showing the considerably greater clearness which is introduced into the whole question by the distinction of unconscious and conscious psychical activity. I am convinced that many a one, who was obliged to maintain a negative position owing to the previous mode of treatment, will be reconciled to the doctrine of plant-animation when the notions of the Unconscious and Consciousness are kept quite apart.

1. *The Unconscious Psychical Activity of Plants.*—The plant has, like the animal, organic plastic activity, *vis medicatrix*, reflex movements, instinct, and the impulse towards the beautiful; and if in the animal the phenomena must be regarded as unconscious effects of a soul, ought they not also so to be in the plant? If the unconscious psychical performances of the plant do not rise to the mental processes of the animal, but remain entirely sunk in corporeity, should therefore their soul be less soul, if that which it accomplishes is just as perfect in its sphere as that achieved by the animal in its sphere, nay, even far superior, because it builds up the refractory inorganic substances into higher and higher stages, whereas the animal, on the whole, only guides and watches over their natural degeneration? Let us consider the several movements in their order.

(*a.*) *Organic Formative Activity.*—This works, as in the animal, according to a typical generic idea, which, it is true, allows a great latitude in respect of number of branches, leaves, &c., but nevertheless is still perfectly definite in the law of arrangement of the leaves, the form of leaf, inflorescence, and internal structure. This morphological type possesses the greatest constancy and unchangeability, although the nearer definition of the same for the physiological functions is tolerably indifferent. Accordingly, one cannot look upon this constancy as a result of useful adaptation in the struggle for existence; rather one has to perceive in the morphological type of the vegetable kingdom essential results of an ideal formative impulse of the Unconscious.—As in the ascending organisation of the animal kingdom typical anticipations are especially remarkable which only become suitable at higher stages, we have to mark such anticipations of the unconscious formative impulse of Nature in the vegetable kingdom likewise. Thus, *e.g.*, higher Algæ exhibit an axis with lateral regularly arranged expansions which would at once be designated by the ignorant as stem, root, and leaves, whilst according to the dogma of the botanical system the Algæ are root and leafless plants. Hence the botanist calls the leaves of the Sargassum only "leaf-like expansions," and the roots "root-like structures," which want at the apex the "root-cap,"—and we will not disturb him in his faith.

It is true one can divide the plant as one may divide lower animals, so that each part still possesses the capability of again completing the type from itself. But as in animals, so also in plants, the division is by no means unlimited, if a completion is to remain possible. In the plant, too, all parts are in reciprocal connection. Every part nearer the earth works up the materials precisely as the proximate part must receive it for further elaboration. The root of an oak would never nourish a beech, nor a tulip-bulb a hyacinth. There takes place also in the plant a harmonious interaction of all the parts, and this can only conduce to the end of the exhibition of the specific type in all the successive stages of development.

If in winter one conducts a branch of a tree standing in the open air into a hothouse, the tree unfolds its leaves and flowers, whilst the rest of the tree retains its rigidity. The water required by the tree for this purpose is absorbed by the roots, as observation shows. Thus the latter are stimulated to increased absorption by the increased vital action of a branch (Decandolle, "Vegetable Physiology," i. 76). How far a direct union by conduction takes place between the several parts of the plants we do not know, although the spiral vessels appear to point to that; but we just as little know in the case of the animal how far the harmonious interworking of the performances of the single parts is effected by conduction, and how far it is due to direct clairvoyance, as that of the individuals in the commonwealth of bees or ants.

Propagation takes place in the animal and vegetable kingdoms on precisely the same principles, by cellular division, spores or budding, and sexual generation. The similarity in both provinces is, especially in the first stages of generation, so striking, that precisely the same reasons necessitate the assumption of an unconscious psychical influence in the origin of the plant as in the origin of the animal. The embryonic states certainly part company very soon after, as is not otherwise to be expected, according to the difference of the types to be produced; but in both the progressive development is a continuous struggle of the organising soul with the tendency of the material elements to decomposition, degeneration, and destruction of form. Only by the constant prevention of these degenerating processes and ceaseless reinstatement of the circumstances urging to continued formation, is it possible at any moment for the formed organic matter to get the better of the relatively formless inorganic matter, for a new higher stage of the specific type to be realised.

Every single cell takes part in these operations; for the living part of every plant, as of every animal, consists of the sum of the living cells, except that in animals on the average the changes of form and fusion of the cells are somewhat more extensive, and the intercellular substance secreted and nourished by the cells is more copious. The cell is the chemical laboratory for the preparation of the various organic combinations; the division and amalgamation of the cells are the sole means for the setting up of the external form. At the same time just as strict a division of labour is carried out as in the animal; one kind of cells has to form this material, another that. As in the animal the cells are elaborated into bones, muscles, sinews, nerves, connective tissues, and epithelial cells; so in the plant into medullary cells, wood cells, cortical cells, sap cells, starch cells, &c. Each cell absorbs only those substances which it can make use of, or if it takes up aught else, it sends this on unassimilated. A circulation of sap takes place in each single cell, and likewise in the whole plant. It is true open vessels do not exist, but the circulation of the sap is effected by the endosmose and exosmose of the several cells; still, however, a perfect circulation of ascending and descending juices takes place, as a similar circulation takes place in all the parts of the animal body that are wanting in nutritive vessels (*e.g.*, in the deciduous parts of the umbilicus, the bones, sinews, cornea, &c.), or with which the nutritive vessels do not directly communicate. Hales cemented a tube to the upper end of a lopped vine seven inches long; in the first experiment the height of the sap which had risen from the surface of the section into the tube amounted to 21 feet; in the second, quicksilver poured in from above was raised to the height of 38 inches. Hales calculates from this the energy of the ascending sap to be equal to five times the force of the blood in the femoral artery of a horse. One sees what in the higher animal is due to the heart's action is in the plant the sum of the united absorption of all the sap cells. This difference frequently recurs, that the same actions in the animal are produced by centralisation, in the plant by decentralisation: in the animal monarchically, in the plant in republican fashion. But the absorption by the cells is by no means merely mechanical; it takes place rather with selection of direction and material, for otherwise no circulation and no distribution of nutritive matters to different cells could take place.

The directions of the growth of plants and parts of plants are, as a whole, conditioned by gravitation and light, now in the sense that they coincide with the directions of these forces; now in this, that they strive to place themselves in a transverse position with respect to the latter; now in such a way that both forces neutralise one another. The complications hence arising become, however, still more intricate by this: that certain plants change their behaviour to these determining forces according to the phases of their stage of development, if they are brought by special circumstances into a position where their normal behaviour would be inappropriate in respect of their vital needs. Thus Duchartre found, under the bottom of a water-butt, numerous fungi of the Mushroom family which had been compelled to grow from above downwards, but had deviated from the perpendicular at least 30°, and of which those more developed with opening and spreading caps exhibited a geniculate bending of the stalk upwards, about 5^{mm} from its end, through which the normal position of the opened cap was restored. Seven examples of Clariceps, which were artificially brought into the inverted position in a glass tube, showed an analogous behaviour, only that the stalks formed here no angle but an arc of 3 to 5^{mm} ("Der Naturforscher," 1870, p. 194).

In organic adaptation, likewise, the vegetable will bear comparison with the animal kingdom. There is even much which in animals is cared for by instinct, but which in plants, on account of their greater weight, is provided for by organic mechanisms, which again can be set up only by unconscious psychical activity. Here, too, the transitions are of such a kind that we cannot always sharply distinguish mechanisms and instincts.

First there is a series of phenomena for the better nutrition of plants by retaining putrefying animal matters. The aborted leaves of the common Teazel—*Dipsacus fullonum*—form about the stem a kind of basin, which is filled with rain-water, and in which many accidentally drowned insects are often found. The like is found in a tropical parasitic plant—*Fillandsia utriculata*. The Sarraceniæ have leaves which, latterly rolled together, form an ochrea, and are in part provided with opercula. Short, stiff hairs prevent imbibing insects from returning from the water-holding ochrea. *Nepenthes destillatoria* has the urn with an operculum as appendix of the shallow leaves. It closes the opercula by night and secretes sweetish water, enticing insects, which by day is again gradually evaporated from the open urn. The sweetness of the water is produced by hairy, glandular, excretory organs. *Dionœa muscipula* has a lobed divided appendage on each leaf, which is closely set with small glands, with six aculeæ in the middle and setaceous cilia at the edge. When an insect, attracted by the juice, sits on the two lobes, these shut up, and only again open when the animal has become quiet, *i.e.*, when it is dead. Curtis sometimes found the captured fly enveloped in a slimy substance, which appeared to act as a solution on the same. The sun-dew, *Drosera*, has very red bristly hairs on the leaves, each of which terminates in a gland, from which in hot weather a small viscid pearly drop is exuded. This viscid sap retains small insects; the hairs quickly curve over the same, and gradually the whole leaf bends back with the apex towards the base (A. W. Roth, "Beiträge zur Botanik," 1 Thl., 1782, p. 60). This sap is at the same time poisonous for insects (also unwholesome for sheep), and thereby compensates for what the plant wants in quick irritability. Roth often found in the open air leaves of the Sun-dew bent together, which always enclosed insects more or less in a state of decay. " Let any one imagine in boggy water small utricular leaves, bent together into a hollow tube with open mouth, irritable at their borders, with hair-like soft threads, whilst the opening acts at the same time venomously on small animals, and the inner surface of the cylindrical tube adapted for absorption. One would thus have an image, which would be compounded of the convolute or urn-shaped leaves of the Sarracenia and Nepenthes, of the irritability of the leaf-appendages of the Dionæa, and of the irritable but poison-secreting hairs of the Drosera. One gets, however, also at the same time the actual picture of the organisation of a small insect remarkable for its instinct—the green hydra of sweet water, *Hydra viridis L.*" (Autenrieth); for the touch of the mouth of this creature also acts poisonously. That such plants thrive more luxuriantly on products of animal putrefaction absorbed by the leaves is experimentally proved in the case of the Dionæa.

Very wonderful also are those contrivances in plants which subserve sexual propagation. In erect flowers the stamens are generally longer than the pistils; in pendulous ones, the reverse. Where the pollen grains cannot without assistance fall on the stigmata, and the wind is not sufficient to carry them away, insects have to perform this office. Hence the attractive bright colours of flowers, their far-reaching scent, which is always developed most strongly in the daytime, when the insects most suited to the particular flower swarm; hence the sweet sap at the base of the flower, which compels the dainties-loving animal to creep deep enough within, so that it brushes off with its bristly body the pollen, which then comes to adhere to the pistil, either of the same or of another flower. In the Asclepiadeæ and Orchids the pollen adheres to the insect by means of a sort of bird-lime. *Aristolochia clematitis* has a bellied flower with a narrow entrance, which by means of lateral hairs prevents the exit of the little midges that have crept in. These swarm about in their prison until they have stripped off the pollen with their feathered antennæ and brought it to the stigma. Immediately after fructification the hairs begin to dry up and fall off, and release the flies from their prison.

If the pollen grains become wet, they expand and burst; then fertilisation becomes impossible. In this way rainy weather becomes very injurious at the blossoming of the grain. The precautionary measures of the flowers for escaping the wet are very numerous. In the Vine and the species of Rampions fertilisation takes place under the protection of the petals cohering by their tips; in the Leguminosæ the standard (*vexillum*) accords the same protection; in the Labiatæ, the upper lips of the corolla; in the species of Calyptranthe, the operculate calyx. Many plants close their corolla when it is about to rain (this is instinct); many also by night to protect themselves from the dew; others at night-time bend round their flower-stalks, so that the open side of the corolla is turned aside. *Impatiens noli me tangere* hides even its flowers under its leaves by night. In most aquatic plants dry fertilisation is rendered possible by this, that they do not bloom before their stalks have reached the surface of the water. The Alga fixed to the sea-bottom flowers in leafy folds, which it is true are open laterally, but hinder the entrance of the water by means of excreted gases. The Water-crowfoot (*Ranunculus aquaticus*), whose flowers are flooded at high water, is protected by the pollen dropping out of the anthers at a time when the flower is still a close, air-containing bud. The Water-nut (*Trapa natans*) lives at the bottom of the water until flowering time, when the petioles, ranged side by side into a kind of leaf-rose, swell to cellular bladders filled with air, and raise the whole plant to the surface of the water. Thus florescence and fructification take place in the air. When this is over, the bladders are filled with water, and the plant sinks again to the bottom, where it then brings its seed to maturity. Still more complicated is the arrangement of the species of Utricula for the same purpose. Their strongly ramified roots are covered with a multitude of small round bladders (*utriculi*) possessing a kind of movable lid, and filled with a mucus that is heavier than water. By means of this ballast the plant is retained at the bottom of the water, until at flowering time the mucus is got rid of by excreted gases. It now slowly rises to the surface, flowers and fructifies, and is then again drawn down, whilst the root again secretes mucus, which now on its part drives out the air from the little sac (Decandolle, "Vegetable Physiology," ii. 87). The Vallisneria is an aquatic plant with distinct sex (diœcious), which grows attached at the bottom of the water. The flower of the female plant sits on a long screw-shaped stalk, which subsequently extends and lifts the flower above the water. The male plant has a shaft tending straight upwards. The four-leaved spathe is split into four pieces through further expansion of the inner parts, and now the male organs of fructification swim freely about in the water in thousands. As soon as a female flower is fertilised the stem again spirally contracts, and thus the seeds are brought to maturity below.—Also in *Serpicula verticillata* the male flowers, when near rupture, are released from the opened spathes and swim to the female, whereby they rest on the apices of the replicate sepals and petals.

"One species of plant jerks ingeniously far and wide the ripe seed-grains by means of the elasticity of the capsule which flies open spontaneously. The beards of oats are, on the contrary, wound round spirally, and are so hyproscopic that the first rain unrolls them, and compels the thereby backwards-thrust grain to creep under the nearest clod, and so to betake itself beneath the earth for future sprouting. Other plant-seeds are provided with wings or plumose pappus, in order to be borne through the air. Others even have little hooks, in order to cling to passing animals, that they may be again dispersed by these means to other places" (Autenrieth, 151). The ripe fruits of the Stork's-bill are jerked off, by the curling back of the indurated styles, three to four feet from the plant. The extending style, by becoming damp, makes a spiral revolution, which chiefly causes the sharp point of the seed to strike the earth somewhere, into which it must now penetrate. If drier weather occurs, little bristles on the seed-corn, which act as barbs, prevent a recoil, and the shortening is followed by a drawing of the style towards the grain, so that now, with repeated moistening, the newly gained point of support for the end of the style permits a deeper penetration into the ground. Since the lower part of the style itself is also provided with barb-like bristles, on change of weather the fruit can interpenetrate the soil even to complete disappearance in the manner of a corkscrew.

Many seeds cover themselves for protection with a hard shell, and in order to be devoured and carried farther by animals, which in their excrements directly supply them with manure, they envelop themselves in savoury pulp (stone-fruit, grapes, gooseberries, currants, &c.), or they peripherally surround a carnose nucleus (strawberries, &c.) The seeds of aquatic plants are usually heavier than water, and accordingly sink to the bottom. Those of most lofty trees, on the contrary, are light, and are transported on the surface of the water far and wide to new stations by wind and current. The mango-tree (*Rhizophora mangle*) grows, at the mouths of rivers and on flat sea-shores, in the mud, so far as the same is covered over by the salt flood, thrives therefore only on a narrow strip, wherefore the seeds must take firm root beside the mother tree. On the receptacle of the flower of this tree now there is gradually produced a pulpy hollow growth, by which the seed, with the help of a stalk $1\frac{1}{2}$ inch long, is pushed out, so that after about a year it depends perpendicularly. The seed itself is 10 inches long, thicker and heavier towards the free end, but terminating with a puncheon-shaped point. It sprouts within its covering, and even develops an important root. Through its form and weight the falling seed penetrates water and mud three to four feet, and penetrates the ground yet one inch more, where it can then soon fasten itself with its root.—These examples may suffice to show, that even the vegetable soul performs sufficiently wonderful works in setting up appropriate mechanisms, whose end is even in part tolerably remote.

(b.) *The Recuperative Power of Nature.*—Animals have each organ only just as often as the whole organism requires it for its maintenance; hence the endeavour to replace a lost one in the same way. The Idea of the plant demands a numerically unlimited repetition of the same organs; wherefore also a partial loss usually is not prejudicial to the persistence of the whole. Here, then, no reason exists for restoring the lost parts at the same place and in the same manner, since the plant finds it much easier to accomplish the replacement at other places by means of the already existing buds. Nevertheless, sufficient opportunities are afforded for seeing that in the plant likewise the *vis medicatrix* is active, it is only necessary to deprive a plant of a certain class of organs which is essential for its existence, *e.g.*, all the roots, when it will immediately put forth new roots, or die when it has no longer the requisite force. Also the process of cicatrising wounds or cut surfaces is altogether analogous to that of animals.

Finally, in the plant as in the animal, the whole life is an infinite sum of infinitely numerous acts of the *vis medicatrix*, since at each moment the destructive physical and chemical influences must be paralysed and met.

(*c.*) *Reflex Movements.*—The physiologists distinguish reflex movement and "simple stimulation of contractile tissue." This is correct when one inquires where the reflexion of the stimulus into motion takes place; namely, whether the seat of reaction lies at the stimulated spot itself or at another; it is, however, a mistake to try to find herein a difference of principle. The essence of reflexion in both cases is conversion of an active stimulus into reactive motion; an absolute restriction to the irritated point is at the same time never met with; but whether the conduction proceeds a little further or not can make no difference in principle. That which stamps a reactive movement as reflex action is the inadequacy of merely material natural laws for its production; only when we can rest content with these (*e.g.*, elasticity, chemical reaction), only then can we deny reflex action, whose essence is an unconscious psychical, an instinctive reaction. Whether a reflexion is effected by nerves and muscles, or by other equivalent mechanism, can by no means justify a difference in principle, since the strictly active matter is still always the protoplasm, whether free or enclosed in various kinds of cells.

If the water inhabited by a polype be shaken, the polype contracts into a bundle. This will be called by every one reflex action, no matter whether in future, in the homogeneous slimy mass of the polype, the analogues of nerves and muscles be discovered or not. And when the *Mimosa pudica*, shaken by the tread of the passer-by, shrinks along with its leaves, is this not reflex action? When the irritated penis is erected in virtue of change of blood-circulation, this is admitted to be reflex movement, and in the case of the plant is not the altered sap-circulation to be considered just as good a means to reflex movement? For the plant indeed does not need the continuous quick movements for which the animal requires its muscles, accordingly muscles would be a useless luxury for it. In the animal the sign of reflexion is that about the same reaction occurs, whether one applies a mechanical, chemical, thermal, galvanic, or electric stimulus; the same is, however, also the case with plants, whereas dead mechanisms are wont to respond only to a quite definite stimulus. Strong electric shocks annihilate animal as well as vegetable irritability. If a needle, connected with the positive pole of a galvanic battery, be stuck through the stalk of a barberry flower, and the wire of the negative pole be united with a petal by means of a lightly affixed moist piece of paper, at the moment of closing the chain the stamen belonging to the leaf springs over to the pistil. If the pole be changed, the current is less active, just as animal preparations more powerfully react when the negative pole is united with the peripheral end. On opening the chain no movement takes place, just as with frog's thighs. According to Blondeau the constant current, with application of the necessary precautions, acts on the *Mimosa pudica* just as little as on animal muscles as a motor stimulus, whilst the intermittent induction current proves to be a very violent stimulus. The part of an irritated animal slowly returns to its position on the abolition of the stimulus; thus, *c.g.*, an irritated oyster or polype quickly shrinks, but opens slowly. A repetition of the stimulation blunts the irritability, rest restores it. Further, the irritability manifests itself differently according to condition of health, age, sex, season, state of the weather, and other circumstances. All this occurs with plants precisely as with animals.

The reflex movements of the *Dionæa muscipula* I have already mentioned above. If an insect deposits itself on a leaf of the same, it is first of all retained there, being caught by the hairs, and then gradually the whole leaf coils round it. Here we have upon a simple stimulus at a single spot a partly simultaneous, partly appropriate successive participation of many places of the leaf, precisely as we are accustomed to find in animals, only that instead of the monarchical command of a nerve centre, a republican participation of all the parts in harmonious agreement has place. The phenomenon is more centralised, and therefore more animal-like in all leaves, anthers, &c., where the seat of reaction is to be sought in the joints, by which these parts are fastened.

In many flowers the ripe anthers gradually spontaneously incline towards the pistil, in some a joint is formed, which, on the stimulus of some insect, jerks the pollen on to the stigma. In others the crooked stigma is also irritable, and extends on a stimulus affecting it, whereby it carries off pollen from the anthers. *Mimosa pudica* has bipinnate leaves, and the leaflets, nerves, the chief leaf-stalk, nay, even the branch, have each their special movement. If cautiously avoiding all shaking, some strong acid be applied to a leaflet by degrees, all the adjacent leaves close up; according to Dutrochet, the velocity of propagation amounts from eight to fifteen millimetres in a second in the leaf-stalks, in the stigma, at the most, from two to three millimetres. Here the conductivity is actually visible. The same result is reached when a leaflet is gently scorched; the leaves fold up much beyond that required by the effect of the heat. Brücke, and subsequently Bert, proved that in this remarkable plant the spontaneous movements, which consist in a raising and lowering of the petioles according to the time of day, are to be well distinguished from the movements resulting from stimulation, since the capacity of the plant for the latter is paralysed by ether vapours, which, indeed, act likewise narcotically on the nervous system of the animal, whereas the former are propagated unchanged. That the diurnal elevations and depressions depend on regular alternations of the sap-circulation is undoubted; by what means the tension of the upper and lower knots on the petioles is changed on occasion of a stimulus has indeed not been directly established for *Mimosa pudica*, but certainly for the above-mentioned pollen of *Berberis vulgaris*. Here, namely (as in most vegetable parts), an opposite tension on the part of various tissues takes place, in that the exterior coating strives to shorten the filament, the underlying protoplasm endeavours to lengthen it. If, now, a suitable stimulus approaches the inner side of the filament, the protoplasm contracts; and while, in this way, the previous equilibrium of the tensions is changed in favour of the exterior coating, this can realise its tendency to shortening, and by this means bends the filament. The action, which liberates the play of existing forces, is thus here a contraction of the protoplasm, precisely as in lower animals or as in muscles of higher ones.

It is impossible to mistake the thorough-going analogy between the reflex actions of animals and plants; the differences reach only just as far as the general arrangement of the organisms and as the special ends of each reaction differ. If, now, the reflex actions in animals have once for all been recognised as in the last resort acts of a psychical nature, one cannot avoid claiming this unconscious psychical element also for plants, just as one must reckon it to every animal part, which is still *per se* capable of reflex movements.

(*d*) *Instinct.*—We saw already in the animal kingdom the inseparability of instinct, reflex movement, and organic formation; in the vegetable kingdom they can still less be separated, for, on the one hand, on account of the defective means of movement for the plant, organic formation must accomplish much by appropriate mechanisms which the animals perform with instinctive movement (think of coition and the dissemination of the seeds), and on the other side the consciousness of plants stand so low, that the difference between the stimulus of reflex movement and the motive of instinctive action must shrink to a minimum. Nevertheless we shall still find abundant traces, which unmistakably confront us as the same as that which we call instinct in the animal kingdom. A polype instinctively betakes itself from the shaded half of its vessel to that illuminated by the sun, and when Oscillatoriæ do the same, when the sunflower almost dislocates its neck in order to turn its face to the sun, is that not to be called instinct? Dutrochet relates in his *Rech.* p. 131 : " I saw the leaf of a plant standing in the open air, whose upper surface was covered with a small board, try to withdraw itself from the screen by means which were not always the same, but were always of a kind which must most easily and quickly lead to the goal; thus this happened now by means of a lateral bending of the leaf-stalk, now by a bending of the same leaf-stalk towards the pedicle."

Knight saw a vine-leaf, whose under side was illuminated by the sun, and whose approach to a natural position he had blocked in every way, make almost every possible attempt to turn to the light the right side, with which it was mainly necessitated to respire. After it had for a few days attempted to approach the light in a certain direction, and by bending back its lobes had almost covered its whole under-side therewith, it spread itself out and removed further from the window of the glass-house, in order to approach the light in the opposite direction

(Treviranus, Beiträge, 119). Frank (Die natürl. wagerechte Richtung, &c., Leipzig, 1870) has recently confirmed this, and extended it to a number of other plants. According to him also it is noticeable that this movement is always executed *by the shortest course*, the leaf turning now up, now down, now right, now left. The wonder is not diminished by the circumstance that the leaves, or leaf-stalks, lose this capability when their growth is complete, except when they are provided with special cushion-like swellings at the base of the stem, which on every occasion may again receive changes of dimension, which during the period of growth are to be looked upon as relatively violent modifications of the same.—Dutrochet covered the terminal leaf of a three-leaved bean-leaf (*Phaseolus vulgaris*) with a small board. As the shortness of the special leaf-stalk made retreat impossible to the leaflet, this took place by the *bending of the joint petiole*, whereas in the dark the board was not evaded. "If," says the investigator, "one sees how many means are here applied to attain the same end, one will be almost tempted to believe there dwells here a secret intelligence which chooses the most appropriate means for the attainment of the end." So, driven by the simple power of facts, does a naturalist utter a truth, which is only incomprehensible to him, because he is not acquainted with unconscious psychical activity. That there is here no mere reflex action on a stimulus is easy to see, for it is just the *want* of a necessary stimulus which is *evaded*.

Tolerably familiar are the phenomena of vegetable sleep, whereby the leaves are partly lowered, partly inverted, the flowers lower their heads or shut up. In fact, these phenomena have been already mentioned and find their end in protecting the pollen grains from the dew. That the depression of the petals, however, does not depend on mere exhaustion, we may easily convince ourselves; in their bent condition they are rather in a state of tension and elastic. *Malva peruviana*, by rearing the leaves round the stalk at the tip of the branches forms in the dormant condition a kind of funnel, under which the young flowers or leaves are protected; *Impatiens-noli-me-tangere* forms out of the depressed upper leaves an arch for the young sprouts, some others enclose the flowers by folding the leaflets of their compound leaves. The time for sleep and waking are as different for plants as for animals. Many of our plants bend towards the sun, others punctually keep fixed times, no matter into what climate they are transferred, no matter whether it be summer or winter. One sees from this that these periodical movements also are partially independent of external stimuli and arise purely from internal conditions of the plant itself; they are simply instinctively regulated efforts.

In many plants the stamina incline towards the pistil for purposes of fertilisation, shed their pollen, and then return to their position; in others the pistil moves towards the stamens; in yet others, both mutually seek each other (Treviranus, Physiologie der Gewächse, ii. 389). In *Lilium superbum, Amaryllis formosissima*, and *Pancratium maritimum*, the anthers successively approach the stigma. In *Fritillaria persica*, they alternately bend towards the style. In *Rhus coriaria*, two or three filaments simultaneously protrude, describe a quadrant, and bring their anthers quite close to the stigma. In *Saxifraga tridactilytes, muscoides, aizoon, granulata*, and *cotyledon*, two stamens approach each other from opposite sides above the stigma, and again spread, after they have scattered their pollen, in order to make room for others. In *Parnassia palustris* the male parts move to the female in the same order in which the pollen matures, and indeed, when they approach the stigma, quickly and at once, when they again separate after fertilisation, in three periods. In *Tropæolum* they elevate themselves one after the other from the originally depressed filaments at the period of full bloom, and after the anthers have shed their pollen on the stigma bend down again, in order to make room for others. One cannot wish for a clearer indication of instinct than is presented in these examples; for here the motive is the presence of the stigma, and the maturity of the pollen, but the order in which, and the fashion in which the stamens move to and fro wears just as much the semblance of caprice as any animal movement can.

Remarkable are the instinctive movements of climbing plants (*vide* Mohl, On the Winding of Tendrils). Such a plant first grows somewhat perpendicularly upwards, then its stalk bends horizontally, and describes circles, in order to seek a support in the environment, just as an eyeless caterpillar describes circles with its anterior parts to seek a new leaf. The longer the pistil grows the larger, of course, become the circles; that is, if the plant finds no support in the environment it seeks it in a wider circuit. Finally, if the stalk can no longer support its own weight it falls to the ground, and now creeps further in a straight direction. If it now finds a support it might either take no notice of it, or, for convenience sake, run indeed further along the earth in order not to be obliged to climb; in point of fact, however, it immediately grasps its support and climbs up by it spirally. Yet here, too, the plant still proceeds by way of selection; the flat side (especially in the young stalk) does not wind itself about dead organic or inorganic supports, but only about living plants, by which it eagerly climbs upwards, for the roots cleaving to the earth soon die, and it is then entirely assigned to the food, which it imbibes with its papillae from the clasped plant. Every creeping plant by nature either moves to the right or to the left. If one unrolls a young *convolvulus* from its support and winds it round again in the opposite direction, it will return into its original spiral direction, or will surrender its life in the endeavour. This too answers to the animal instincts. If however, one allows two such plants mutually to embrace without foreign support, and so to climb by one another's aid, the one voluntarily changes its solitary direction in order to make this mutual embrace possible (Farmer's Magazine, repeated in the *Times* of the 13th July 1848). Thus, instead of adapting itself to the powerful change, the plant prefers to sacrifice its life; but when this change is judicious, it anticipates it of its own accord. Here one finds even the variability of animal instinct in the most remarkable form.

(c) *The Instinct for Beauty* in plants cannot in this place be further proved. I hold the assertion to be correct also for the vegetable kingdom, that every being builds itself up as beautifully as is compatible with the ends of its existence, and so far as it can subdue the stubborn material. Whether one considers the greatest or the least in the vegetable kingdom, the stately oak or the microscopic moss; whether one looks to the whole or the individual, to the glorious primæval forest or the fir cone, everywhere that truth will be found confirmed.

Thus we have again found the five moments in the vegetable kingdom in which, as in the animal kingdom, we perceived the effects of the Unconscious in bodily life. Accordingly, we are no longer warranted in refusing to the plant unconscious will and unconscious presentation. That we perceive no higher mental phenomena in the plant need not surprise us, since, indeed, the purpose of the vegetable kingdom is altogether only this—to prepare the ground, the food, and the atmosphere for the animal kingdom, although we must also admit that at the same time the creative principle works itself out independently in the vegetable kingdom in its own fashion.

2. *Consciousness in the Plant.*—The result thus far was not difficult to foresee, and needed no great penetration. More difficult, however, is the question whether in the plant there also dwells a consciousness.

Old as Natural Science is the dispute concerning the vegetable or animal nature of certain organisms, and even at the present day it is as little capable of decision as in the time of Aristotle, for the simple reason that as an alternative it does not admit of decision.

Plants and animals have, as organic beings, certain attributes in common; by other attributes they are distinguished according to their different offices in the household of Nature. But now, if all vital phenomena are reducible to so simple a form, that those distinguishing qualities more or less disappear, and essentially only those common to the two kingdoms remain, the differences between plant and animal must also disappear, and it is foolish to maintain a dispute which in its nature must be without result. Microscopic observation is so far advanced that, if there were criteria for the vegetable or the animal nature, they could certainly not escape the investigator, and the dispute would have ended long ago; that there are, in fact, no criteria mutually admitted by the two contending parties, is a proof that there is no distinct agreement as to the point of dispute itself. Were the facts accepted without prejudice, the inference could only be that one had hitherto narrowed too much the sphere of the qualities common to the two kingdoms, that there are far fewer differences between animal and plant than one had previously supposed, and that these differences became only in their extreme forms so striking that nobody can mistake them. Quite recently this way of looking at the matter has also gained ground in scientific circles, the strictest development of the same being the attempt of Häckel to set up a third kingdom of Protista before the vegetable and animal kingdom, although he may perhaps have extended its borders too far, and his criterion of non-sexual reproduction may turn out to be untenable, because the possession of sexual generation alike by animal and plant points to a *common origin, i.e.*, to its existence already in the realm of Protista. Altogether the attempt to give fixed definition to the naturally fluctuating boundaries between the Protist kingdom on the one hand, and the animal and vegetable kingdom on the other, must be just as vain as the earlier endeavour in respect to the two latter kingdoms.

This mode of regarding the matter is also the only one which can be approved by geology. Whilst the terrestrial creation now subsists by the equilibrium of the productions of the animal and vegetable kingdom, manifestly the first foundation-stone of organic nature could only be laid by such beings as contained this equilibrium *in themselves*, and accordingly stood still at the point of indifference between animal and vegetable. One of the most important of these wonderful beings, to which the history of this earth appears to owe the whole chalk formation, has been dragged to light by recent explorations of the sea-depths, and been called Bathybius. In what way this slimy gelatinous net with interspersed protoplasmic nuclei filling up the sea-bottom, and secreting little heaps of microscopic calcareous shells (Coccoliths) is fed and thrives in the absence of every ray of light, is up to this time a riddle. Only from such an insignificant commencement could the development begin on different sides, in that marine animals arose, which lived on these undifferentiated Protista (Polyps, &c.), and as their counterpoise the first stages of decided vegetable structures became possible. The more the two kingdoms became peopled, the more were means of subsistence placed at the disposal of the higher animal classes, the more higher classes of vegetable could again exist on the living and dead products of these animals, and the evolution thus kept pace in the two kingdoms, as geology teaches, whilst within each kingdom the lower grades generally always preceded the higher. From this one should, however, draw the conclusion that vegetable kingdom and animal kingdom are not subordinate, but co-ordinate departments of creation, and that the animal kingdom, when it holds itself entitled to take rank above the vegetable kingdom in virtue of the higher development of consciousness, owes this power entirely to the pre-eminence of the latter in organic reference, since the latter forms for it the materials, to the leisurely consumption of which it owes its own higher consciousness. If, now, the consumption of material, which is formed in foreign organisms, suffices to define the action of parasitism (for the dwelling of the parasite is indifferent, as, for example, the chamber-bug), the animal kingdom as a whole may be called a *parasite of the vegetable kingdom.* In this respect the animal kingdom resembles the great class of fungi, which, although, according to morphological analogies, hitherto reckoned to plants, yet can only be termed vegetable parasites. There are wanting to them, namely, the vegetable "philosopher's stone," the arcanum, by whose help the vegetable converts inorganic matter into organic *chlorophyll,* and they are therefore just as much as the animal kingdom consigned to the consumption of ready-formed organic matter.

This contrast of formation and consumption is now, however, not to be taken so strictly, as if the plant *merely* produced, the animal *merely* consumed, rather do we see in every animal also processes partly of the higher elaboration of received material (*e.g.*, the formation of cerebral fats), partly of the conversion of the same without relapse, partly of decomposition and recomposition in the course of the process of digestion and assimilation. On the other hand, we see in every plant a consumption here and there of the products, which it has itself formed at other places (we have only to think of the processes of retrogression in flowers, their inspiration of oxygen and excretion of carbonic acid). In yeast, fungi, and some other unicellular plants, we even find a remarkable ambiguity of such a kind, that they are able to take up, indeed, the nitrogen requisite for their organic production from ammonia, the carbon, however, only from higher ternary combinations. There can, accordingly, on both sides be a dispute only of a *more or less;* every animal is in part of vegetable, every plant, in part, of animal nature; where one side clearly dominates the other, we rightly term the whole according to that side; but where both are in tolerable equipoise, a one-sided designation is difficult—nay, even inadmissible. We can now also find it no longer wonderful, if one and the same being exhibits for one part of its life an eminently vegetable, during another part an eminently animal nature. There is no greater metamorphosis at those stages near the point of indifference, than that of insects, frogs, or fishes. Certainly, whoever regards animals as animated organisms, but plants as merely empty soulless husks, such an one must be brought to despair by that fluctuation of the boundary of the two kingdoms, and the harmless passing over from the one to the other. We shall, however, see in these facts, in conjunction with the previous considerations of this chapter, only one more proof that plant and animal have much more in common than our age is accustomed to suppose.

As concerns the external general form, plants lose at lower stages their foliate type, and assume simply articulated, or rotundate, more or less enclosed forms (*e.g.*, Confervæ, Fungi). On the other hand one finds striking similarities with higher vegetable forms among the lower animals. "Some (coral animals) grow as leaves rolled one over another, like a cabbage-head, others consist of delicate, crisp, irregularly arranged leaflets. The surface of every leaf is covered by polyp-blossoms, by whose growth and secretion it has arisen. Not less may we detect resemblances with an oak or acanthus twig, with fungi, mosses, and lichens" (Dana in Schleiden's and Froriep's Not., 1847, June No. 48).

The chemical substances can certainly not establish a difference. Linnaeus thought we must regard several calcareous marine plants, such as corallines, as animals, just because he regarded the formation of chalk as a monopoly of the animal kingdom. Silicious coats of mail are found both in vegetable (Diatomaceæ) as in animal (Infusoria) organisms. The similarity of the vegetable and animal proteids is well known; the Fungi especially are rich in animal-like compounds; in the mantle of the Ascidians and other salpae-like Tunicata is found ligneous fibre; chlorophyll (leaf-green) has been proved to exist in Turbellariæ (rotifers) and in Infusoria.

Often different species of a genus were reckoned partly to the vegetable kingdom, partly to the animal kingdom, *e.g.*, the species of *Alcyonium* are all in the main of so similar a nature, that Linnaeus certainly was not wrong in including them in one genus. Nevertheless, some of them are the not inaptly named *Animalia ambigua* (according to Pallas), which accordingly are very well ranked among the Amorphozoaria, *e.g.*, *Alcyonium cidaris* (Donati), *cydonium* (Leba), and *ficiforme* (Sotander, Ellis, and Marsigli). Others were generally reckoned to the vegetable world, thus, especially, *e.g.*, several specimens of the synonymous genus *Peziza*, so rich in species. In yet others not only the animal, but even the polyp nature is so decidedly evinced, that they have been separated from the Sponges and ranked among the Polypifera at the same time with the addition of a second generic name, so that *Lobularia digitata*, *palmata*, and *arborea*, from the Alcyonaria of the animal corals, are synonymous with *Alcyonium lobatum*, *palmatum*, and *arborcum*. The primæval species *Manon peziza* is compounded of an animal and a plant name. Here we find only phenomena from other departments of the animal kingdom again, where, *e.g.*, some rotifers are reckoned to the worms, others to the infusoria, a species *Cercaria* to the worms, other species of the same genus to the spermatozoids (?)

The small vesicles of which the red-colouring matter of snow consists (*Protococcus nivalis*), were regarded by Agardh, Decandolle, Hooker, Unger, Martin, Harvey, Ehrenberg, as Algae; the latter sowed them even on fresh snow and observed their propagation; the tiny young plants bore a finely-grained, lobed receptacle and rootlets, but no trace of animal character. Voigt and Meyen subsequently found, that the red-colouring matter presented rather the form and movement of infusoria, and Shuttleworth finally distinguished therein partly Algae, partly Infusoria. These contradictions are cleared up by Flotow's careful observations on a quite allied little plant or animal (*Hæmatococcus pluvialis*) living in rain-water. This showed at first merely a vegetable nature, was converted however in infusions under suitable circumstances by different intermediate steps clearly traceable, into an infusory animalcule (*Astasia pluvialis*) with proboscidiform, sometimes even furcate feelers and all the signs of independent movement. Shuttleworth's *Astasia nivalis* showed itself related in red snow. Kützing (" On the Metamorphosis of Infusoria into the lower forms of Algae, Nordhausen 1844 ") observed, that the infusorium *Chlamidomonas pulvisculus* changed many times, *e.g.*, into a decided species of Algae, *Stygeolconium stellare*, and into other formations of an algous character, which certainly in form partially resembled sedentary forms of infusoria (*Tetraspora lubrica* or *gelatinosa*, *Palmella botryoides*, species of *Protococcus* and *Gyges*). The same asserts the conversion of the infusorium *Enchelys pulvisculus* into a Protococcus and finally into an Oscillatoria. In a whole series of algae (*Zoospermae*) and yet other lower plants (Fungi, Star-jelly), the germinal granules, spores or sporidia have an infusorian-like form, and move by means of cilia or whip-shaped organs, and there are even certain forms among them, which Ehrenberg recognised as infusoria. An altogether similar state of things is observed in the embryos of many polyps and Medusæ, they too go through a period, in which by means of cilia they produce a simultaneous rotatory and progressive movement, before they settle themselves for further evolution, they have also the form of infusoria and no mouth. Unger (" The Plant in the Moment of becoming Animal ") observed of the sporidia of a small Alga (*Vaucheria clavata*, or *Ectosperma clavata*), that, when liberated from the mother cell, they at first raise themselves in the water and revolve several times in quick movement similar to an infusorium, that then moments of repose arbitrarily alternate with movement, and that they carefully avoid all obstacles in the most surprising manner, wind themselves extremely cleverly through the threads of the Vaucheria, and always avoid each other in such a way that two never collide.

The emission of mucilaginous filaments indistinctly formed and again coalescing, which is characteristic of many kinds of inferior animals, is also found in certain plants (*Mycomycetes*).—A small thread-like species of Algæ exhibits, as long as it actively vegetates, a threefold movement—an alternating slight curvature of the anterior filament, a half-pendulous, self-elastic, to-and-fro bending of the anterior half, and a gradual advance. "These movements have something strange, I might say uncanny, about them" (Schleiden, Grundzüge, ii. 549). The Oscillatoriæ and the Zoospores of several kinds of algæ (*e.g.*, *Vaucheria sessilis*) move just like polyps to the illuminated part of the vessel; other Zoospores (*e.g.*, of *Ulothrix speciosa*) flee from the same, yet others (those of the families of *Stephanosaura*) avoid both intense illumination and darkness, and collect at semi-dark places.—Pandorine, an Alga living in fresh-water pools, affords an example of the family of the Volvocineæ; it consists of sixteen pyramidal cells, which, with their bases turned outwards, form by their close attachment to one another an ovate collective body. Every cell has at its base a colourless spot on which rest several cilia, by means of which the organism swims about. From this mobility its animal nature was for a long time inferred, and Ehrenberg called the red pigment granule found beside each ciliated part, an eye.

We see that all the marks which have been set up on different sides as decisive do not hold, such as partial or total locomotion, spontaneous movement, morphological and chemical differences, mouth and stomach. As concerns the oral aperture, it is in the sea-blubber (*Rhizostoma Cuvieri*), a Medusa of the Mediterranean one to two feet in diameter, replaced by numerous openings and canals in its eight arms; further, a mouth is entirely wanting in many intestinal worms, Cercariæ, infusoria, and embryos; the Gregarinæ, which are found in abundance as parasites in the digestive canals of insects and other animals, have not only no oral aperture, but also no cilia—no visible organs at all; they are simply cells with visible nuclei. To speak of a stomach where the mouth is wanting is without meaning, for then we may call the interior of every cell its stomach.

These statements may suffice to justify the previous general remarks.—What is now contributed by this examination to the solution of the question regarding the consciousness of plants is as follows:—We have seen that plant and animal have something distinct, somewhat in common, and that we may fairly well collect the total of the common characters, if in both kingdoms we descend so far down the scale of organisation, until we come to those structures where the differences disappear, and essentially only the common element remains. If we now find that in this common element sensation and consciousness is still included, that thus the lowest vegetable organisms possess sensation and consciousness, we shall look round for the material conditions to which here sensation and consciousness appear to be linked; and supposing these material conditions are fulfilled in higher plants in the same or still higher degree, we shall consider ourselves warranted in ascribing also to the higher plants a similar, but higher, measure of sensation and consciousness to that which we may suppose to exist in those lower ones. Since we do not directly know how the plant feels, but only how we ourselves feel, we descend the animal scale guided by analogy, turn round again at the indifference-point of animal and plant, which forms the connecting link between the two kingdoms, and likewise under the guidance of analogy ascend the scale of plants.

Further, we call to mind the result of the conclusion of

the first introductory chapter and of C. Chap. iii., according to which each sensation excited by material movement, as soon as it at all arises, also arises consciously, whilst if the material movement lies below the threshold of stimulation, not only no conscious, but altogether no sensation at all comes to pass. So far then as we can trace signs of a sensation excited by material stimuli, so far shall we also be obliged to regard sensation as conscious, and thus must allow the existence of a consciousness, no matter how barren its content may be.

We must here recur once more to the already frequently repelled prejudice (comp. A. Chap. vii. 1. a., vol. i. pp. 173, 174), according to which nerves are the *conditio sine qua non* of sensation. That on this globe, and up to this time, they are the form of matter most suited to the production of sensation is certainly not to be doubted. It by no means, however, follows from that that they are the sole form; on the contrary, a multitude of facts prove that other forms may be substituted for them. The tactile papillæ in the epidermis are found at several parts of the body at tolerably wide intervals (as the sizes of the ellipses prove, within which two contacts are felt as one). Nevertheless every spot of the skin is alike sensitive, even to thermal and chemical stimuli, where the mere propagation of mechanical pressure or conduction of heat is excluded. Burdach states that even nerveless parts of the human body may become sensitive as soon as, with increased blood-pressure and loosening of the tissue, their vitality is increased; so that, *e.g.*, the new flesh formed in healing wounds may be highly sensitive without any nerves, and an inflammation of the nerveless cartilage and kidneys may be even much more painful than an inflammation of the nerves themselves. Wundt shows (Beiträge, pp. 392–395) that these pains are always accompanied by specific organic sensations. Here certainly the pain of which the man is conscious is localised only in the brain, but the nerve-like function of those parts is thereby proved, *i.e.*, their capacity to propagate currents of molecular vibrations which are similar to those in nerves. Where, however, forms of vibration exist similar to those of the nerves, they will also excite sensations which are similar to those excited by nerves, supposing that they do not lie beneath the threshold of stimulation. The latter is in no case to be assumed, since the part reaching the brain after so great a resistance causes still so many violent pains. Further, we have often seen the mind act on the body without nerves; *e.g.*, in the embryonic states before elaboration of the nerves, in the action of the nerves beyond their own limits in muscles, secreting glands, everywhere where the mass of the organs concerned must themselves undertake the last portion of the conduction, in the sudden turning grey of the hair after emotion, &c. But now, if the mind can act upon the body even without or beyond the nerves, yet in the thoroughgoing reciprocal action of the relation of body and mind, the body also, without or beyond the nerves, can act upon the mind, *i.e.*, evoke sensation.

Then it is almost certain that the lowest animals (polyps, infusoria, several intestinal worms) have no nerves, for nerves and muscles go everywhere hand in hand; and according to Dujardin and Ecker they have no muscles at all: in place of muscular fibrine and nerve matter, only the fibroine of Mulder is found in them. This substance comports itself pretty much as the neoplasm of wounds, and is therefore at the present time generally called protoplasm. It is becoming continually clearer that the proper support of life is in every cell its protoplasm, and that the protoplasm of the cells of the grey matter of the brain, mediating the highest functions of thought, is altogether not different in type, but only in degree, from the protoplasm of the lowest organisms. This nitrogenous, albuminous substance, called protoplasm, is thus the special substance in which the organic and motor acts of will of the animal mind operate in conformity with its ends;

in it alone can we therefore look for that constitution of organic matter, which is adapted and able to allow material effects to directly influence the mind.

Add to that the relatively high psychical manifestations of these animals; for the fresh-water polyp distinguishes, even at the distance of a few lines, a living infusorium, a vegetable, a dead and an inorganic object. Of all these he only draws to himself the first mentioned by a whirlpool created by his arms, whilst he does not trouble about the others; or if he by chance grasps one of them, he immediately lets it go again. The polyp must thus, indeed, have different perceptions of these different things, and these can only be given as sensations above the threshold, *i.e.*, as conscious sensations. Further, it moves out of the shadow towards the part of the vessel illuminated by the sun, and often two polyps struggle over their prey. The latter is only possible if the polyp possesses the consciousness that the other will deprive him of his booty. If, then, a nerveless animal displays such high manifestations of consciousness, we should not be surprised to find manifestations of consciousness at the next lower grade of the infusoria, and its many lower plants at the same level. This, however, one would hardly venture to maintain, that with the penultimate animal grade sensation and consciousness ceases; for why precisely at the penultimate, which yet exhibits so rich a content of consciousness that indefinitely many poorer stages can be imagined before complete disappearance, to which nothing in the world would correspond except just those infusoria and simple plants? In fact, however, a more exact observation of the lowest animal genera of all renders evident quite distinct perceptions, as follows from the appropriate use of the given (perceived) circumstances for the vital purposes of the animal. I need only mention the manifestly voluntary movements of *Arcella vulgaris* by means of appropriately developed air-bubbles (in vol. i. pp. 93–95).

What makes the protoplasm of nerves so well adapted

both for mediating the execution of acts of will and for the production of sensations is the semi-fluid consistency of the whole mass, which furthers the displacement and rotation of the molecules, and the polar nature of the individual molecule, which has a high degree of chemical organisation of matter for its condition. The former is equally well shown by the protoplasm of lower animals and plants. In every cell there is to be made out at least a fluid content and a solid wall, commonly also a nucleus; both the nucleus, or at any rate its environment, as well as the boundary of wall and content, frequently, however, the whole content of the cell, exhibit this semi-fluid consistency of high chemical organisation, from which physical and chemical elements one may conclude with probability to a polar constitution of the molecules, if also in a less degree than in nerves, and of the central ganglion cells, which likewise consist of nucleus, wall, and content, especially if one takes note of the phenomena of contraction of all animal and vegetable protoplasm after electrical stimulation. These conditions, however, recur in all properly living parts of higher plants, probably even in heightened forms, since the chemical organisation of matter manifestly increases in higher organisms, but in no case sinks. But quite specially vegetable protoplasm, which, as we have seen, brings to pass the quick reflex movements of the higher plants, shows apparently a perfect identity with the protoplasm of the Protista and lowest animals, as is proved by the same behaviour with respect to the most different stimuli and narcotics. This protoplasm has, however, also in *higher* animals a very wide distribution; and if attention was at first turned to its vital action by those examples, where its movements achieve results which become visible and startling even to the naked eye, at the present moment vegetable physiology already studies with zeal the movements of protoplasm going on *within* the *cells* on the irritation of light, heat, and other stimuli, which manifestly stand in the closest relation to the life and propagation of the cells.[1] There is thus quite certainly no ground for the assertion that the sensation and the consciousness of higher plants stand *below* that of the lowest plants and animals; on the contrary, we may presume that, although the total and partial mobility of plants of higher forms decreases in conformity with their vital conditions, the sensations, at least in certain privileged parts, rank *above* that of the lower plants.

The lower we descend in the animal scale, the more does the importance of the sensations related to digestion and the genital region increase in comparison with those arising from outer stimuli. In plants where the surface is more and more secluded from the insignificant external stimuli, this augmentation will go still further. For the plant, the outer world, except light and the chemical constitution of the atmosphere, is continually losing all interest, and we only owe to special cases the knowledge that also higher plants take notice of certain events which obtain for them importance, *e.g.*, the plants which capture insects, of stimuli which affect the leaves, the climbers of supports, &c.

After the foregoing it will no longer surprise us if we attribute to plants a sensation (and of course conscious sensation) of the stimuli on which they, whether reflectorially or instinctively, react; if we assert that the

[1] As in lower animals (*e.g.*, Amœbæ), so also in the protoplasm of living vegetable cells, there are to be distinguished a state of activity and another of perfect rest, which may alternate with one another even several times. Although both states uniformly belong to *life*, yet only in the former does there appear to be present a distinct sensibility, whereas there is in the latter a lowering of irritability, which resembles the anæsthesia of protoplasm brought about by narcotic vapours, and perhaps forms an analogue of animal sleep, or still better of hibernation. As certain infusoria, after a period of active vitality, enter upon a period of incrustation, so also do many vegetable cells that at maturity surround themselves with a thicker cell-wall, which cell-wall may even remain after their death (*e.g.*, ligneous cells). The acme of sensibility in every vegetable cell one must therefore only seek in a particular, sometimes perhaps very short, epoch of their life, which forms the culminating point of their vital activity, and accordingly for the most part falls into their youthful period.

Oscillatoria as well as the polyp *feels* light if it wanders towards the illuminated part of its vessel, and that just in the same way the vine-leaf feels the light, to which it endeavours by all means to turn its right side, and every flower feels the light, to which it on expanding turns its tiny head. We maintain that the leaf of the *Dionæa* and of the *Mimosa pudica feels* the struggling of the insect before it reacts on this sensation by folding up; for it lies indeed in the notion of reflex action, as a psychical reaction, that a psychical perception must precede the same. This is, however, conscious sensation. We further maintain that the plant has a sensation of the physical events of the organisation which answer to animal digestion and of sexual life; that the latter especially takes place in parts where the higher vitality of vegetable existence is concentrated, where the plastic activity during flowering time effects no longer compounding, but decompounding chemical processes (as the inhaling of oxygen and exhaling of carbonic acid of the flowers proves); whence it follows that here the formative forces have withdrawn from material construction into a certain animal-like internalisation, and become disposable for more receptive processes. That the content of this consciousness must always be still very poor, much poorer, *e.g.*, than that of the wretchedest worm, hardly admits of doubt; for whence should wealth and definiteness come, such as is afforded the animals through the lowest sense-organs?

We have thus, in fact, found consciousness in the plant. But now how far can a UNITY of consciousness exist in the plant?—We have seen that the unity of the consciousness of two ideas or sensations depends on the possibility of comparison, and this on the presence of a sufficient communication between the two places producing sensation. The question then is this: Does such a communication exist in the plant? Already in the animal the converse between different nerve-centres, although mediated by nerve-cords, was exceedingly deficient and the unity of consciousness in fact only extant for very energetic excitements. The velocity of propagation of the nerve-current in man, according to Helmholtz, amounts to about a hundred feet in a second; that in the *Mimosa pudica*, as before mentioned, only to a few millimeters. One can draw from these velocities a tolerable conclusion as to the resistances to conduction, and accordingly to the disturbances and changes of the propagated results. It is possible that the spiral vessels serve such purposes of communication, but it is not proven. At all events, with regard to the unity of consciousness of two neighbouring anthers, the connection must be infinitely weaker than with that of brain and ganglia in man. A sufficiently faithful and strong conduction will always only be able to exist between the parts lying quite near to one another. I would not affirm that one is at liberty to speak of the indivisible consciousness of a flower,—hardly perhaps of that of a stamen. The plant does not, however, need such a unity of consciousness as the animal; it needs to institute no comparisons, and does not need to reflect on its actions. It needs only surrender itself to the single sensations, and let the same serve as motives for the incursions of the Unconscious. Then have these fulfilled their purpose; and this is accomplished just as well by sensations with separate consciousness as by those with one indivisible consciousness.

V.

MATTER AS WILL AND IDEA.

PHYSICAL science is concerned with three inter-connected objects: *laws, forces,* and *matter*. This division is entirely deserving of approval, for it summarily embraces different groups of phenomena under single points of view and facilitates expression. The question now is, whether these three are really of different nature; or whether, strictly speaking, they are only *one*, which, looked at merely from different points of view, *appears* in three different modes? Of the *laws* this may well be allowed without discussion, for it is obvious that they are not existences hovering in the air, but mere abstractions of forces and substances. Only because this force and this matter are so and so, only on that account do they *act* in a particular manner; and as often as we meet with such a force, we must find it acting in just such a way. This constancy of the *so-acting*, however, it is which we call Law. This relation is also pretty generally acknowledged, and we hear, in fact, materialists always speak of *force and matter* as their principia, as something which of course includes laws. We have in C. Chap. ii. defended Materialism, so far as it maintains organised matter to be the *conditio sine qua non* of conscious mental activity; we have in the preceding inquiries established an unconscious psychical principle as superior to matter, and thereby already shown the one-sidedness of that Materialism which knows no other than material principles. We have now arrived at the point where we must occupy ourselves with that, which this one-sided Materialism sets up as exclusive principles of all existence, i.e., as philosophical first principles, *force* and *matter*.[1]

I should consider it useless to enter here into a dialectical discussion of these conceptions; one would thereby neither be sure of actually treating of precisely the same notion as Materialism, nor would a materialist ever be induced to change his opinion by such a method. I hold the deepening of the natural scientific investigation of matter to be the only suitable course. It is true the future may yet bring inestimable light in this direction which we have not hitherto suspected, yet I believe that the outlines of the only possible mode of apprehending Matter are not only rendered so certain by the most recent results of physics and chemistry that no time will ever shake them, but that they offer also perfectly satisfactory resting-places for penetrating into the last depths of this mystery. If this

---

[1] As we shall see that force is only a pseudo-materialistic, but in fact a spiritualistic principle, the consequential Materialism, which, however, has been nowhere advocated in this form, should before all things deny force. *i.e.*, regard Motion as an ultimate, requiring no explanation, as an eternal and original quality of matter. The circumstance that many derivative forces (as magnetic attraction or repulsion between wires traversed by galvanic currents) are, in fact, only results of peculiar combinations of movement, might seduce us to go farther on this road, and to try, whether also the elementary forces of the general attraction of masses (gravitation) and of repulsion in ether could be explained as results of the forms of movement. For this purpose the ether is first of all denied, and a filling of space with very rarefied gases supposed; then repulsion is regarded as a result of heat-vibrations, and finally gravitation is sought to be explained either according to the analogy of the attraction of galvanic currents as a bye-product of transverse (heat or other) vibrations, or as a phenomenon resulting from the repulsion of peripheral strata. (In both cases, certainly, gravitation would not be proportional to the mass of a body, but to its plane of intersection at right angles to the direction of gravitation.) The whole theory is still too much in an embryonic condition to admit of criticism. Only this much stands firm, that *matter*, with all its contradictions, to be pointed out farther on, is here indispensable, since possibly force, but not motion itself, may be the mobile, and that accordingly this theory stops at *two* incomprehensible principles, matter and motion; whilst we get along with force *alone*, which is free from the contradictions of matter, and is itself again not an incomprehensible ultimate, but resolvable into the spiritual principles will and idea; thus in this manner closely joins the material world with the spiritual as consubstantial.

has not been the case hitherto, or at least not yet on the part of physical science, the reason simply is that physical science has at bottom always only so far an interest in hypotheses as the latter either afford it guidance to new experiments, or as they are indispensable for the application of the calculus: in what goes beyond that it sees no *practical* value, and therefore is indifferent to it. We shall thus have first to recapitulate what physical science knows of the constitution of matter, and the forces inhering therein, and then see whether these results are capable of being fathomed in a simple and unforced way.

If we imagine a chemically homogeneous body, *e.g.*, chalk, continuously divided, we arrive at parts of a certain size which cannot be further divided *if they are to remain chalk;* if we succeed in splitting them up, we get as separate portions one part carbonic acid and one part lime. These smallest parts of a body are called molecules.[1] These act in different directions with different force, because they have in general the crystalline ground-form of the particular chemical substance, or such an one from which this can be easily formed. The molecules of different substances are thus distinguished by different forms, also, moreover, by different weight (molecular weight); on the other hand, in their grouping into bodies in the gaseous state they fill equal spaces with equal temperature. If two bodies of different kinds come together, the forces of the molecules differently active in different directions, mutually disturb one another at the borders of both

---

[1] Not to be confused with atoms, as is done by the older physicists. Philosophical readers who come to this chapter with a certain prejudice against the physical atomic theory, I refer to Fechner's memoir "On the Physical and Philosophical Atomic Theory" (Leipzig, 1855), especially pp. 18-63 and 129-141, although since then the physical atomic theory has been very much further developed by the working out of the Theory of Heat. Comp., in reference to the present chapter, my essay, "Dynamism and Atomism (Kant, Ulrici, Fechner)," in the Ges. Phil. Ablandh., No. vii.—In this place only this much need be remarked by way of preliminary, that the splitting up into atoms in a metaphysical sense represents nothing else than the special form in which, in the department of matter, the general philosophical principle of *Individuation* obtains its realisation.

bodies in their conditions of equilibrium, which disturbances are presented as electrical excitement, or are propagated as galvanic vibrations; if the disturbance is sufficiently strong, a permanent rearrangement and chemical union of the different molecules into more compound molecules takes place. The various chemical compounds are distinguished by the number and position of the combining molecules. Those molecules which we have not as yet succeeded in decomposing we call chemically simple, although we know with tolerable certainty of several that they are compound (*e.g.*, iodine, bromine, chlorine are possibly combinations of oxygen, as the change of their spectra at very high temperatures appears to indicate; the metals perhaps are all combinations of hydrogen), so that possibly the number of chemical elements may be very much simplified. Moreover, modern chemistry distinguishes the elementary molecules according to their behaviour in chemical combinations into univalent and multivalent molecules, and conceives the latter as compounds of several equivalent parts, each of which is chemically equivalent to a univalent molecule. It calls these parts atoms, and their relative weights atomic weights. But already this difference of weight proves that even these chemical atoms can just as little be the ultimate elements of matter as the chemical molecules in their manifold morphological fundamental forms. The simple numerical relations of the atomic weights permit us to conclude that all these parts of matter are in the last resort only different dispositions of a varied number of homogeneous primitive elements or primitive atoms, as only in this way does the agreement of the atomic weights with the specific heat and that of the molecular weight with the specific weight of gases appear intelligible. These homogeneous primitive atoms, which I shall immediately call without ceremony atomic bodies, must act in all directions with *equal* force, and can thus, *if* they are to be conceived as material, only be imagined *spherical*.

Besides these body-atoms there are ether-atoms, which

are distributed both in every body between the corporeal molecules and also between the heavenly bodies, and which are perceived by their property of radiating heat. (A certain part of the thermal scale is, owing to the structure of our eyes, only perceived by us as light.) The ethereal atoms it is which, as environing envelopes of the corporeal molecules, produce electrical phenomena, and by revolution of the corporeal molecules (Ampère's molecular current) magnetic phenomena; further, it is these which, in the mutual rebound of the molecule of a gas, cause the elastic repulsion; in short, they are a hypothesis which is nowhere to be dispensed with when manifestations of energy are to be explained, in which, besides attraction according to the Newtonian law of gravitation, repellent forces also play a part.

Bodies and corporeal atoms attract one another, and that too in the inverse square of their distance; *i.e.*, the force of a corporeal atom, in all directions of space taken together, remains equal at all distances.

Ether and ethereal atoms repel one another, and that too in the inverse ratio of a higher than the second power of the distance, the third at least; *i.e.*, the force of an ethereal atom, in all directions of space taken together, increases at least inversely as the distance.[1] All bodyatoms would converge to a point if the environing etheratoms did not form, as it were, envelopes round every material molecule, preventing actual contact. Two etheratoms can never collide, because their repulsion at infinitely small distances becomes infinitely great. Two body-atoms, however, could never separate again, supposing they once touched, because then their attraction would be infinitely great. Therefore the corporeal molecules must also be

---

[1] According to Briot (Lehrb. d. mechan. Wärmetheorie, p. 271), the doubtful power of the distance must be even higher than the fourth, if the transversal light-vibrations are to propagate themselves in the medium of the ether; and it follows from the laws of the propagation of light in doubly-refracting media, as from the absence of dispersion in empty space, that it is probably the sixth power of the distance to which the repulsion of the ethereal atoms is inversely proportional.

kept asunder within the chemical combinations by ether-atoms, because they can again be separated by ethereal vibrations (heat, electricity).

Body and ether atoms probably repel one another at molecular distances. It used to be assumed that they attracted one another at the ordinary molecular distances, and that this attraction was only converted into repulsion in the most immediate vicinity; this supposition is also still the common one in the elementary manuals. Up to a certain point, the phenomena are equally well explained by either of the hypotheses; but since, for the sake of calculation, a decision must be made in favour of one, attraction was *accidentally* chosen. Wiener has shown (comp. Poggendorff's "Amalen," vol. cxviii. p. 79, and Wiener, "Die Grundzüge der Weltordnung," first book) that the hypothesis of repulsion offers essential advantages for the explanation of the fluid state of aggregation, and that this generally agrees better with our other physical views. There is, according to this supposition, not as in Redtenbacher's "System of Dynamids," a thick envelope of ether-atoms about every material molecule, but, on the contrary, the ether is thinnest in the immediate neighbourhood of the corporeal molecules, accordingly thinner within the body than in empty space, because the densely packed corporeal molecules partially repel the ether. As we shall see later on that at all events attraction takes place at greater distances between body and ether atoms, the difference of the two opposed views in strictness only consists of a divergence in respect of the *magnitude* of that distance where attraction is converted into repulsion; and, moreover, according to *both* views, this distance must be so small that it must be designated molecular distance.

The atomic theory, in the present phase of its development, explains in a surprising way the laws of heat and the different states of aggregation induced by changes of heat (see Wiener, "Grundzüge der Weltordnung," first book; and for a more mathematical treatment, Ch. Briot,

"Lehrbuch der mechanischen Wärmetheorie"). It has the advantage of representing all the many so-called forces of matter, as gravitation, elasticity, heat, galvanism, chemistry, &c., as manifestations of molecular and atomic forces—*i.e.*, that one also actually sees and calculates the evolution of the one from the other,—whereas that Dynamism, which, like the Kantian, will know nothing of atoms and atomic forces, only merely asserts the origin of the higher material forces from attraction and repulsion, but cannot in the least say how it comes to pass.—

There still remains one material force to be mentioned, *vis inertiæ*, of which Atomism has hitherto wrongly denied that it comes under the conception of force, or which it has treated as an additional force, whereas it might have already learnt from Kant ("New System of Rest and Motion," comp. Kant's Werke, vol. v. pp. 282–284, 287–289, and 409–417) what *vis inertiæ* is, namely, that it *depends* simply and entirely *on the reciprocity or relativity of movement*, which had been previously clearly stated by Leibniz (Mathemat. Werke, vi. p. 252). To wit, if one imagines an atom alone in space, the notion of rest or motion cannot at all apply to the same, *because it has no definite place in space;* thus also cannot *change* this place. There is, accordingly, no absolute, but only relative, rest and motion. It follows from that, that one has no *more* right to say, A moves towards B, than B moves towards A; the ball moves towards the target, than the target moves towards the ball; that thus the resistance which the target opposes to the ball is not so much a resistance of the resting as of the moved target, or its *vis viva*. What here in the case of impact immediately strikes the eye takes place again in pushing and pulling, only as an integration of infinitely numerous single moments of repulsion or attraction of atoms and molecules. In both cases the resistance of the *vis inertiæ* to be overcome depends on the reciprocity of attraction and repulsion and the relativity of motion.

To explain Inertia we thus, in fact, need, notwithstanding that it itself acts as an opposing force, no *new* force; we can get along perfectly well with the attraction and repulsion of corporeal and ethereal atoms.—Let us now see how, on closer inspection, the principles previously adduced assume of themselves a simpler form.—

If we imagine two corporeal atoms, A and B, they would even then still move towards one another if *only* A possessed attractive power; for in that A attracts the atom B, it necessarily, on account of the relativity of motion, just as much moves towards B as it draws B towards itself. The same holds good, however, for B. Since now both A and also B possess attraction, each of them produces the mutual approximation, thus their actual attraction will be the sum of their individual forces. The same holds good for the repulsion of ether-atoms. But now curiously one and the same corporeal atom is said to possess two opposite forces, namely, energy of attraction for corporeal atoms, and repulsive force for ether-atoms. An ether-atom has thus either a corresponding *special* repulsive force for ether-atoms, and a *special* repulsive force for corporeal atoms; or, however, its repulsive force is equally great for corporeal and ether atoms, *i.e.*, *one and the same*. The latter supposition has nothing against it; it will therefore, as the simpler, in any case deserve the preference, for *principia non sunt multiplicanda præter necessitatem*. According to the latter assumption, then, an ether-atom is similarly repellently related to *every other atom*, no matter what other forces may belong to this atom; *i.e.*, if a corporeal atom meets it, it repels this just as much as an ether-atom, no matter how great the force may be with which the corporeal atom repels the ether-atom, as compared with the repulsive force of an ether-atom. Of course the total *mutual* repulsion is the sum of the two forces. But if the magnitude of the repellent force of the corporeal atom is indifferent with regard to the repulsive force of the ether-atom, it must also be indifferent to it if this force becomes $= 0$, or if it becomes *negative*, *i.e.*, *attractive*, always supposing that the total repulsion of the two is the sum of the single forces. In the latter case the total result would remain repulsion, as long as the repulsive force of the ether-atom is greater than the attractive force of the corporeal atom; in the converse case it would be attraction. But herewith we at once get rid of the unnatural assumption of two mutually contradictory forces in this corporeal atom; for the repulsion between ethereal and corporeal atom remains as such for all small distances, when the repulsion of the former is stronger than the attraction of the latter, and the body-atom is similarly related to *every* other atom by attraction, just as the ether-atom is repellently related to *every* other atom in the same way. That, however, in fact, ethereal and corporeal atoms do *not* repel one another *at all*, but only at smaller, distances, seems to me evidently to result from the following: The *material* system is unconditionally to be regarded as *finite*, both from *à priori* considerations and on astronomical grounds.[1] The ether, however, must extend into the infinite, if there be no limit, where the attraction of all the corporeal atoms prevails over the repulsion of all the ether atoms; a rotation of the system about one or more axes (so far as such an one is at all conceivable under the supposition of the relativity of motion) would only strengthen the continual efflux of the ether-atoms by centrifugal force; and even on the inadmissible assumption of an infinite number of ether-atoms to a finite number of corporeal atoms, the constant efflux of ether-atoms in infinite space would induce a continuously increasing rarefaction of the ether in the world-system, for which there is nothing to be said.

Accordingly, if we are compelled by the finiteness of the material world-system to assume a definite *finite* distance,

---

[1] Comp. Zöllner, "Ueber die Natur der Kometen," 3 Aufl.

where the repulsion of the ether-atom from the corporeal atom is *equal* to the attraction of the corporeal atom to the ether-atom, we immediately get what we want, namely, that at less distances repulsion must *prevail* over attraction, since the repulsion of the ether-atom diminishes much more quickly with diminution of the distance than the attraction of the corporeal atom. However, then, one may regard the matter, in every respect the simplest assumption most recommends itself, that the corporeal atom has *only* attractive force, the ether-atom *only* force of repulsion, which is *uniformly* manifested towards both kinds of atoms. At a particular distance (which manifestly must be determined by the magnitude of the intended world) they are equal to one another; the different law of their change with the distance causes at greater distances attraction, at lesser repulsion increasingly to predominate. At the distances at which they exist between the molecules of a body, repulsion probably *immensely* preponderates. This is, however, also necessary if, according to the assumption of Wiener, the ether-atoms are distributed within the body *far more sparsely* than in empty space, and nevertheless must suffice to hold in *equilibrium* the mutual attraction of the so thickly packed corporeal molecules.

Since, if one steers clear of the contradiction of an already existing, *i.e.*, *completed infinity*, the number of the ether-atoms, as that of the corporeal atoms, must be *finite*, we have no ground at all to assume that the number of both is different; we may, on the contrary, rather hold them to be equal, since what the ether-atoms seem to gain in greater distribution through space the corporeal atoms acquire in density of cohesion. We have then *for every body-atom an ether-atom*, which are distinguished, apart from the law of their change of force with distance, only by the positive and negative direction of their forces. If one conceived every corporeal atom and every ethereal atom fused together, all force would suddenly disappear from the world, for their antagonism would have been *neutralised*. Thus we see here the sundering into a *polar dualism* to be the principle which produces the material world.

Let us further inquire what we are to understand by the *mass* of a *body*. We chiefly measure mass by *weight*. As soon, however, as science reached the assumption of the ether, which, because it has no attraction, can also have no weight, it was necessary to take something else instead of weight as the measure of mass, and, moreover, somewhat that is *common* to ether and body; as such, only *vis inertiæ* is offered. But now, even if we can thus *measure* mass, we still get no *notion* of mass unless we are content to grasp it as *the unknown substratum of equal persistent forces*. But assuredly no one is really satisfied with this. Physical science explains mass to be *the product of volume and density*, and this certainly leads to the mode in which all unprejudiced thinking conceives the notion of mass, provided that, in the explanation of density, one avoids the circle and does not again employ the notion of mass. Then is density only to be apprehended as the *keeping asunder of equivalent particles*. If, now, the product of volume and density remain unchanged, it is clear that this is only possible by the number of equivalent particles remaining unchanged. We may then define *mass* absolutely as the *number of equivalent particles*, supposing that in all things to be compared we continue the division until we everywhere come to equivalent particles. It is immediately evident that only the original atoms answer this requirement; but this they really do: even the ethereal and corporeal atoms are to be regarded as equivalent, since each ether-atom just as much repels each body-atom as each ether-atom, and inversely; consequently the reciprocity of their forces, *i.e.*, their *vis inertiæ*, is equal. We have, then, now to define the mass of a thing as the *number of its atoms*, and herewith furnish the only possible strictly scientific expression for that which each one more or less clearly conceives by the word *mass*. It follows, however, directly from this, that there is no longer any sense in talking of the mass of an atom, for one would then have to imagine the same again decomposed into equivalent parts, and thereby would get no farther than one already is. One may possibly speak of the mass of a *molecule*, for this just consists of atoms; one may also say, by way of comparison, a corporeal molecule is of very much greater mass than an ether-atom; but the masses of two atoms cannot be compared, for each of them is the mass-unit. Further, it would be conceivable that, without interposed ether-atoms, n body-atoms should unite into a single one, so as to become inseparable; then an ether-atom would repel each of these united atoms with a single, the compound with n-fold force, and the compound would certainly have the mass n; but just on that account would it be erroneous to call it One atom with n-fold mass; there always remains, so long as the atoms are conceived as material, impenetrable balls, a complex of n atoms.—For the rest, we have no occasion at all to believe in the real existence of such direct fusions of body-atoms, for it is to be assumed that the body-atoms in the molecule of a so-called chemical element are just as much kept asunder by ether-atoms as the molecules of the chemical elements in the molecule of their chemical compound, which last is proved by this, that they may be again separated by ether-vibrations (heat, galvanism, &c.) With respect to the great differences of the atomic weights, we must also imagine the number of the body-atoms united in an elementary molecule to be *very great*, in conformity with the fact that often hundreds of elementary molecules are united in the molecule of a higher organic combination.

The result of all this is, that the atom is the *unit* of which every mass is composed, just as all numbers are compounds of One; that it is therefore just as sensible to ask what is the mass of an atom as what is the number of unity.—

We come now to the last and most difficult question: Is the atom anything else but force? has the atom *substance*, and what are we to understand by this term?—Let us recall the way in which we arrived at the atom. As children, we knock our heads and feel pain; we touch things, and get visual and other impressions from them. For these instinctively localised projected perceptions we just as instinctively suppose causes which we call things. We suppose things outside us which act upon us, but especially that *against which we push outside* we call *matter* or *substance*. Science does not stop at this crude, instinctively sensuous, and practically sufficing hypothesis, but pursues the causes of our perceptions *farther*, and examines them more carefully. It shows us that visual perceptions are excited by ethereal vibrations, auditory perceptions by aerial vibrations, olfactory and gustatory perceptions by chemical vibrations in our sense-organs; that thus all these perceptions by no means concern a matter, but a motion, for whose explanation it must again suppose *forces*, which in the last resort turn out to be *manifestations* of combined molecular and atomic forces. It shows us further that the foundation of all our tactile perceptions, the so-called *impenetrability* of matter, or the resistance which it opposes to foreign bodies in attempting to approach beyond certain limits, may be the *result of the repulsion of the ether-atoms*, which at infinitely small distances become infinitely greater than the attractive force of the corporeal atoms; that, however, a direct *contact* of the atoms, therefore an impenetrability, not as consequence of force, but inhering in matter as such, nowhere occurs at all. All the explanations which physical science gives or attempts to give rest on *forces;* substance or matter remains thereby, at the most, a spectre idly lurking in the background, which, however, is always only able to assert itself at *obscure* places, where the light of knowledge has not yet penetrated; the further knowledge, *i.e.*, the explanation of phenomena, spreads its light, the more in the course of history does matter, which in the *naïve* sensuous intuition still occupies the whole outer space of perception, withdraw into the background.

Never, however, as far as physical science reaches, or will reach, can it require anything else than forces for its explanation. On the contrary, where, at the present day, it wants the word *substance*, it understands thereby, as by *matter*, only a system of atomic forces, a dynamic system, and only employs the words *substance* and *matter* as indispensable summary signs or formulæ for these systems of forces.

As, now, scientific hypothesis should never extend farther than the need of explanation requires, but the concept Matter serves and can serve no scientific need of explanation, it follows from this that a concept Matter which means anything else than a system of forces has no warrant and no place in physical science, since it has indeed itself proved all that which sensuous apprehension calls effects of matter to be effects of forces.

Undoubtedly nothing is more difficult than to free ourselves from the immediate ideas of sense, which we have imbibed, as it were, with our mother's milk, which have been instinctively laid hold of as first crude but practically sufficient hypotheses, and which by the habit of a lifetime have become a part of ourselves. There is need of industry, tranquillity, clearness, and force of thought to perceive the prejudices of sense and other prejudices of thought as such; still more courage does it require to break for good and all with that which has been once surmounted in *all its consequences;* but even when one has done all this, there is still required an almost superhuman energy of intelligence and character never again to be prejudiced, or at least secretly influenced, by what has been absolutely discredited; for there is no task more difficult than this, to conquer for ourselves only a full, negative freedom of thought. Precisely because the prejudices springing from sense are not conscious conclusions of the understanding, but instinctive, practically sufficing suggestions, are they so difficult to be destroyed and set aside by conscious thought. One may say to oneself a thousand times that the moon at the horizon has the same angular magnitude, has the same apparent size, as high up in the sky; that it is an error of the understanding to hold it to look smaller up in the sky than down at the level—the same error which does not allow the vault of heaven to appear as hemisphere, but as flattened spheroid—all that cannot bring a single individual to see the moon in both cases as of equal magnitude, just because, in spite of better conscious knowledge, the instinctive assumption asserts itself.

Such an instinctive prejudice springing from sensibility is Matter. No natural philosopher has, in his science, anything to do with matter, except in so far as he decomposes it into forces, whereby accordingly the apparent material effects turn out energies, *i.e.*, matter is more and more resolved into force. Thus, even at the present day, few natural philosophers will be found who would grant the final consequence of their own science, that matter is nothing but a system of forces; and the reason of this lies simply in sensuous prejudice. One forgets that we indeed just as little directly perceive matter as atoms, but only its pressure, impact, vibrations, &c.; that this matter is indeed also merely a hypothesis, which must justify itself before the tribunal of physical science; but this justification is not merely never forthcoming, but instead of it after every inquiry instituted in any quarter whatsoever evaporates into forces. This is forgotten because one accidentally knocks one's elbow, and instinctive sensibility shrieks at once "Matter" into the reasoning.—If, now, we seriously attack such a prejudice, it tries to maintain itself with sophisms; the natural philosopher forgets the rules of his method, and even advances *à priori* reasons in order only to save his favourite prejudice.

But then we hear it exclaimed, " I cannot imagine force

without matter; force must have a *substratum* by which, and an object on which, it acts, and just this is matter; force without matter is a non-thing."—Let us also consider the *à priori* side of the speculation, after having perceived that on the empirical side the hypothesis of a substance has no warrant.

In the first place, it may be asserted that man is so organised that he may think everything which is not self-contradictory, *i.e.*, that he may unite all conceptions given in words, provided that the meaning of the conceptions is clearly and precisely given to him, and the required combination contains no contradiction. The above assertion says: "Force cannot be imagined in independent real existence, but only in indissoluble union with matter." Force is a clear conception, independent real existence likewise; accordingly every sound understanding must be able to unite the two notions, unless this combination contains an inherent contradiction. To prove the latter would doubtless be difficult, consequently the first part of the negative assertion is false. Properly understood, the only question is: Is the combination thinkable? not whether it really exists; otherwise the speculation would be no longer *à priori.*—The second positive part of the proposition asserts "that force is to be conceived in union with matter." This part is just as false; one cannot think the union of force and matter, because one cannot think matter, for all conception is wanting to this word. Let us go through the different meanings which might possibly be ascribed to the word. The sensuous meaning is, it is true, quite definite: cause of felt resistance; but it is resolved into repulsive atomic forces, and can thus not be opposed to the notion Force. The notion Mass, which, in a perverse fashion, might be subsumed under the notion matter, has further above been decomposed into atomic force; of it, accordingly, the like holds good; its confusion with matter is, besides, only possible in respect of the crude sensuous meaning of matter by means of the notion of density.

The physical notion of impenetrability has likewise been resolved into the infinitely great repulsive power of the ether-atoms at infinitely little distances; and, moreover, only appertains to the repulsive ether-atoms and to bodies, *i.e.*, systems of dynamids, in virtue of the ether-atoms contained therein, *but not* to the attractive corporeal atoms, since it would not be apparent why, in fact, a perfect interpenetration and blending should not take place between two body-atoms which are not sundered by ether-atoms.

Finally, there still remains the meaning, "*substratum of force;*" however, I must confess, to my misfortune, that I am just as little able to think anything by substratum as by matter. Schelling says ("System of Transcend. Idealism," pp. 317, 318; Werke, i. 3, pp. 529, 530): "Whoever says that he cannot imagine action without substratum, just confesses thereby that that putative substratum of thought is itself a mere product of his imagination; thus again is only his own thought, which he in this way is compelled to presuppose as independent *ad infinitum.* It is a mere illusion of the imagination that after one has taken away from an object the only predicates which it has, still something, one knows not what, remains of it. Thus, *e.g.*, nobody will say impenetrability is implanted in matter, for impenetrability is matter itself" (which certainly is only half the truth). Substratum sometimes means the same thing as subject; one will, however, still not maintain that dead matter is something more subjective than force. Sometimes substratum means "the underlying," *i.e.*, a *causal* moment; of which there can be no question here. Usually it signifies *prop*, plainly in a sensuous meaning of the word; the crude sensuous idea must, however, here be excluded, and so our list ends. In short, we can think here nothing at all by substratum. But even if this were possible, the defenders of matter would always still owe the proof of the validity of their hypothesis of a substratum of force; for I cannot see the need of still supposing something *behind* force, as I maintain that one can quite well think force to be independently existing. It still remains: Matter is for science an empty word, for one can name no single quality which shall appertain to the notion thereby designated; it is simply an insignificant word, unless we are contented with the notion of a "system of forces," for which we would rather put "matter." Accordingly, it is settled that those who assert they cannot think force as independent can assuredly not think it in combination with matter.

Further, it is asserted, "Force must have an object to act upon, otherwise it cannot act." This is unconditionally allowed; it is only disputed that this object must be matter. "The force of any atom has other atoms for its object;" that is all the physical scientific hypothesis requires; what that is in the atoms which serves as object, about that physical science does not trouble itself at all. *We*, however, have to show that we as yet know in the atom *only force;* that nothing stands in the way of regarding force as that in the atom which serves as object to the force of the other atom; that thus for this reason all occasion is wanting for setting up the new hypothesis of matter. In addition to this, there is still the analogy of the mental forces, which likewise have one another for objects, *e.g.*, the idea acting as motive has the will as object, the will again has the idea as object, and so on. The pure reciprocity in the relation of atomic forces to one another should serve as a warning against the assumption of another object than force itself.

But now, let us really assume for one moment that the atoms consisted, beside force, also of matter, and consider what difficulties thereby arise for this idea in the mutual action of two atoms, A and B, and how the one unauthorised and superfluous assumption must always be supported by new and just as arbitrary ones. The force of A is to act upon the matter of B and *vice versa*, thereby the matter of A and B approach one another, whilst the forces stand out of all relation to one another, the converse of which one indeed would expect, since it is force which acts at a distance, but not matter, since force and force are of homogeneous, force and matter, however, of heterogeneous nature. The matter of A and B then approach in consequence of the momentary attraction of the mutual forces. What follows from this? Manifestly that the force and matter of every atom must be separated, for matter is caused by the foreign force to change its place, but not force. If, now, still the force and matter of every atom remain together, and nevertheless force cannot be necessitated by the force of the foreign atom directly to a change of place, it follows with logical necessity that the force of A must be compelled by the matter of A to change its place. Therewith, however, acting, consequently activity is ascribed to matter, whereas it is in general absolute passivity which must be represented in opposition to the activity of force. The mode and manner of this action is, however, perfectly incomprehensible, for if matter becomes *actively acting* it becomes indeed again force. Instead, then, of force A, as would be natural, attracting force B, it moves the matter of B, and the matter of B moves the force of B.

How force is to be "bound" to matter, which is the favourite expression of the partisans of matter, I must confess I cannot at all imagine. It would also be difficult for them to answer the following: Is one to imagine force bound to the centre of the material atom, or uniformly distributed over the whole matter of the same? For a material atom must surely have a certain size!

The former assumption certainly evades the difficulties connected with the other, but then force is no longer strictly bound to matter, but to a mathematical point, which yet cannot possibly be material, and which only accidentally coincides with the centre of a material ball. Then the action of matter on the movement of force is not at all comprehensible; rather the material ball is a fifth wheel in the waggon, since only the point, the ideal centre of the same, is in question. On the second assumption the difficulties are, however, far greater, for then indeed from *every point* of the material atom acts a *part* of the force, and each of these points has another distance from the atom which is acted upon. There is then the resultant to be taken of all these partial forces, whose point of attack now on action at finite distances by no means falls upon the centre of the material atomic sphere, but becomes different according to each direction of action. In this speculation, however, one must manifestly imagine the atom decomposed into an infinite number of parts, each of which is burdened with an infinitesimal part of the force. Let one think such an atomic particle as small as one will, it is still always matter, and still no mathematical point; thus the union of the same with force can yet again only be comprehended by imagining the force uniformly distributed within the same. We are thus again constrained to infinite division, and so on, *i.e.*, the material atom must be divided infinitely an infinite number of times, and in spite of it all it can never be comprehended how the force is distributed to matter, since one can absolutely only imagine the manifestation of simple force referred to the mathematical point, and this again is no longer material. (This the most considerable physicists and mathematicians, as Ampère, Cauchy, W. Weber, &c., have recognised, and therefore admitted that the atoms must be conceived as absolutely without extension.)

Let us, on the other hand, consider how the case stands without matter. We have nothing else to do but to retain the idea of atomic force, which the defenders of matter also possess, that it is the final unknown cause of motion, whose paths prolonged backwards cut one another in a mathematical point. Even he who assumes the atomic force to be equally distributed over the whole matter of the atom can, as said, not get rid of this mode of viewing the matter, for he must apprehend the total force of the atom as resultant of an infinite mass of punctual forces within the atom, however contradictory this requirement may be.

Further, the defenders of matter also assume the possibility of a relative change of place of this point, in which the directions of the manifestations of force intersect. We leave, provisionally, the question undiscussed whether force as such, apart from its manifestations, is something to which one may attribute spatiality or a place in space; if it has a place, it is in any case this point of intersection, and we will therefore provisionally call it the *seat* of force. Further, we assume that the atomic forces mutually serve as objects, *i.e.*, that the mutual attraction of A and B produces local change at the seat of the forces in the sense of the latter approaching one another and separating on repulsion. I do not see where difficulties could be found here. According to the assumption of science, forces act at a distance and are homogeneous; why should they not act *upon one another*, if one indeed has hitherto granted an action of force on the matter heterogeneous to it and an action of dead matter on the force heterogeneous to it? We only need assumptions which were already there, strip away from these several as superfluous and unauthorised, and arrive notwithstanding not only just as well, but much more simply and more plausibly, at the goal, and avoid all the difficulties which appeared in the train of those useless assumptions. If we reckon, in addition, that those assumptions rest on an *empty word without any thought*, the gain proceeding from the simplification of the principles cannot be rated lightly.

There is, besides this, the crucial test, that our present rendering of Matter reconciles the two previously distinct parties of atomists and dynamists, since it has arisen from the conversion of Atomism into Dynamism, retains unimpaired all previous advantages of Atomism, which have assured it its exclusive authority in current physical science, purifies it of all the warranted reproaches of the dynamists, and gives birth to the fundamental principle of Dynamism, the denial of matter in a new, and more thorough fashion. We may therefore rightly call this conception *Atomistic Dynamism*. Dynamism in its previous form, apart from the want of an empirical proof, could never be accepted by physical science, because its formlessness made all calculation impossible. If forces are to act locally, they must determine their effects in space, and thus refer the same to definite starting-points. With this the point is directly given as starting-point of material force, wherefore Dynamism also, as soon as it tried to assume a more definite shape, was necessarily converted into Atomism, for it only then gained for the first time a tangible form, when it referred the play of opposite forces to *force-individuals*, *i.e.*, atoms. This point of view was advocated by Leibniz in a tolerably pronounced fashion:—"Il n'y a que les *points métaphysiques*, ou de substance, qui soient exactes et réels.—Il n'y a que les atomes de substance, c'est à dire, les unités réelles et absolument déstituées de parties, qui soient *les sources des actions* et les premiers principes absolus de la composition de choses, et comme les derniers élémens de l'analyse des substances." ("Système Nouveau de la Nature," No. 11.)—Leibniz altogether comprehends "substance" only as force, and force is to him the only and genuine substance. Comp. *De Primæ Philosophiæ Emendatione et de Notione Substantiæ*. That he does this, and with the notion of force *implicitly* insinuates the notion of the Will into substance, is his main philosophical advance beyond Spinoza. Undoubtedly physical science was then too much behindhand for him to put himself into active alliance with it. Schelling would have succeeded far better, who very decidedly confesses to a dynamic Atomism; but on principle deduces his assertions *a priori*, wherefore also his mode of looking at the matter has not been able to obtain any influence over physical science. He says (Works, i. 3, p. 23):—

"What is indivisible cannot be matter, and, conversely,

it must then lie beyond matter; but beyond matter is *pure intensity*, and this notion of pure intensity is expressed by the conception of action."—(P. 22): "The original actions, however, are not themselves space, they cannot be regarded as part of matter. Our assertion may accordingly be called principle of Dynamic Atomism. For every original action is for us, just as the Atom for the corpuscular philosophers, truly *individual;* each is in itself whole and self-enclosed, and represents, as it were, a natural monad." (P. 24): "In space, however, only its effect is representable; action itself is earlier than space, *extensione prior."*—

If thus, on the one hand, Dynamism, even when it attained atomistic individualisation of force, was not able to prove itself to be something empirically authorised, on the other hand, at no time could Atomism defend itself against the reproach of logical contradiction, which was always brought against its *material atoms.* If, notwithstanding, physical science has inclined to it with ever-increasing confidence, this certainly proves a strong inner compulsion, with which, in spite of the acknowledged contradiction, the force of facts ever and again urged the natural philosophers to the atomistic explanation. Atomistic Dynamism satisfies all requirements by uniting the positive principles of both sides in itself.

If we once more briefly recapitulate these principles, they run thus: There are as many positive as negative, *i.e.,* attractive and repulsive, forces. The directions of action of every force intersect in a mathematical point, which we call the seat of force. This seat of force is movable. Every force acts upon every other in the same way, no matter how it be designated. Positive force is called body-atom; negative, ether-atom. At a certain (molecular) distance the repulsion of an ether-atom and the attraction of a body-atom are equal to one another; but as the law of their change varies with their distance, between ether and corporeal atoms at lesser distances there prevails repulsion, at greater distances attraction. Corporeal atoms with interposed ether-atoms keeping them asunder unite to form the molecules of the chemical elements; these in the same way the molecules of the chemically compound bodies; these the material bodies themselves. Matter is thus a system of atomistic forces in a certain state of equilibrium. From these atomic forces in the most different combinations and reactions arise all the so-called forces of matter, as gravitation, weight, expansion, elasticity, crystallisation, electricity, galvanism, magnetism, chemical affinity, heat, light, &c.; nowhere, as long as we confine ourselves to the inorganic sphere, do we need to call to our aid any other than atomic forces.

We have accordingly seen that of the two materialistic principles, force and matter, the latter dissolves and disappears beneath our hands into the former; and now we know exactly what we have to understand by force, namely, an attracting or repelling, positively or negatively acting *point of force*. Now the notion of force is made so precise that we are able directly to consider the same, without in our investigation having any cause to fear that we apprehend it otherwise than physical science and Materialism intends. Let us see what this conception involves.

The attracting atomic force strives to bring every other atom nearer to it; the result of this endeavour is the completion or realisation of the approach. We have thus in Force to distinguish the *effort itself* as pure act, and that which is aimed at as the goal, content, or object of the endeavour. The endeavour lies *before* the execution; so far as the execution *is already posited*, so far is the effort *realised*, *is* therefore no more; only the *yet to be realised*, that is, *not yet* realised effort *is*. Consequently, the resulting movement cannot be contained in the effort as reality, since their times are separate. Were this, however, *not at all* contained in the endeavour, there would be no reason why the latter should produce attraction, and not something else, *e.g.*, repulsion; why it varies according to this and not according to that law with the distance. It would then be empty, purely formal endeavour, without definite goal or content; it must thus remain aimless and without content, and accordingly resultless, which contradicts experience. Experience rather shows that an atom does not accidentally now attract, now repel, but remains perfectly consistent and always equal to itself in the aim of its endeavour. Nothing more is wanting, then, than that the effort of the attractive force contain in itself the approximation and the law of change according to distance, *i.e.*, the whole variable determination of its mode of action; and yet not contain in itself their reality.

Since the striving or the force of the atom is the primitive element constituting matter, and as such in itself simple and immaterial, there can here then be no more talk of material predispositions; the above requirements must be combined in an immaterial way. This is only possible if the striving possesses all the uniformly variable definiteness of its mode of manifestation as an appearance resembling reality—as *image*, as it were; *i.e.*, however, if it possesses the same *ideally* or as *presentation*. Only if in the striving of the atomic force the "what" of the endeavour be ideally prefigured, only then is a determination of the endeavour at all given; only then is a *result* of the endeavour, only then that consequence possible which in the same force-individual always retains the same positive or negative goal of endeavour, but still acts on a second atom from this particular distance with this particular strength, on a third from that distance in that strength. Without itself changing, the atomic force changes the extent of its action according to circumstances, and that too with *logical* uniformity (mechanics = applied mathematics, mathematics = applied logic). This necessitation by circumstances leaves its activity, its spontaneity untouched, and requires therefore, nevertheless, the direct procession of action from *inner* determination; thus requires ideality as *prius* of reality, and causes the necessitation to be perceived as a logical necessitation (from the logical determinateness of the Idea).

But now, what then is the striving of *force* other than *will*, that endeavour whose content or object forms the unconscious idea of what is aimed at? Let one only compare A. Chap. iv. Vol. I. pp. 117–112; what we have here derived from force we have there derived from will. That the will is in its nature and immediately regarded eternally unconscious we have shown, C. Chap. iii. pp. 96–104; that it here also must be mediately unconscious, since its content is an unconscious idea, is matter of course. Not violently have we so far extended the notion of the will as to include in it that of force; but in that we proceeded from the will of the cerebral consciousness, acknowledged as such, has this notion of itself broken through the limits drawn for it by consciousness in an authorised manner (vol. i. pp. 69-71), and evinced itself gradually as the efficient principle in *all* activities of the animal and vegetable kingdom. Now we see, to our astonishment, that if we would think anything under the notion of a (no longer derived, but independent) force, it can only be what we have thought in the case of will; that thus both conceptions would be *identical* if force were not by *conventional* limitation of its content narrower, and, moreover, were used quite especially for *derived* forces, *i.e.*, for particular combinations and manifestations of atomic forces, *e.g.* elasticity, magnetism, muscular force, &c. To replace the notion Will by the notion Force, or at all to subsume it under the latter, would therefore be bad, because force is properly derivative, only in the special scientific sense original; will, on the other hand, *always* original; and because force, in the ordinary acceptation, and in the view of common sense, is a much more incomprehensible conception than will; one is also accustomed by the crude sensuous mode of apprehension to think something especially material by "force," since the notion is only carried over from the feeling of muscular energy to other external objects. So much more inward as is the will than the feeling of muscular energy, so much more significant is the word Will to express the essential truth than the word Force. (Comp. Schopenhauer, "Welt als Wille und Vorstellung § 22, and Wallace, 'Contributions to the Theory of Natural Selection.'" Wallace declares himself just as decidedly against the retention of matter along with force as for the volitional nature of all force, and herewith of the whole universe.)

The manifestations of the atomic forces are thus individual acts of will, whose content consists in the unconscious representation of what is to be performed. *Thus matter is in fact resolved into Will and Idea.* Herewith is the radical distinction between spirit and matter abolished; their difference consists only in higher or lower forms of manifestation of the same essence, the eternally Unconscious, but their identity is perceived in this, that the Unconscious manifests itself equally in mind and matter as the intuitively—logical Ideal, and dynamically realises the conceived ideal anticipation of the actual. The identity of mind and matter herewith ceases to be an uncomprehended and unproved postulate, or a product of mystical conception, by being elevated to scientific cognition, and that, too, not by killing the spirit, but by vivifying matter. There were only two standpoints hitherto which actually avoided this dualism, but both could only do this by boldly denying the truth of one side. Materialism denied spirit; Idealism, matter. The former regarded mind as unsubstantial appearance, resulting from certain constellations of material functions; the latter regarded matter as unsubstantial appearance, resulting from the peculiarity of subjective conscious psychical function. The one is as one-sided and untrue as the other, and the unconquered strict dualism of co-ordinate spirit and matter to be preferred to both. Not merely to evade this dualism by the denial of one aspect, but really to overcome and absorb it, is only in the power of a philosophy which sees in the subjective conscious mind, as in matter, only phenomena of one and the same principle in the subjective or objective sphere respectively —a principle which is higher than both, and at the same time less differentiated than either; in a word, a philosophy of the Unconscious (whether Hegel's Unconscious Idea, or Schopenhauer's Unconscious Will, or the substantial unity of both in Schelling's Eternally Unconscious).

Let us now consider how the atomic will is related to space. Without in any way needing to enter upon the question concerning the essence of space, we may say this much: Space may have a twofold existence, one real in bodies or bounded voids, and one ideal in the mental representation of bodies and bounded voids. If the *ideal* space is in the *representation*, the representing cannot be *in the* ideal space which it first creates; if cerebral vibrations constrain the Unconscious to a reaction with conscious perception, this perception has nothing to do with the place of the vibrating spot in the brain, or the place of this perceiving man upon the earth; the idea is thus also not in the *real* space. Will is the *translation of the ideal into the real;* it adds to the ideal its content, that which bare thinking cannot give it, by *realising* it. Whilst this its content, which is always an idea, also contains ideal-spatial determinations, the will at the same time also realises these spatial determinations, and this also puts space out of the ideal into the real, posits thus the real space. (How space arises in the ideal does not here concern us; enough that it is the will that posits real space.) That which is only created by the will cannot be present before completed willing; the will as such cannot then be real-spatial. With ideal space, however, the will has nothing at all to do. For it exists merely in the idea, *i.e.*, in the mental representation. In short, *Will and*

Idea are both of non-spatial nature, since it is the idea which first creates the ideal space, the will by realisation of the idea the real space. It follows from this that also the atomic will or the atomic force can be *nothing spatial,* because it, as Schelling says, is *extensione prior.*

To common apprehension this may for the moment appear strange, but the strangeness immediately disappears if we compare it with the spatial effects of the will in organisms. The will moves in me certain nervous molecules in such a manner that by transmission of the current and employment of the polar forces in nerves and muscles my arm lifts a hundredweight. The will has thus directly produced certain spatial changes of position, which we, it is true, do not more exactly know, but of which we can say this much, that their movements of direction by no means meet in a common point of section, but probably consist of revolutions of a certain number of molecules about their axes. Movement ensues just in this manner because the unconscious idea, which forms the content of the will, ideally contains just this kind of movement. Did this representation, on the other hand, ideally contain such movements or intersect in a common point, the will would also realise such movements, and this it does in the atomic will. One sees, then, that this common point of section of all manifestations of the atomic will is something purely ideal,—I might, not to be misunderstood, rather say is *imaginary,* and only by a considerable license of speech can be called the *seat* of the will or of energy; for the only spatial elements in the whole affair are the *manifestations* of force, which never reach the common point of section, in that this always lies only in its *ideal* prolongation. Nevertheless this point must be definite in relation to others, *i.e.,* the distance of the ideal point of section from all similar points of intersection is determined. Hence it of course follows that this distance may also be changed, *i.e.,* that this point is capable of motion.

What, then, actually happens when two attracting forces approach one another? In the first place, the attraction increases; secondly, the actions on all laterally situated atoms so change their direction that their prevailing ideal points of intersection must be conceived brought nearer to one another; the first and the second change stand in such a relation that the attraction increases n^2 times if the diminution of the distance of the points of intersection due to the displacement in direction of the lateral manifestations of force amounts to n. The *reality* is thus always only the *manifestations* of force which have a certain direction and strength, and the change of this direction and strength, whereas the points of intersection are and remain something *ideal*. But the two former, as mental representation, form the content of the atomic will; and one will now understand how the will *itself* may be somewhat *non-spatial*, and by no means need reside in the ideal point of intersection, and move about with this, whilst yet the realisations of its content are of spatial nature, and have a common ideal point of intersection, whose position with reference to other ideal points of intersection are definite and variable.—

The question might here be raised whether the atoms have a consciousness. However, I think that data are all too lacking for any decision to be come to thereupon, since with regard to the means required for the production of consciousness and the degree of movement necessary for overstepping the threshold of sensation we still know next to nothing. Thus much, however, we may assert with confidence: *if* matter has a consciousness it is an atomistic consciousness, and between the consciousnesses of the several atoms no *communication* is possible. Wherefore it is decidedly erroneous to speak of the consciousness of a crystal or of a heavenly body, for in inorganic bodies can at most the atoms each for itself possess a consciousness. Of course this atom-consciousness would, by reason of poverty of content, assume the lowest place conceivable.—Leibniz, who was not acquainted with the phenomenon of the threshold of sensation, thought himself warranted in deriving from the law of continuity (*natura non facit saltus*) and from that of analogy (σύμπνοια πάντα) a certain degree of consciousness for each, even the lowest, monad. However this authorisation disappears through the law of the threshold. When carbonic acid gas, *e.g.*, is more and more compressed, it takes up, indeed, a smaller and smaller space, but still always remains gas; suddenly, however, one reaches a point where it is no longer compressible but becomes liquid; this is, so to speak, the threshold of the gaseous condition. So in the scale of individuals or monads, consciousness may become ever poorer and poorer, but always still remain consciousness, until suddenly a point is reached where the decrease is at an end and consciousness ceases, the lower limit of the threshold of sensation being exceeded. But who can in Nature assign this point with certainty?

We shall, in conclusion, have to take notice of the question whether, in our present mode of regarding the atoms as acts of will, we may look upon them as so many substances, or not rather as phenomena of *one* substance? whether to every atom there corresponds a separate, independent, substantial will,—as a matter of course these also endowed with separate faculty of perception,—or whether a single identical will underlies these many counter-working actions and activities? After having perceived only the opposition, the contradiction of actions, to be the spatially real, but having comprehended the forces themselves as something absolutely non-spatial, every reason disappears for the splitting of will and idea in the eternally non-spatial into an innumerable multiplicity of single substances, and rather the impossibility of the reciprocal action of such isolated and non-contiguous substances compels us to assume that the atoms, just as all individuals, may be altogether merely objectively-real phenomena or manifestations of the All-one, in which, as in their common root, their real relation to one another may be effected (comp. C. Chap. vii. and xi.) Were the atoms substantially separate and different, the spaces fixed by their unconscious ideational functions would be as numerous as the atoms, and accordingly the spaces *realised* by the atomistic functions of will would be as *numerous* as the atoms. There would then not at all come to pass that which makes possible the community of the spatial relations of the atomic functions to one another, namely, the one *objectivo-*phenomenal, *i.e.*, objectively-*real* space. Such can only arise by the realisation of the unconscious space-ideas, if these latter in all the atoms only compose the inner multiplicity of the content of a single collective idea; and this, again, is only possible if all the atomic functions are functions of one and the same essence as modes of an absolute substance. For him, who elects to stop short at the pluralism of the atoms regarded as substantially different, there will always remain an inexplicable residue even with our conception of matter; this disappears, however, as soon as the final unavoidable step to metaphysical Monism has been taken.

VI.

THE CONCEPTION OF INDIVIDUALITY.

INDIVIDUAL means indivisible (as does atom); but every one knows that individuals may be cut into pieces and divided. We can thus only think of something as individual which in its nature cannot be divided if it is to remain what it is; but this is the notion of unity—Greek *monas* (not to be confused with the numerical concept of the *one*, Greek ἕν). According to this, the conceptions unity or monad and individual coincide; but one very soon sees that unity is a wider notion than individual, *i.e.*, every individual is a unity, but not every unity is an individual. Thus every connected form, in virtue of the continuity of space, is a unity. I cannot divide it without annihilating it; still I shall not call the accidental unity of form of a clod, *e.g.*, an individual. Further, every movement or every occurrence possesses a unity in virtue of the continuity of time, *e.g.*, a tone; this unity likewise is not an individual (comp. V. Kirchmann, "Philosophie des Wissens," vol. i. pp. 131–141, 285–307). The unity of coinherence or of interpenetration, as it appears, *e.g.*, in colours, mixtures of taste or smell, and in different qualities of the same thing, is reducible partly to *existence in the same place*, partly to the *temporal coexistence* of different qualities, partly to the *causal* unity of succession, and can accordingly not be regarded as a particular species of unity. The unity of the causal relation is the strongest that there is. We have to distinguish in it three kinds: (1) Unity by identity of the cause (as in the different perceptions of a thing); (2) unity by reason of identity of the purpose (as in the many contrivances of the eye for seeing); (3) unity by mutual action of the parts, so that the function of each part is cause of the persistence of the other.—These unities also do not suffice for the conception of individuality. An example of the first is the unity of the many perceptions of a thing, so far as they do not directly contain the identity of place and time, but are only referred to the thing as identical causes. Nobody will maintain that the unity of the perception of a thing is an individual. In the second place, if the unity of purpose consists in the construction of a building, we should not call the sum of the workmen which have this purpose an individual. Thirdly, if a country lives on the natural products of its colonies, and the colonies only exist by reason of the importation of the artificial productions of the mother country, there is here a perfect reciprocity, and yet nobody will call the sum of colonies and mother country an individual.

Each of these unities, then, shows itself as insufficient to fix the notion of the individual. Just as insufficient are the external characteristics which are set up here and there as marks, e.g., the origin from a germ or an egg (Gallesio and Huxley). According to that, all the weeping willows of Europe must be an individual, since they can be shown to be historically derived from a single tree introduced into England from Asia by means of offshoots; thus all spring from one germ. According to that, further, all the plant-lice (perhaps several millions) which are produced by parthenogenesis in ten or more generations in the course of a summer, represent collectively a single individual. Just as little as the derivation from a single egg can the typical idea of the race pass as mark of the individual; for the typical generic idea is the idea of the normal individual, which represents the race because it is free from accidental peculiarities; and one gains this idea of the normal individual by allowing the accidental peculiarities to be stripped from all individuals of a species, and only retaining the uniform common element in abstraction. It is here at once evident that one must already *possess* the mark of the individual in order to be able to compare the several individuals and to single out the normal type; that thus this type cannot possibly hold good regressively as criterion of the individual, since one would thereby only revolve in a circle. But, in addition, we have undoubted individuals, even where the same do not, or imperfectly, represent the generic idea. Thus the root belongs to the idea of the plant, the tentacles to the idea of the polyp; but if I cut off the twig of a plant or a piece of the tube of a polyp, these have no roots or tentacula, and yet continue an independent existence, since they carry about with them all the conditions of the continued existence; we cannot possibly denude them of individuality. Derivation from an egg and the typical generic idea thus appear altogether unsuitable to serve as marks of the individual; let us therefore return to the conception of unity as we formerly conceived it.

It is true the several kinds of unity considered were likewise insufficient, but if each taken singly is too wide for the limits of the concept individual, yet the combination of all these species of unity in a thing afford the necessary limitations. We had, namely, demanded unity for the individual, because it was of its essence that it should be indivisible; but now it is clear that this requirement is only fulfilled, if not merely in this or that relation, but in all possible relations it is essentially inseparable, *i.e.*, if it combines in itself all possible modes of unity. That the five above-mentioned varieties of unity are in fact all possible and alone possible, it is not difficult to see, for they exhaust the three subjective-objective forms: Space, Time, and Causality.

We have, then, gained a satisfactory definition of the individual: the individual is a thing which unites in itself all possible modes of unity: (1) *Space* unity (of the form); (2) *time* unity (continuity of action); (3) unity of the (intrinsic) *cause;* (4) unity of *purpose;* (5) unity of *reciprocal action* of the parts (so far as such are present; otherwise, of course, the last disappears).—Where the unity of the form is wanting, as in a beehive, one says notwithstanding that all the other unities are most strikingly present, but not that of the individual. Where the continuity of action is wanting, as in frozen and re-thawed fishes, in dried-up and again softened Rotifers, there exists, it is true, a unity of the thing, but I should consider it an error to speak of unity of the individual; there are in that case just two individuals, which are distinct owing to the pause in their vital activity, as I am different from a man living a thousand years ago. That of the three causal unities none can be wanting to the individual is doubtless self-evident.

It is decidedly of importance for the conception of the individual that no one of these unities is anything absolutely fixed, outwardly rounded off, but all the inferior unities of the same kind can be included and be taken up together with several of their like into a higher unity. It is altogether a vain endeavour to seek for a definite boundary to any kind of unity whatsoever; there are always, again, higher unities conceivable, which include them at the same time, as everything finally is taken up into the unity of the world, and this may again be crowned by a metaphysical unity of different co-ordinated worlds imperceptible to us. If this holds good of the conception of unity, it already shows that it also holds good for the conception of the individual, and that for this, too, the external rounding off and strict separation is only in appearance. This appearance to superficial observation, namely, arises from this, that the individual first comes into being through this composition of *all* the above-mentioned unities. If, now, several individuals are said to be contained in an individual of a higher order, there appertains to that, both in the individuals of the lower and in that of the higher order, a coincidence of all these kinds of unities; if, on the other hand, any mode of unity is wanting in the former or the latter, there remains, it is true, the subordination of the other unities under the higher ones, but there is then no longer an embracing of several individuals by a higher. Even Spinoza, the monist of purest water, says (Eth. Th. 2, Prop. 7, Post. 1): "The human body consists of several individuals of various nature, each of which is very complex;" and Leibniz carries this idea farther in his Monadology.

Let us first look at the matter in the case of immaterial individuals, where the relations are much simpler. So far, namely, as we have hitherto spoken of individuals, the discussion has only been of material individuals; something quite different to these, and by no means coinciding with them, are the immaterial individuals, which therefore require a quite special investigation. Had a resolution been earlier taken to separate the investigation of spiritual and material individuals, the present terrible confusion would by no means have prevailed with regard to this conception.

We have here again to distinguish between consciously-spiritual and unconsciously-spiritual individuals, and speak provisionally only of the former. Locke asserted that the identity of a person exclusively depends on the identity of consciousness, and this truth has been readily admitted by all later philosophers. The unity which may not be divided, constituting the individual, is accordingly here the unity of consciousness, which we have considered in C. Chap. iii. pp. 113–118. For only by this, that the consciousnesses of two ideas temporally or spatially separate in the brain are taken up into the common consciousness of the comparison, *i.e.*, find in this their higher unity, only hereby does it become possible that the subject or the *instinctively* supposed cause of the one and the other idea is recognised as one and the same, and accordingly both referred to a common internal cause

(Ego). Only so far as the unity of consciousness extends does the unity of the mental processes by causal reference to a common subject extend, only so far extends the consciously-mental individual.

Now we know that in the subordinate nervous centres of men and animals conscious mental processes go on, which, owing to the excellence of the communications, are united into an intimate unity; we shall then be necessarily obliged to recognise in these unities spiritual individuals. It cannot be objected that these other centres are mentally too low to attain to self-consciousness, to the Me. This Me is only *instinctively* presumed, *i.e.*, it does not at all need to emerge as self-consciousness; but all goes on as if self-consciousness existed, and referred all actions to the Ego. This we still see, indeed, in the lowest animals and plants, and call it zoopsychological sensibility. There is, therefore, nothing in the way of comprehending the lower nerve-centres as supporters of conscious mental individuals; but when we further see that sensations of different nerve-centres can be taken up into one consciousness under particular circumstances, which more or less occurs in common feeling, one cannot avoid acknowledging this unity of consciousness as a higher spiritual individual, which comprehends the lower individuals in itself. Further, if we consider that the properly active parts of the white nerve-fibres merely destined for conduction, namely, their axis cylinders, are quite the same as the grey matter, and that the white appearance is merely produced by the medullary matter destined for the isolation of the fibres deposited between axis cylinder and fibrous membrane, one cannot avoid the conclusion that the active parts even of the white nerve-matter have a consciousness of their own of some sort or other of the vibrations, which they are certainly only destined to transmit as their share in the general economy. In like manner, the contracting muscular fibres, or the secreting glands responding to nerve-stimulation, beyond a doubt possess a certain sensation of these events, since they are, indeed, adapted to propagate the nervous vibrations exciting them beyond the limits of the nerve-fibres to the neighbouring parts. (Thus, according to Engelmann, the peristaltic movements of the ureter are spontaneous functions of its unstriped muscular walls.)

If we further remember the results of C. Chap. iv., where we came upon cell-consciousness in plants, the supposition is very plausible that even the animal cells, in part still more highly organised than the vegetable cells, have their separate consciousness; an assumption which later on in this chapter will receive yet further confirmation. This much is certain, that the animal cells in great part live, grow, increase, and pay their specific contribution to the preservation of the whole, just as independently as the vegetable cells. Why, if they lead just as independent a life, should they not have just as independent a sensation ? Virchow says (" Cellulorpathologie," 3d edit., p. 105): "Only when we conceive the absorption of nutritive material as a consequence of the activity (attraction) of the tissue-elements themselves, do we comprehend why the several districts are not every moment flooded with blood, that rather the offered material is only taken up into the parts according to the real need, and carried to the several districts in such proportion that, in general at least, as long as there exists any possibility of conservation, the one part cannot be essentially injured by the others." If this proper activity of the cell holds good for the *reception* of the nutritive materials, how much more for their chemical and formal conversion ! There are, indeed, large districts of the animal body which are entirely devoid of nerves and vessels, *e.g.*, the substance of the epidermis, tendons, bones, teeth, fibrous cartilage; and yet a circulation of moisture through the cells takes place as in plants, and a life and an increase of cells without stimulation of nerves. If the animal cells are capable of performances so individual, just as in the plant, must they not be, like those, supporters of an individual consciousness? The difference is only this: in the animal the importance of the individual consciousness of the cells *is evanescent* in comparison with the individual consciousness of higher orders, but in the plant the cellular consciousness is the principal thing, because it is altogether only in certain sensitive and privileged parts, as flowers, &c., that there can be any individual consciousness of a higher order worth speaking of.

Lastly, should ever the question with regard to the consciousness of the atoms come to be affirmatively decided, the atoms would, in fine, be the conscious individuals of lowest order. Thus for *conscious-spiritual* individuals we have found the *superposition* of individuals of higher and lower orders to be a correct representation; we have now to consider the case of *material* individuals.

Recurring to the organic individuals, the difficulty of deciding the question, what is the individual, is still more evident in the case of plants than in that of animals. In the case of the higher plants, the layman especially designates as individual what the botanist calls the *stem* (cormus). Linnæus, Goethe, Erasmus Darwin, Alexander Braun, and many others sought for the individual in the *shoot*, which answers to a single axis of the plant. Ernest Meyer and others declared the *leaf* in its different forms (discovered by Goethe) to be the true individual, and the pedicle as lower part of the leaf. Gaudichaud, Agardh, Engelmann, Steinheil, and others thought they had found the same in the *pedicle*, as whose upper offshoot they regarded the leaf or the calyx. Schulz-Schultzenstein, on the other hand, tried to find it in the cell groups, called by him anaphytons, as presented in the developing buds. Schleiden and Schwann took the next step, setting up the *cell* as the sole individual in the life of the plant. Each of these views has important reasons in its favour, and, in fact, each of them is so far right in maintaining this or that to be individual, but wrong in combating the other views; for the question is here not about an *either, or,* but about a *both, and.* The whole plant as well as each branch and sprig, and also every leaf and every cell, combines in itself all the unities which are necessary for individuality. This indeed is coming to be perceived more and more; thus Decandolle distinguishes *five* orders of individuals (cell, bud, offshoot, stem, embryo); Schleiden, *three* (cell, bud, stem); Häckel,[1] *six* (cell, organ, counterpart, afterpart, shoot, stem).

It would be altogether wrong and perfectly untenable if spatial separation and seclusion were asserted to be the condition of individuality, for then twins, only externally connected at some part of the skin (as the Siamese pair, who have lived to upwards of sixty years), would always have to be regarded as only one individual, which would be altogether too absurd. Just as certainly is it erroneous to require in an individual independence [2] of existence

---

[1] Comp. his "Generelle Morphologie der Organismen." Berlin, Reimer, 1866, vol. i. p. 251. Chapters viii. and ix. of this work, which unfortunately I only became acquainted with after the appearance of the fourth edition of the "Philosophy of the Unconscious," form the best and most thorough confirmation of the opinion I have here expressed concerning the conception of individuality.

[2] On this ground I cannot assent to Häckel's distinction between morphological and physiological individuality, since the latter is only an ill-selected expression for vital self-sufficiency or biological independence. Certainly one must ascribe individuality to every independent and self-preserving living being, but not because it is physiologically independent, but because the physiological independence *presupposes* the coinherence of those various unities in which individuality consists. Häckel himself declares ("Generelle Morphologie," vol. i. p. 333) the "physiologic individual" to be in its nature *divisible*, in contrast to the infinitely *indivisible* "morphological individual," and therewith openly allows the contradiction of the notion in respect of its name. Certainly it is physiologically important to settle with what order of individuals in each class of animals and plants biological independence begins; but why substitute for this perfectly sufficient and clear notion of the "Bion" or independent vital existence that of the "physiological individual"? On the other hand, Häckel's conception of the morphological individual itself contains physiological elements, which are smuggled in unnoticed by means of the indispensable unities of purpose and of the reciprocal action of the parts. We, therefore, do not think we are going far astray when we stop at the unitarian conception of the organic individual, and reject Häckel's attempted division of the same.

without the support of other individuals; one has only to think what would become of the infant if the mother did not offer it her breast, or of young beasts of prey if the parents did not take them with them on the chase; and nobody will deny individuality to children and young animals.

In lower organisms that coalescence which in the higher only appears as abnormity of the fœtal life uniformly occurs. A unicellular Alga, *Pediastrum rotula*, appears in the adult condition only as a complex of cells or a cell-colony of middle cell and peripherally deposited marginal cells. The green protoplasmic content of each of these cells parts for the end of propagation into four, eight, sixteen, thirty-two, or sixty-four globular branch cells, which on emergence possess an independent motion lasting a tolerable time; but then lie beside one another, eight for every surface, in order by growing together with one another to form a new rosette-like colony, which, although consisting of eight unicellular Algæ, yet comports itself entirely as an individual. Similar processes are found in a few other Algæ, *e.g.*, the water-net (*Hydrodictyon*).—In a polyp-stock, every single animal is as certainly an individual as the whole stock is an individual, since its parts, like the members of a so-called simple animal, are related to one another through the community of the nutritive process, and nevertheless maintain their morphological independence. "Every compound zoophyte springs from a single polyp, and grows (like a plant) by continued gemmation into a tree or a dome. The trunk of an Astræa twelve feet in diameter unites about 100,000 polyps, each of which takes up a square half inch; in a Porites, whose animalcules are hardly a line in breadth, their number would exceed five and a half millions. In it, therefore, there are an equal number of mouths and stomachs to a single zoophyte, contributing together to the nutrition, gemmation, and growth of the whole, and also united laterally to one another" (Dana in Schleiden's and Fror. Not., 1847, June, No. 48). Whoever ascribes individuality to an oak-tree must grant it also to such a polyp-tree.

The globular animal, *Volvox globator*, is (although not belonging to the corals) a polyp-stock formed of several animalcules, which, sitting on the circumference of a sphere, are only united by feather-like tubes. "If one puts some red or blue colouring matter into the water under the microscope, a powerful current round the balls is very distinctly perceived. This is a consequence of the collective action of all the single animalcules, which, like herds of animals, flocks of birds, even singing or dancing human beings and crowds, possess a common rhythm and a common direction, often even without the word of command, and without being clearly conscious of a purpose. Thus float all polyp-stocks, and the sympathetic as the more coldly judging naturalist sees herein a social impulse, which consists of force and pliability for common purposes, a condition requiring a mental activity, which one may be betrayed into, but not justified in rating too lightly. One must also never forget that all the single animalcules possess organs of sensation which are comparable to eyes, and that they accordingly do not turn themselves blindly about in the water, but, as citizens of a great world very remote from our estimation, share with us the enjoyment of a highly sensitive existence, however proudly we may bear ourselves" (Ehrenberg in his great work on the Infusoria, p. 69). This judgment is so interesting just because it shows how the modest but great naturalist, overpowered by the simple facts, recognises an instinct of the masses and a stirring mental life at those lower animal grades.

"In the Mediterranean there is a rich family of splendid swimming-polyps, which Carl Vogt in particular ("Recherches sur les Animaux inférieurs de la Méditerranée") has brought to the knowledge of the scientist. A young polyp is developed from an egg. It begins its life freely floating in the sea. At its upper end it forms a bubble, in which the air is set free which supports it, at its lower end there are formed, in ever richer and fairer measure, feelers and prehensile threads with special urticating organs. On its stem, which is continually elongating, there is formed a filtering tube. From this stem arise bud-like shoots. Some of them form swimming bells, which propel themselves, and consequently the whole mass. The others are metamorphosed into fresh polyps, which possess mouth and stomach, and not merely collect, but also digest food for the whole, to deliver it finally into the common trunk-tube. Finally, yet other buds attain a nettle-like aspect, and provide for propagation; they bring forth ova, from which again proceed freely-floating polyps." (Special polyps with long sensitive tactile threads represent the sense-organs or the intelligence of this state.) "What is here individual? The young polyp appears to us simple, but out of it there is formed a stem like a plant. The stem sends out tentacles like roots, but they move voluntarily, and grasp prey; it forms a trunk with a digestive sac, but it has not any more than the plant a mouth to make use of the sac. It sends forth buds and sprouts like the plant, but every bud has a special task, which it performs with the appearance of original activity. Special sprouts or branches endowed with movement of their own manage, some the reception and digestion of the food, others propagation. The trunk is nothing without the limbs, the limbs nothing without the trunk" (Virchow, "Vier Reden," pp. 65, 66). Whoever holds fast to the "either-or," certainly such an example must reduce to desperation; but we see in the several members individuals partly of polyp-form, partly medusoid, and, in the whole, an individual of higher order, which includes in itself all these individuals. Even in the bee- and ant-hive there is nothing wanting to complete the view of the whole as an individual of higher order but spatial unity, *i.e.*, the *continuity* of the form; here this likewise is present, and therefore the individual is indisputable.

This widespread phenomenon in the animal and vegetable kingdom of a varied physiological development of morphologically originally similarly constructed individuals of the same species is termed Polymorphism (even the separation of the sexes comes under this conception). Kölliker recently discovered an interesting example in the family of the sea-pens (*Pennatulidæ*). Without entering into the morphological significance of the organs of the trunk, which serve as supporters of the several animals, it is to be said that here the sex-animals, devouring animals, and feeling-animals are not different, but one; on the other hand, stunted individuals without tentacles and sexual organs occur, which used to be regarded merely as warts (granulation) of the skin, but which otherwise possess altogether the structure of the sex-animals, and perhaps have a particular relation to the imbibing and venting of water. It is one and the same principle of *division of labour*, of the facilitation of a collective performance by distribution to various one-sidedly endowed organs, which, in the organised state of the bees, and still more in that of the ants, conditions the different development of from three to five separate individuals, and that here he assigns the system of movement, of assimilation of food and digestion, of perception and propagation to diverse individuals coalescing into an individual of higher order. It is just this principle, however, which we find also carried out in the higher plants, where the roots provide for the reception of nutriment, the leaves for respiration, the flowers for propagation, whilst a trunk or stalk gives support or cohesion to the whole, as the middle stem of the floating polyp commonwealth. As in the bee-state the sexual activity is personified in drones and queen, so also in the diœcious plants, *i.e.*, in those in which the one plant bears merely male, the other merely female flowers; and in the monœcious, where male and female flowers are on one plant, are these flowers not to be called individuals, because they happen to be united in space by other parts of the plant?

But not merely in the remote region of lower marine animals do we thus manifestly find compound individuals. The comprehension of the tape-worms, in which the head, by means of so-called nurse-generation, produces an entire colony of hermaphrodite sexual animals, leads us to the correct estimation of the anatomical structure of the annelids, and these guide us to that of the articulata. In the lower Annulata each segment has its gills, its expansion of the intestinal canal, its contractile distension of the large blood-vessel, its ganglia, its ramifications of the nervous and vascular trunks, its organs of propagation, its locomotor appendages, and sometimes even its special pair of eyes. Among the Articulata the Myriapoda stand nearest to the Annelids; the process of gemmation of segments, which is characteristic of the compound individual, is here in part to be very distinctly observed in the embryological history of development; the larva of the milliped, which is hatched with eight segments, forms, even in the first moulting, between the ultimate and penultimate segment six new ones. In the degree in which the division of labour and perfection of the type progresses from the tape-worms to the Annelids, to the millipeds and from these to the higher Articulata (crabs, spiders, insects), in the same degree is there exhibited an intensified differentiation of the segments of which the compound insect consists; but even in the most perfect insects, with the assistance of the individual and the palæontological history of development the composition from segments, which are conceived as originally independent, is still more certainly to be made out, and however far the d'ferentiation may otherwise be carried, there yet remain certain functions (*e.g.*, respiration) here always decentralised.

The successive segments of the Vertebrata, which consist of a vertebra with its osseous processes, 'er with the appertaining muscular, vascular, and nervous pairs, unquestionably exhibit a certain analogy with these successive pieces of the compound worms and millipeds. Nevertheless this does not seem to me sufficient to place, with Häckel, both forms on the same level of individuality, because in the compound worms the manifold of the collective individual arises by aggregation of many single individuals, but in the Vertebrata by *internal differentiation*. It makes no difference here whether the several individuals are the result of sexual congress, or whether, as in the tape-worm, they are produced from an originally simple individual by way of nurse-generation; both form a mutual contrast to the interior, gradually progressive differentiation of the vertebrate organism, whose prototype, the Amphioxus, forms by no means the analogue of a compound, but of a simple worm. The course of development in the Invertebrata and Vertebrata is accordingly an exactly opposite one. In the former it is the manifold, which concretes to unity in increasing measure by means of unlikeness and closer connection of the parts; in the latter unity is the starting-point, which unfolds to the wealth of the manifold by enhancing the inner multiplicity; in the former case the individuals of lower order grow together to an individual of higher order; in the latter case an individual unfolds into individuals of lower order, and thereby at least relatively enhances the degree of its order of individuality. Thus it becomes intelligible that, in spite of the opposite starting-point, both courses of development approach one another so much nearer in their *results* the farther they have progressed, *i.e.*, the more closely on the one side the composing members have coalesced, and the more they have converted their functions, fulfilling originally merely particular aims, to serviceable functions of the higher whole,—the farther on the other side the inner differentiation of the successive portions, organs, and systems of organs has advanced.

As the above-mentioned floating polyp-stocks and

Pennatulidæ are remarkable for the several individuals composing them being entirely lowered to the rank of differentiated organs of the higher collective organism, so conversely we see that in the higher animals the organs obtain the more sharply defined individuality, the more strongly they are differentiated in their functions and their constitution. One may again distinguish within the organs three essentially different grades of individuality of organ; the simple, the compound organs, and the systems of organs. The simple organs (Häckel's organs of first and second rank) consist of a tissue of one kind; the compound of that of several kinds; the systems of organs are the indivisible union of a number of single and compound organs in the whole organism, so far as they serve a particular functional purpose. Simple organs are, *e.g.*, the epidermis, whose appendages (hairs, nails, scales, cutaneous glands, crystalline lens), cartilage, and several other vascular and nerveless forms of the connective tissue; compound organs are such as the several muscles, nerves, bones, blood-vessels, mucous membranes. The sense-organs are mostly of so complicated a nature that they conduct us from the organs to the systems of organs, *e.g.*, the sum of the endings of the tactile nerves beneath the epidermis. As system of organs one may further cite the protective system of the surface of the body (epidermis with appendages), the system of the skeleton, the muscular system, the nervous system, the vascular or circulatory system, the intestinal or digestive system, the respiratory system, the generative or reproductive system. Of course between these different systems in the higher animals there takes place a very intimate interpenetration and interlacing; still even morphologically their separation can very well be accomplished, and there is no apparent reason why the more intimate fusion should afford a motive for doubting the relative individuality of these systems, which is so glaring in the floating polyps in spite of the local fusion, and in the communities of bees and ants is developed even to the partition of functions among *discrete* individuals. In the spatially more sharply defined simple or compound individual organs the acknowledgment of individuality should meet with still fewer difficulties; as certainly as to the single leaf or stamen of the plant belongs a kind of individuality, so certainly to a hair of a man's head does a sort of individuality appertain. In lower animals single organs sometimes testify their individuality by releasing themselves from the collective organism, and yet go on living and regularly perform the office for the sake of which they are there; thus, *e.g.*, in several kinds of Cephalopods (Argonauta, Philonexis, Tremoctopus) the males have a hectocotylus, *i.e.*, an arm elaborated into a sexual organ, which performs the procreative act by being liberated from the male and penetrating into the female. This hectocotylus was at first regarded as a parasite, afterwards as the rudimentary male of the respective cuttlefish, until it was perceived to be the individualised organ of the male.

Of importance for our theme is likewise the pathological conception of *parasitic* formations. I shall let an authority in this field, Professor Virchow, speak for me. ("Cellular Pathology," pp. 427, 428): "Let one only remember that parasitism only *gradually* comes to mean something else than the notion of autonomy of each part of the body. Every single epithelial and muscular cell leads in relation to the rest of the body a kind of parasitic existence, just as every single cell of a tree in relation to the other cells of the same tree has a special existence belonging to it alone, and withdraws from the rest of the elements certain matters for its needs (ends). The notion of parasitism in the narrower sense of the term is developed from this conception of the independence of the several parts. As long as the need of the remaining parts presupposes the existence of any part, as long as this part is useful in some way or other to the other parts, so long one does not speak of a parasite; it becomes so, however, from the moment when it is foreign or injurious to the rest of the body. The conception of the parasite is therefore not to be confined to a single series of excrescences, but it belongs to all plastic (formative) forms, but before all to the heteroplastic, which in their further elaboration do not produce homologous products, but new formations, which are more or less unsuitable in the composition of the body (at this particular place)." From the unmistakable individual independence of the parasites and the purely gradual difference between them and normal formations one may also regressively conclude to the individual independence of the latter.

Still more distinct is the individual independence in those structures which exhibit also morphologically a certain local separation from the rest of the body, and yet in their independent functions produce an effect subserving the ends of the entire organism. I may mention, *e.g.*, the seminal filaments. The time has gone by when the spermatozoids were regarded as independent animals analogous to the intestinal worms destitute of mouth and stomach, for the purpose of their existence and above all their developmental history testify to the contrary. Nevertheless we cannot deny to these structures an individuality. In the diluted semen the filaments may be seen to contract, to revolve on their axes, lash with their tail, jerk forwards the head, and freely float about in all directions, the wriggling or screw-like motion of the tail effecting the movement. These movements appear most arbitrary in the spermatozoids of the animal species where fertilisation is most difficult, *i.e.*, in the mammalia, and become the more simple and regular the more easy in the ascending animal scale fertilisation becomes by the number, size of the ova, and arrangement of the place of fertilisation. That a certain dependence of existence on particular surrounding external relations, or even a linking with the existence of other organisms, does not disprove individuality, we have already mentioned before (one has only to think of parasitic animals); but the spermatozoids have also a tolerably long life outside the seminal fluid in every blood-hot, chemically indifferent fluid, if they are only not hygroscopically deformed by the same. In the female organs of generation of the mammalia they continue to live for days, nay, weeks; and in the seed-pouches, *e.g.*, the male river-crawfish, which, in the rut, attach to the females in autumn, or in the seminal vessels of humble-bees and wasps that have copulated in the autumn, they continue to live until the spring, to then fertilise the ova which have in the meantime become ripe. This already proves a high degree of independent vital capacity after the separation of the organism producing them. The morphological type of all spermatozoids of the whole animal kingdom are the zoö spores of the Protist kingdom, structures of whose individuality hardly a doubt could well be suggested. It is just the zoö spores of the lower organisms which exhibit the extremest degree of individual independence (in the Myxomycetes the spores even increase for several generations by fission), and nevertheless many of them surrender the same in the act of *copulation*, in which two or more individuals lose their individuality and blend into one new individual. In the copulation of the zoö spores we have to see the prototype of the fertilising act, in which likewise two individuals (ovum and seed-filament) allow their individuality to become lost in that of a single new individual. When the plasmodes of the Myxomycetes in their apparently lawless creeping about now disintegrate, now flow together into one, we shall perceive therein a phenomenon merely of life and growth. We see, then, how near procreation stands to growth even in reference to the act of copulation of the materials of generation, if we compare with the confluence of two plasmodes the congress of a number of zoö spores to form a plasmode. If here only a summation of like individual forces appears to be intended, the thought is forcibly suggested of a neutralisation of invisible individual differences in a copulation of *two* zoö spores, until in sexual generation this difference rises to the height of a characteristic contrast of the generative substances.—If one should attempt to dispute the autonomous movements of the spermatozoids by a parallel with the movements of cilia, I should reply that in my view conversely the autonomy of the former makes for that of the latter. An alternating movement of a structure separate in form, which demonstrably neither follows on mere external stimulus nor is even produced by central parts, since it persists after the isolation of the smallest portion of ciliated epithelium, must arise from a cause inherent in the structure itself, *i.e.*, bears the character of a certain individuality. That the movements of the ciliary hairs of a surface frequently agree with one another in such a way that regular total movements, continuous waves, &c., arise, cannot weaken this opinion. The like is also found in the bundles of spermatozoids, where in each bundle regular waves flow on one after another, or in those which are deposited together in a thickly packed mass (*e.g.*, in the earth-worm), where the beautiful, regular waving is said to be comparable with that of a cornfield. It is just the same co-operation of many individuals towards a goal as in the organism in general.

There are Protista (*Amœba diffluens* and *porrecta*) whose sole locomotion consists in this, that they shoot out rays in which the substance of the animal combined with the points flows after one, or even several, whilst the previous centre is thereby narrowed to the ray remaining behind, which now withdraws to the new centre of gravity. On precisely the same principle (according to Van Recklinghausen) pus corpuscles move as long as they are living; they too shoot out radiated processes at the periphery, and withdraw the same; and at times one observes that the viscous content of the cell darts after into such a ray. The identity of these pus corpuscles with the most common form of the white lymphatic bodies was subsequently demonstrated by Cohnheim, and their exit at the place of suppuration established. Then Virchow observed similar phenomena of movement in the large-tailed cells which are found in a just excised cartilaginous tumour. Movements had already been discovered in the blood corpuscles of several animals. Without desiring to place the pus corpuscle and similar freely moving structures morphologically, chemically, or physiologically beside the corresponding lower animals in any way, from which they are so entirely distinguished by their historical development, I yet think that they may lay claim to an equal right of individuality with those, since they, if not animals in the zoological sense, are yet beings which move about in their environment just as purposively and with the same appearance of voluntariness and animation as the lower infusoria. That the circumstances of nutrition are accommodated to the medium entirely answers to the general processes in organic nature, and that they have accordingly no mouth and stomach, cannot detract from their individuality, since there are indeed animals also in whom both are wanting.

The most recent discoveries on the immigration and emigration of these amœboid corpuscles from the blood circulation into the tissue and back again lift the process of nutrition out of the inorganic into the organic sphere, in that, quite analogously to the procreative process, they may be perceived to be conditioned by the living individuality of their substrata. The nutritive fluid absorbed from the intestine as it enters into the lymphatic vessels as yet contains no formed elements, but doubtless it copiously receives such from the lymphatic glands; similarly the vascular glands, above all the spleen, are breeding-places of these amœboid elements. They pass through the walls of the blood-vessels into the tissue of the body, in that at first a fine thread-like process is pushed through a pore of the vascular wall, and if the process, which lasts for hours, remains undisturbed, the total content of the corpuscle gradually follows. These points have been most certainly established, as the eagerness of these corpuscles for the reception of finely divided pigments facilitates observation. As connective tissue corpuscles they now penetrate into all organs, and the cell-wanderings of the connective tissue enveloping all the organs have been even longer known. When they have fulfilled their office, they retreat through the walls of the blood-vessels or lymphatic vessels again into the circulation. Unfortunately we do not yet know anything more particularly with respect to the chemical differences on entrance and exit, and their possible regeneration into a condition capable of nutrition. This much is, however, certain, that the colourless blood corpuscles must also be regarded as the origin of the red blood corpuscles, which are the substrata of the respiratory process in the widest sense. The passage from the one to the other form is guaranteed by numerous intermediate stages. The red blood corpuscles now present, it is true, at their periphery no visible phenomena of movement; but according to the investigations of Brücke, which have been found to be confirmed also by other distinguished histologists, the red-coloured amœboid individual (zooid) is here only limited with its movements to the interior of its case, which consists of a porous, immobile, very soft, colourless, and vitreous substance (oikoïd). In the normal condition the zooid pervades the whole oikoïd, and leaves in the centre a colourless nucleus; placed in water, it withdraws, however, from the periphery to the centre, so that now the former appears colourless, the latter red; not rarely one sees amœbiform processes radiate from the red centre to the periphery.—In the face of such results in regard to a living individuality of the supports of the nutritive and respiratory process in animal organisms, the naturalists in question have seen themselves constrained to the admission that only the view of the organism as a complex of living elementary beings is capable of doing justice to the phenomena. Each of these individual beings floats about independently in the lymph or the blood, and autonomously executes its functions pre-designated for it by its own individual nature, and yet the results fit as organically together as if a secret tie united these beings, or a secret commander guided their performances according to a higher plan.

But even before these recent surprising clues to the supports of nutrition and respiration, thinking naturalists, on considering the *cell* as the elementary fundamental form of all organic construction, have felt themselves compelled to the acknowledgment of living individuality *within* the externally limited organism. "All life is bound to the cell, and the cell is not merely the vessel of life, but it is itself the living part" (Virchow, "Vier Reden," p. 54). "What is the organism? A community of living cells, a little state, well provided with all appurtenances of upper and under officials, servants and masters, great and small" (p. 55). "Life is the activity of the cell; its special character is the special character of the cell" (p. 10). "Peculiar appears to us the mode of activity, the special function of the organic matter, but yet it happens in no other way than the activity and function which Physics reveals in non-living nature. The entire speciality is limited to this, that the greatest multiplicity of material combinations is packed together in the smallest space; that every cell represents in itself a seat of most intimate effects, most manifold material combinations with one another, and that therefore results are attained which nowhere else occur in nature, since nowhere else is a similar intimacy of effects known" (p. 11). "If we will not make up our minds to distinguish between collective individuals and single individuals, the conception of individual in the organic branches of physical science must either be abandoned or be strictly confined to the cell. To the former result both the systematic materialist as well as the spiritualist must logically come; the unprejudiced realistic view of Nature appears to lead to the latter, in as much as only in this way is the unitarian conception of life assured for the whole sphere of vegetable and animal organisms" (pp. 73, 74). This is the final result of Virchow; one sees that he grazes the truth, without having the courage to grasp it firmly. What concerns us here is his well-established conception of the cell, which he has further elaborated according to the suggestions of Schleiden and Schwann, and therewith has raised animal physiology and pathology to a new level, so to say; comp. Virchow, "Cellularpathologie," especially chaps. i. and xiv. That organisms in general consist of cells, and moreover of so many microscopically minute ones, for that there is the teleological ground that nutrition can only be effected by endosmosis. Endosmosis is only possible through very thin, firm walls. Thus if with these thin walls the necessary solidity is to be attained, the whole system must be a complex of very small cells. How great is the number of cells is proved by the following quotation:—

"At Zürich, near the Tiefenhof, stands an old lindentree; every year, when it puts on its ornament of leaves, it forms, according to the estimate of Nägeli, about ten billions of newly living cells. In the blood of an adult man there circulate, according to the calculations of Vierordt and Welcker, at every moment, sixty billions (think: 60,000,000,000,000) of minutest cellular bodies" (Virchow, p. 55).

After all this, we cannot doubt that we have before us in every cell an individual; but whether with the cell we have reached the lowest grade of the individual, which is still organism, this may still appear doubtful.

We distinguish, namely, in most cells: cell-wall, cell-content, kernel or *nucleus*, and usually also, in addition, kernel-corpuscle or *nucleolus*. These parts are decidedly to be regarded as organs of the cell, having their special functions. The cell-wall regulates the income and outgoing according to quantity and quality; the *nucleolus* takes care for propagation or increase of the cells (cells without *nucleolus* are infertile); the *nucleus* secures the continuance of the cell, and probably directs the chemical transformations and productions in the interior of the cell. If the relative independence of these organs is to be regarded as established, one can hardly dispute whether they are still organic individuals, for undoubtedly within every such sphere there takes place an organic reciprocal action of the parts for the sake of the function to be exercised.

This relative independence of the organs of the cell, inferred by me *a priori*, has recently received a needed confirmation through the inquiries and observations of the botanist Hanstein, which he has made especially on the cells of some vegetable capillaries, but also on the parenchyma cells of different plants. In the large hair-cells of the Cucurbitaceæ and many Compositæ, *e.g.*, one sees the cell-nucleus suspended about the middle of the cell by protoplasmic bands, "like the spider in its web." The protoplasmic bag-like covering of the nucleus, the bands, and the cell-wall exhibit the most varied movements, by means of which the main and side currents of the fluid cell-content circulating in the cell must be explained. Independent of the latter, however, because without reference to their direction, and often even opposed to it, are the movements of the cell-nucleus, which require now a few minutes, now, however, even several hours, to traverse about the space of the cell. Now they are rectilinear, now frequently interlaced, now the nucleus intersects the cell crosswise, now it creeps along clinging to a wall. By this both nucleus and nuclear envelope and bands constantly change their form, and the nuclear corpuscle changes its situation in the nucleus.—In the division of the cell, also, characteristic modes of movement take place. In the first place, the nucleus repairs to the centre, and the bands draw nearer to form a heap of plasma. Then the nuclear corpuscle first divides into two, and thereupon the nucleus is halved by a fine, just perceptible border, until the division reaches also the protoplasmic mass, in which gradually a new wall of cellulose is formed. Now the two new nuclei (in medulla-parenchyma-cells of Dicotyledons) betake themselves tolerably quickly to the wall, creeping to opposite sides of the old cell-wall, where they rest a certain time before they again begin their normal life. "Thus, then, the cell-nucleus, through the changeability of its own form, as well as through the still greater one of its covering, and through the restless shifting and remodelling of the bands which issue from it and keep it in suspension, acquires a striking resemblance to a young plasmode or an amœbiform organism. Nay, it resembles such an one during its creeping about to such a degree, that substantially only the union with the wall-protoplasm serves as a point of distinction." According to this, Hanstein adopts the above-mentioned view of Brücke, " according to which the whole protoplasmic system must be conceived as an *individualised* organism, *i.e.*, a living, moving, proper being, consisting of nucleus, peripheral envelope, and radial or net-like uniting members, and found within its self-formed shell, the cellulose wall, in continual motion, which consists in a gliding hither and thither, and a consequent shifting and constant remodelling of the internal articulation. As the mollusc not only constructs its own shell, but moves within the same, so the protoplasmic body within its cellular membrane. Not the currents in the bands, not the cell nucleus, not the primordial sac *per se* are the seat and cause of the movement. *The whole protoplasmic body*, which is not a substance, but an organism, moves in all its parts, now simultaneously, now alternately, as indivisible, amœbiform, vitalised, proper being, which of course in the higher plants is only partial existence of a larger whole" ("Botanische Ztg.," 1872, Nos. 2 and 3).

If in the Monera or protoplasmic primitive animals the

observation of the microscope cannot establish any morphological differentiation of the apparently homogeneous slimy clot, there still follows from the fact that the essentially different behaviour of the Monera in propagation and nutrition has already necessitated the discrimination of seven different kinds, that doubtless an inner differentiation must exist. If the viscidity or tenacity of an extremely fluid water-drop is at its surface very much greater than in its interior, and this difference increases in an astonishing degree in aqueous albuminous solutions, it must certainly obtain in a viscous protoplasmic drop or clot, even when the condensation at the surface does not reach such a degree as to become visible to the eye as solid cell-envelope, to say nothing of its being separable as isolated membrane; the statements with respect to cells destitute of membranes or plasmic clots are therefore always to be understood *cum grano salis*. Even when an intussusception of solid pigment-molecules is proved by means of amœbiform movements, a certain viscosity of the state of aggregation of the surface is always apparent, but considerable difference of the state of aggregation between surface and content is by no means refuted. (The formation of an envelope in drops has recently been very well observed by Famintzin in solutions of carbonate of lime, by allowing concentrated solutions of chloride of calcium and carbonate of potash to act upon one another with gradual addition of water.) In a similar manner, as a condensation takes place at the surface even before it becomes visible, can a condensation also take place at the centre without being perceptible to the eye. Under all circumstances, however, the superficial condensation must occasion a *functional* difference from the less dense content, as is manifested in the absorption of booty. In the same way the inner condensation of the centre must condition a functional difference, as it appears in the division proceeding from within. Where, then, cell-membrane and nucleus appear to be wanting, whilst yet the cell manifestly performs the functions thereto appertaining, there must necessarily exist analogues of these organs imperceptible to the eye. Only in this way can we understand the development of nucleated membranous cells from simple plasmic clots, as required by the Theory of Descent. How overhasty it were, relying on the mere visible appearance, to deny a differentiation of the Monera into organs of various functions is eminently proved, besides the indiscernibility of an actual membrane at the apices of several cilia, by the analogy with the just fertilised ovum, in whose apparent molecular homogeneity those differences must yet exist, so that in its development to the child "the finest mental and bodily peculiarities of the parents are afterwards manifested in the same. We must here stand still in wonderment and admiration before the almost infinite delicacy of albuminous matter" (Häckel, "Natürliche Schöpfungsgeschichte," 2d edit., p. 179).

These would, then, be the lowest individuals which could be called organic. There is a question, however, whether we are altogether entitled to require of an individual that it be organism. This much is certain, as long as a thing has *parts*, so long must these parts be in organic reciprocal connection, if the teleological unity of relation is not to fail; *i.e.*, as long as a thing has parts it must be *organism*, if it is to be *individual*. But how if a thing has no more parts? If of a thing with parts one requires the most intimate causal relation of the parts only that it may possess the greatest possible unity in all directions, should then this greatest possible unity not exist in yet far higher degree where the thing is in its nature *simple*, *i.e.*, without parts, thus this requirement is from the first rendered superfluous? The unity of place, cause, and purpose is, *eo ipso*, given with the simplicity of the thing; but the requirement of reciprocity of the parts, which in the compound thing was a necessary evil, has here been fortunately superseded, since all the parts are reduced to one, which is at the same time the whole; the unity of the simplicity is thus much stronger than the unity of the reciprocation of the parts. It does not detract from the worth of the present argument when the notion of unity is asserted to be inapplicable to the simple, for we had only reached the notion of unity by seeking what is individual, *i.e.*, what *in its nature cannot be divided*. This is, however, undoubtedly at least as much the case in the *simple* as in the *complex* unity, nay, even still more than in the latter, for the unity consisting of united parts always carries in itself the possibility of resolution into parts, but not the simple.

Such a simple thing, which thus has the highest claim to the conception of the individual, we are cognisant of, however, in the immaterial functional atomic force, which consists in a single continued act of will. Save the atoms there can be no individuals in the *inorganic* sphere, for everything which consists of several atoms has these for its parts, and must accordingly be *organism* if it is to be individual. It is thus wrong to call a crystal or a mountain an individual. On the other hand, we may very well call the heavenly bodies, so far as they are still living, individuals, for they are then in fact organisms; but with their extinction the individuality also perishes, as in animals and plants. Whoever doubts that a *living* Astrum, such as the earth, is an organism, need only study the mutual action of atmosphere and interior in the circulation of water, the reciprocal action of stratification and lower animal kingdom, as well as the strata among themselves in the metamorphosis of rocks, and the mutual action of the organic kingdoms. In short, let him study geology, meteorology, and the household of Nature on the large scale. He will everywhere find revealed the essence of the organic world, *preservation and improvement of form by change of matter*, without it being thereby implied that the direct participation of the will of the Unconscious (beyond the atomic forces in the actual combinations and the organisms concerned in the formation of the strata) is requisite for that end.

Let us now consider how the conscious individual is related to the material, or, better expressed, external individual. It is at once evident that only where an external individual is given can a conscious individual become possible; but a conscious individual need not arise in every external individual. *The external individual is thus a condition, but not the sufficient reason, of the conscious individual.*

We have seen that a certain kind of material motion with a certain intensity is the condition of the origin of consciousness. All those external individuals must thus be excluded from the production of a conscious individual which do not fulfil these conditions in the character or strength of their movements. It is just possible that the atomic forces, perhaps also several cells of a too solid or a too fluid nature, are in this case. Inorganic masses without external individuality have evidently also no conscious individuality, for even if the several atoms are to have their consciousness, this would always remain in atomistic dispersion through lack of a uniting bond, but could never reach a higher unity. Where we first find visible traces of consciousness is in the *cell* with semi-fluid content (protoplasm of the protists); here undoubtedly the unity of consciousness is introduced through the same conditions as its origin, since the part of the cell-content satisfying these conditions is distributed homogeneously to all sides of the cell. We shall then be permitted to assume that where consciousness is present in a cell, an inner conscious individuality also corresponds to the external individuality.

Where several cells coalesce to form an individual of higher order, the consciousnesses of the single cells by no means need be united into a higher unity, for this depends on the presence and excellence of the communication.

However, the assertion may not appear venturesome, that between fresh, vitally active cells there always takes place a certain amount, however small, of communication —at least always between two neighbouring cells; the question is only whether the degree of excitement also exceeds the threshold of stimulation. If through the sensation of a cell there is likewise produced a sensation in the adjoining parts owing to irradiation, there manifestly takes place an indirect influence from each cell to every other; and although so indirect and manifestly minute an influence on several cells, on account of the increasing resistance, must necessarily remain very soon below the threshold, and consequently does not authorise us to speak of a conscious individuality of the whole, yet a certain solidarity of interests is here not to be mistaken. If, according to this, a conscious individual of higher order by no means need correspond to every external individual of higher order, yet this much is certain, that different conscious individuals can only then unite to form a conscious individual of higher order, if the external individuals corresponding to them are fused into an individual of higher order; for the communication necessary for the unity of consciousness can only be set up through the medium of highly organised matter, but this directly sets up the unity of the form, of the organic interaction, &c., in short, the external individual of higher order.

Our assertion is thus verified in every respect—that the external individuality is possibly *condition*, but not sufficient *cause* of the conscious individuality, because the latter also presupposes three further conditions—a certain *mode*, a certain *strength* of material movement, and, in individuals of higher order, a certain excellence of *conduction*. If one of these three conditions is not satisfied, no conscious individual can correspond to the external individual.

I believe that the division and discussion of the outer

and inner individual here worked out may essentially contribute to the clearing up of the question of individuality; it is the necessary complement to the cognition of the relativity of the conception of individuality.

The relativity of the conception of individuality is for the rest no new cognition of the last decennia. Spinoza says, as already mentioned above: "The human body consists of several individuals of various nature, each of which is very composite;" and Goethe: "Each living thing is no single thing, but a manifold; even if it appears to us as individual, it still remains a collection of living, independent existences, which resemble one another in idea, in design, but may phenomenally be like or similar, unlike or dissimilar. The more imperfect the creature is, the more are these parts like or similar to one another, and the more do they resemble the whole. The more perfect the creature is, the more dissimilar are the parts to one another. The more similar the parts are to one another, the less are they subordinated to one another. The subordination of the parts points to a more perfect creation." (The latter observation expresses what we have tried to illustrate by the simile of the monarchical and republican form of government.)

The relativity of the notion of individuality was discussed most thoroughly by Leibniz, although his mode of regarding the matter is essentially distinguished from ours, in consequence of his different conception of "body." With Leibniz, each monad has an unchangeable and imperishable body peculiar to it, which forms its fence, and through which its finitude is established. This body is not substance, any more than the soul of the monads, partially conceived, is substance; and between *this* body and the soul there exists no pre-established harmony, since it would here be superfluous; but they are both only moments, differently directed forces, of one and the same simple substance, the monad, which is its natural unity; and this is Leibniz's identity of soul and body (thought and extension). This inalienable body is, however, something purely metaphysical, and nothing physical; at the most, in the case of the atoms, can we, in a certain sense, allow the Leibnizian conception to pass in physical respects. In all individuals or monads of higher order, on the contrary, the idea of an inalienable body *in addition to* the visible body, compounded of other monads or atoms (an idea which has long made a spectral appearance under the name of an ethereal body), has been happily set aside by science: we now know that all organisms only maintain their existence by means of *change of matter*. We will, however, do Leibniz no injustice; what he conceived by the body peculiar to the monad is, at all events, a metaphysically far more tenable thought. I suppose that he intended thereby to express nothing more than the capacity of the immaterial monad to produce *certain spatial* effects,—a faculty which doubtless pertains to all monads, the highest as well as the lowest, and which only by means of the peculiar reference of the lines of action to a point in the atom-monads, and their combination for sensuous perception from outside, evokes the *phenomenon of corporeity*. But, at any rate, "body" is not a happily selected word for describing the power of acting in space, as only the combination of the lowest kind of spatial forces has a right to this term. Let us leave on one side, however, this inalienable monadic body, and consider how Leibniz conceives the composition of the monads.

When several monads come together, they form either an inorganic aggregate or an organism. In the organism are contained higher and lower monads, in the inorganic aggregate only inferior monads; therefore in the former there takes place subordination, in the latter only co-ordination of the monads. The higher the grade of the organism, the more prominent is the predominance of *one* monad in perfection in comparison with all the others. This is then called central monad. The higher monads are obscurely and imperfectly represented by the lower ones; the lower by the higher, on the other hand, clearly and perfectly. "Et une créature est plus parfaite q'une autre en ce qu'on trouve en elle ce qui sert à rendre raison *a priori* de ce qui se passe dans l'autre, et c'est par là, qu'on dit, qu'elle agit sur l'autre. Mais dans les substances simples ce n'est qu'une *influence idéale* d'une monade sur l'autre" ("Monodologie," Nos. 50, 51, p. 709).

Leibniz denies the *influxus physicus* between the monads when he says these have no windows through which anything could shine; the *influxus idealis* which he puts in its place consists for him only in an *accord a priori* of that which the monads picture, *i.e.*, in a *pre-established harmony*. But now the relation of the central monad in an organism to the sum of the subordinate monads is that which has at all times been called the relation of soul and body. Between *this* body and the soul there exists, then, according to Leibniz, certainly pre-established harmony.

The relation between the soul and the complex changeable body Leibniz adopted from Aristotle. It is the relation of ἐνέργεια and ὕλη, spontaneously operative form or Idea, and the material in which the Idea works. The relation of soul and inalienable proper body, on the other hand, Leibniz adopted from Spinoza, according to whom the one substance everywhere appears with the two inseparable attributes—Thought and Extension. Both relations coincide in a remarkable manner in the lowest, the atom-monads, and that too through the simple artifice of Nature, of referring all the efficient tendencies of such a monad to a point. Unfortunately Leibniz did not sufficiently separate these two meanings of body, tending to confusion, and has therefore been frequently misunderstood.

What is essential for us in the Leibnizian doctrine is the aggregation of several monads or individuals into a compound which (as body) is subordinate to a monad or an individual of higher order (as soul). Had the results of modern physics, anatomy, physiology, been at the command of Leibniz, he would not have neglected to carry further his theory with respect to atoms, cells, and organisms; but as it was, it remained only a stroke of genius without the necessary empirical supports.—What, on the other hand, we can *not* accept is the artificial and unsatisfactory hypothesis of the pre-established harmony, by which all real happening is altogether abolished, and the world-process is disintegrated into an unrelated juxtaposition of separate trains of ideas in inactive isolated monads. If Leibniz expressly excludes all real influence of the monads on one another, yet the *influxus idealis* which he puts in place of the *influxus physicus* is an ill-chosen, because misleading expression. For undoubtedly, according to him, the content of the chain of ideas in each monad must at any given point of time correspond to the ideal chain of every other monad in a certain fashion, but this correspondence (chiming, harmony) is by no means said to result from this, that (say) the idea of a monad determines by an ideal influence the simultaneous idea of another (as one might indeed suppose from the wording *influxus idealis*), but from this, that the content of the flow of ideas has been predetermined or predestined from all eternity and for ever and ever for every monad, and is predestined, moreover, in such a way, that between the various trains of ideas there always exists a certain harmony. The harmony thus predetermined or pre-established is accordingly a sportive mechanism, which, moreover, is quite *aimless;* for if, for example, the various ideal currents had a velocity so different that harmony never took place between them, the monads would notice nought thereof, and would behave themselves just the same as in the contrary case. This theory, which abolishes all influence of the monads on one another, thus all causality, is consequently perfectly useless.

What further distinguishes us from Leibniz is the knowledge we have gained—firstly, that the organic individual of higher order *only subsists in* the particular unity of the individuals of lower order, and that the conscious individual altogether *only arises through* a reciprocal action of certain material parts of the organic individual with the Unconscious. It follows from this that the central monad or the central individual, neither in respect of the organism nor in respect of consciousness, is something standing *beyond* or *outside* the subordinate monads or individuals, but that if, in the higher individual, something else is contained in addition beyond the union of the inferior individuals, this can only be an *unconscious factor*. But in regard to this unconscious factor, which we have come to know as the regent in the organic and conscious life of the individual, the question may arise whether we have to do with a central monad *separate* for each individual, or whether the functions of the Unconscious proceed from a being identical and *common* for all individuals? Since, in conclusion, even Leibniz saw himself compelled to transform the unrelated coadjacency of his windowless monads into their coinherence, *i.e.*, to take up all monads into an *absolute* central monad, one may also put the question thus: Do the bundles of rays of unconscious psychical functions in the different individuals point *directly* to one and the same absolute centre, or do they in the first instance lead to different relative centres, and only *mediately* through these to the universal centre of the world? In this culminates the question with respect to the individuality of the Unconscious, after one has assured oneself in general of the unity of the Unconscious as such. In conformity with the importance of this problem we discuss it in a chapter of its own.

VII.

THE ALL-ONENESS OF THE UNCONSCIOUS.

THAT to the Unconscious, as actively manifested in an organic and individual consciousness, there is not wanting strict unity, is probably at once evident We altogether know the Unconscious only by means of causality; it is just the cause of all those events in an organic and conscious individual which lead us to suppose a psychical and yet not conscious cause. All that we have found within this Unconscious of distinctions or parts is limited to the two moments Will and Idea, and of these we have also indeed again perceived the inseparable unity in the Unconscious. But in case some one should insist that Will and Idea are to be conceived as *different parts* of the one Unconscious, yet their *reciprocity* in the motivation of the Will through the Idea and arousing of the Idea by means of the interest of the Will would be quite unmistakable. What in the organism we were still compelled to apprehend as unity through mutual action of the parts is in the One cause of these events taken up into the unity of the end, to which these several activities of the one and another part are all posited only as common means. The unity of Time in the continuity of action is likewise present. The unity of Space can here, of course, be no longer spoken of, because we have to do with a non-spatial being; in the *effects*, however, it is just as much present as the unity of Time. Thus much, then, is settled, that the unity of the psychically Unconscious in the individual is the strictest one can find. It is, however, not implied in this that there are unconsciously psychical individuals, for if the unity of the Unconscious were so strict that it undividedly embraced in itself all the unconsciously-psychical, wherever it might be operative in the world, there would be only *one* Unconscious, and not *several* Unconscious; then there would be also no longer individuals *in the* Unconscious, but the entire Unconscious would be as *one single* individual, without subordinate, co-ordinate, or super-ordinate individuals. Since also Matter and Consciousness are phenomenal forms of the Unconscious, this being would then be the all-embracing individual *which is all-being*, the absolute individual, or *the* individual κατ' ἐξοχήν.

In organisms we had no occasion to raise the question whether we then had actually *several* things and not *one* before us, because the spatial distinction of the form answered it by anticipation. In the case of consciousness we have answered the question, which could hardly be decided *à priori*, in conformity with internal experience, which teaches us that the consciousness of Peter and Paul, of brain and abdominal ganglia, are not one, but many and different. In the Unconscious, however, this question is robbed of half its force; since the essence of the Unconscious is non-spatial, and the inner experience of consciousness of course says nothing at all about the Unconscious. Nobody is *directly* aware of the unconscious *subject of his own consciousness.* Everybody knows it only as *the in itself unknown* psychical *cause* of his consciousness. What ground could he have for the assertion that this unknown cause of *his* consciousness is *another* than that of his *neighbour*, whose immediate knowledge is just as limited as his own? In a word, *immediate* inner or outer experience affords us no aid in deciding this important alternative, which accordingly is provisionally a perfectly open question. In such a case the maxim carries full authority that principles are not to be unnecessarily multiplied, and that in the absence of direct experience the *simplest* assumptions are always to be entertained. According to this, the unity of the Unconscious would have to be supposed so long as the opponent of this simplest assumption had not satisfactorily relieved himself of the *onus probandi* incumbent upon him. But of this no attempt is yet known to us; for Herbart's proposition, "As much appearance, so much indication of existence," can manifestly only serve to prove the many-sidedness, but not the multiplicity of being, since, as is well known, one and the same being appears for the most part quite different according to different aspects. That the assumption of direct unity is really much simpler hardly needs special proof, since here there is only question of the relations of the actor to his activities, and of the reciprocal action of the activities of one and the same actor; whereas, on the opposite assumption, the relations of *different* actors to their activities, and, moreover, those of the actor and his activities *inter se*, are in question, the latter of which must either be acknowledged to be quite inexplicable, or be explained by the further perfectly inaccessible and incomprehensible relations of these many actors to the Absolute standing over them and including them.

Only because the one part of my brain has a direct communication with the other is the consciousness of the two parts unified (conf. C. Chap. iii. 5. pp. 113–118); and could we unite the brains of two human beings by a path of communication equivalent to the cerebral fibres, both would no longer have *two*, but *one* consciousness. Could a union of two consciousnesses into one, such as actually occurs, be at all possible if the Unconscious, from which consciousness is born as a sequel of natural stimulation, were not already in itself one?

The entire ant has one, the divided ant two consciousnesses; and if one sews together the halves of two different polyps (thus two previously divided consciousnesses), one polyp will result with a single consciousness. Wealth and poverty of consciousness can make no difference in these inquiries involving matters of principle. As little as any one can deny, after the foregoing considerations, that he has as many (more or less separate) consciousnesses as he has nerve-centres, nay, even as he has vital cells, so much will every one rightly oppose the assertion that he has as many unconsciously acting souls as he has nerve-centres or cells. The unity of purpose in the organism, the right operation of each single part at the right moment, in short, the wonderful harmony of the organism, would be inexplicable, in fact, only comprehensible as *pre-established* harmony, unless the soul in the body were *one and indivisible*, acting, however, synchronously in all parts of the organism where its action is required,—unless it were one and the same soul which regulates here breathing, there excretion, which here in the brain conditions the brain-consciousness, there in the ganglia the ganglia-consciousness. If the cutting into shreds of the lower animals shows us that the same mind, which before governed the different parts in the whole animal and produced the different kinds of consciousness, continues also to be functional unaltered after division, can we then believe that the corporeal section may also have cleft the soul and divided it into two parts, can by division of a mere aggregate of atoms the non-spatial soul accidentally governing them be at all conceived as affected, save so far as the conditions of its activity are changed?

But if the soul in two artificially separated pieces of an animal is still one, must it not remain undivided also in the spontaneous throwing-off of buds, claws, &c. ? and likewise in bisexual generation, where one hermaphrodite animal begets with itself (*e.g.*, tape-worm) ? (See more particularly the ninth chapter.) If the unconscious soul in the separate portions of an insect, or in the stem and the detached buds, is still one, must it not be the same also in the insects separate by nature of a community of bees or ants, which even without union of the organisms in space still act as harmoniously on one another as the several parts of the same organism? Should not the clairvoyance, which we have found everywhere recurring in the invasions of the Unconscious, and which is so supremely astonishing in the limited individual, should not it alone invite this solution, that the apparently individual acts of clairvoyance are simply announcements of the everywhere identical Unconscious, wherewith at once everything miraculous in clairvoyance disappears, since now the seer is also the soul of the seen? And if it is possible for the unconscious soul of an animal to be simultaneously present and purposively active in all organs and cells of the animal, why should not an unconscious world-soul be simultaneously present and purposively efficient in all organisms and atoms, since indeed the one as the other must be thought as unlocalised?

What opposes this conception is only the old prejudice that the *soul* is the *consciousness;* so long as one has not risen above this view and perfectly extirpated every obscure remnant of such a belief from his mind, so long must that all-unity of the Unconscious be certainly covered by a veil. Only when one has come to see that consciousness does not belong to the *essence*, but to the *phenomenon,* that thus the plurality of consciousness is only a *plurality of the appearance of the One*, only then will it be possible to emancipate oneself from the power of the practical instinct, which always cries "I, I," and to comprehend the essential unity of all corporeal and spiritual phenomenal individuals, which Spinoza apprehended in his mystical conception and declared the One Substance. It is no contradiction to the all-unity of the Unconscious that the individual self-feeling, which at first is present only as slight practical instinct, with growing elaboration of consciousness is ever more *heightened* and sharpened to *pure self-consciousness*, that thus the appearance indestructible for conscious thought of the individual egoity only emerges the more distinctly, the keener conscious thought becomes; this, I say, is no contradiction to the Monism of the Unconscious, for all conscious thought remains indeed entangled in the conditions of consciousness, and can by its nature never be elevated above them in direct fashion, must rather be the more wrapt round by the deceptive veil of Maja, the more it displays its *proper* nature. The unity of the Unconscious may very well exist at the same time, of that namely, which never can come *into* consciousness, because it lies *behind* it, as the mirror can never mirror itself (at the most its own image in a second mirror). Certainly as long as one has not rigidly separated and explicated the Unconscious, so long that objection exists in full force, and so long can the idea of the all-unity not be rationally comprehended and approved, but only be mystically conceived, *in spite* of the opposition of consciousness.

Another point which is often made use of as cheap ridicule against Monism is the paradox that the One contends with itself as a self-parted being, that, *e.g.*, the One Existence is in conflict with itself, like two hungry wolves, each of whom endeavours to devour the other. Two problems are here intermingled: firstly, the problem of the sundering of the One into the many, and, secondly, the question how the Many, if they are indeed only realisations or objectifications or phenomena of the One can turn against one another in strife and discord. The first problem, that of individuation, will be treated of in a special chapter (C. Chap. xi.), and only under the presupposition that this will be solved in a satisfactory manner is there any sense in occupying ourselves with the second question. Here I shall only say this much, that a self-disunion would only be incomprehensible if the One surrendered its unity (and with it a piece of its essence); that, on the contrary, a self-disunion into a secondary (because phenomenal) plurality, in which unity is preserved in plurality, just brings multiplicity into the abstract unity, or, more accurately expressed, that a sundering of the One into plurality cannot be objectionable, if thereby be meant not a splitting of the one substance into many isolated *substances*, but manifestations of the one existing and abiding being in a plurality of *functions*. But if this plurality of different functions is once given, then, in consequence of the circumstance that they are functions of one being, the ideal difference of their content must necessarily exert an ideal influence on one another striving after equilibrium, which ideal compromise, however, becomes a real conflict through this, that the ideal moments compromising one another are at the same time contents of real acts of will. It is thus altogether the same process that takes place in the consciousness of the individual as a struggle between different efforts, desires, and passions; just as a contest is possible here notwithstanding the unity of the mind, whose functions are the intersecting desires, so also in the all-one Unconscious. The struggle of two passions in a human mind in fury and destructive mercilessness need not in truth shun comparison with the struggle of two hungry wolves. The only difference is this, that what takes place in the subjective field within an individual is withdrawn from the direct observation of another, whereas the struggle of different individualised acts of will of the Unconscious hereby possesses an objective phenomenal reality, that the individuals engaged in conflict directly sensuously affect one another and other unconcerned individuals.

If, on the other hand, the question is proposed in these terms, "Why must the several functions of the One Being be so constituted that they collide with, instead of running undisturbed beside, one another?" the answer is to be sought in C. Chap. iii.: "Without collision of different acts of will no consciousness,"—and consciousness it is that is in point.

Hitherto we have shown, on the one hand, that there is and can be no reason which tells *against* the unity of consciousness, and have, on the other hand, adduced various *a posteriori* grounds of probability for the same. We can, however, also settle the question directly by *deduction* from already established presuppositions, thus *a priori* in the Aristotelian sense of the word.

The Unconscious is not confined to space, for *it first posits* space (the idea the ideal, the will by realisation of the idea the real). The Unconscious is thus neither great nor small, neither here nor there, neither in the finite nor in the infinite, neither in the figure nor in the point, neither anywhere nor nowhere. Hence it follows that the Unconscious can have no difference of a spatial nature in it, save so far as it posits the same in imaging and acting. We are accordingly not permitted to say: that which acts in an atom of Sirius *is* something else than that which acts in an atom of the earth, but only: *it acts in a different manner*, namely, locally different. We have two effects without the right to suppose two beings for these effects; for the difference of the effects only allows us to conclude to a difference of the functions in the being; the difference of two functions, however, by no means to the non-identity of the functioning being. We must reiterate: we are compelled to stop short at the *simplest* assumption (the identity of the functioning essence) until the opponents have furnished proof of non-identity; on them, not on us, lies the burden of proof, since they suppose many, we only one. At any rate, this much has been strictly demonstrated by us, that no plurality of its essence can appertain to the Unconscious *by means of space-determinations*, simply because no space-determinations appertain to it. In temporal differences this is much clearer still, since we are indeed thus accustomed to acknowledge the identity of the continuously acting being despite all temporal difference, in spite of the earlier or later occurrence of the effects. But now there are, objectively speaking, none other than spatial differences; for what we else know as differences, the difference of ideas *inter se* and the difference of willing and thinking, are internal subjective differences of different activities of the same essence or subject, but not a difference of different essences or subjects. Of the difference of different ideas *inter se* this is at once clear, but it also holds good of the difference of the two fundamental activities willing and thinking, pervading all individuals of the realm of nature, for the Unconscious is one in willing as in conceiving, only that it here wills and there thinks; it is related to those activities as Spinoza's substance to its attributes. (More in detail in C. Chap. xiv. 4.) All distinction known to us between existing things turns upon spatial and temporal determinations. Space and time are the sole *principium individuationis* known to us. To assert with Schopenhauer that they are the only *possible principium individuationis* would be to assert too much, for there might be worlds in which other forms of existence than space and time obtain. But apart from this, that the burden of proof of the existence of such falls on the shoulders of opponents, and until the impossible production of this proof we have not to trouble ourselves about such empty possibilities, yet even such forms of existence in their particular worlds, just as space and time with us, would only have phenomenal existence, *i.e.*, it could be shown that they can just as little be determinations of the Unconscious as space and time with us, and they would accordingly be just as unsuitable as these would be for establishing a plurality of essence in the Unconscious. If, then, the Unconscious can be burdened with a plurality of being neither by spatial nor other differentiæ, it must just be a *simple unity*.

We may further add an indirect proof to this direct one from admitted presuppositions. Suppose the case, namely, that the phenomenal separation of individuals did not rest merely on a plurality of functions of the existence underlying them, but on a non-identity of the essence, on a plurality of existing substances, no real relations would be possible among the individuals as they in fact exist. This is one of the greatest achievements of the great

Leibniz, that in spite of its extremely fatal (and for his system even ruinous) consequences, he admitted this proposition honourably and candidly. Herbart occupies here a far inferior position, for after having made from the plurality of appearance the false inference to the plurality (instead of the many-sidedness) of existence, he posits the mutual disturbances of these many existences (simple reals) as something self-evident, instead of, like Leibniz, conceding it to be something impossible. Whoever once recognises several substances (*i.e.*, several beings, each of which is self-subsistent, and would continue to subsist even if everything else round about were suddenly to cease to exist), must also confess that these monads can not only have no windows through which an *influxus idealis* could shine, but also that there is no possibility of seeing how entities, which participate in nought and have nothing in common, should be able to come into any metaphysical contact whatsoever. Each individual must rather represent an isolated world for itself. If one tried to suppose a metaphysical bond, to which would fall the part of a mediator, the difficulty to resolve would be, how this newly added substance should be able to enter into real relation with each of the existing substances. For if one tried to imagine this tie somewhat as a function of the Absolute or as the Absolute itself, it is to be remarked, on the contrary (apart from the circumstance that in *many* substances the discussion, strictly speaking, cannot be of One Absolute, but only of as many absolutes as substances), that a real relation between a so-called Absolute and one of several substances only appears less incomprehensible than the relation between two of the many substances, because fancy is more readily inclined to ascribe to the so-called Absolute the power of incomprehensible achievements. The influence of the Absolute on the many only, however, becomes comprehensible if the so-called Absolute is converted from a substance actually limited by the many into an unlimited, genuinely all-embracing substance, which thus contains the many as integral parts of itself. But then, in truth, the many are denuded of their independence and substantiality, and degraded to sublated moments of the one absolute. This step, which again in the last resort dissolves the intended Pluralism into Monism, both Leibniz in the all-embracing central monad, as well as Herbart in the credited god-creator, saw themselves necessitated to take, without however recognising the incompatibility of this change with the retention of the foundations of their systems, and without employing this step for the explanation of the *influxus physicus*, or the causality of the monads among themselves, which must necessarily miscarry without it, but results in a perfectly unforced manner from the essential identity of the many in the One.

Although Pluralism is not able to maintain itself in its proper form as soon as it realises its own consequences, it yet tries to maintain itself in the illusory light of consciousness in a more modest form as it were *within* a reluctantly admitted Monism. The inherently contradictory conception of *derived substance* is especially employed for this purpose. Substance is that which is *in itself* (not in another) and subsists *through itself* (without the aid of another); the derived substance, however, is said not to be in itself, but in the absolute substance, and not to subsist through itself, but only through the absolute substance. Derived substance thus evinces itself as not-substance; it evinces itself as particular mode and manner (*modus*) of the manifestation of the Absolute, or, as we now say, as *phenomenon*. Now Pluralism further tries to at least raise the phenomenon of the individual mind to a higher category of phenomena, or to lower the rest of phenomena one degree, as if they were mediate results of that phenomenon. This is, however, so incorrect, that in a certain sense the contrary is true, so far, namely, as the individual mind results on the one side only from the material phenomena. The light radiating from the unconscious central sun strikes upon the concave mirror of organisms, and is reflected and united in the focus of the self-conscious mind. In this way arise the separate centres of the individual conscious minds, but with these the absolute centre does not communicate directly, but only by means of the unconscious rays (functions) affecting the organism (the brain), which are reflected from this to the focus of consciousness. None of those functions which are ascribed to the unconscious rule of the organism proceed from *these* separate centres; if there is in respect of the latter a separate centre still to be assumed for every individual, there must be a *second beside* that first one; in this second one then we must imagine the functional rays issuing from the absolute centre to be bent or broken. How such a refraction is to take place in such an imaginary centre would be here quite unintelligible, whilst reflection on the organism or its organ of consciousness is a perfectly intelligible image. Through the accumulated difficulties of these separate centres, however, the explanation of the facts would not be in the least assisted, *i.e.*, these mathematical points of refraction of the function-rays of the absolute centre, not to be conceived as substantial but ideal, form a *merely embarrassing and uselessly* interpolated hypothesis.

However we may try to save for the individuals a reality and independence exceeding that of simple phenomenality, it is love's labour lost if intended to favour the unphilosophical partiality of the consciousness doting upon its own ego. As all plurality of individuation belongs to the sphere of phenomenality, everything placed beyond phenomenality also falls outside the plurality of the individuals into the all-one Unconscious and its *direct* activity. Only in this way has the absolute central monad of Leibniz the power to strip off the contradiction which clings to it, namely, by identifying itself again with Spinoza's One substance, in which the many individuals or monads are reduced to dependent phenomenal forms or *modes*.

This going back of Leibniz on Spinoza is, however, as little a retrogression as the falling back of modern physical science: in both cases, through the progress of experience and induction, one is enabled to comprehend and to prove *a posteriori* the mystical conceptions of genius of an elder mind. Such a falling back upon great predecessors is thus a genuine progress and a permanent gain, for it may be allowed me once more to mention that the course of philosophy is the transformation of the mystical conceptions of genius into rational cognition. (Conf. B. Chap. ix.)

Wherever we may look among the original philosophical or religious systems of the first rank, everywhere do we meet with the tendency to Monism, and it is only stars of second or third magnitude which find satisfaction in an external dualism or still greater division. Even in declared polytheistic religions, as the Greek and the different Northern mythologies, one perceives this tendency to Monism, both in the oldest conceptions, and in the later modes of feeling of deeper religious minds; and even in the more philosophical ways of thinking of Christian Monism, the world is only a phenomenon posited by God, which has only continuance (subsistence) so long as it is preserved, *i.e.*, is being continually renewed. All systems tending to Monism have not succeeded in really reaching it, yet one feels the unmistakable need of a unitarian world-conception, and only the shallowest religions and philosophical systems have rested contented with an external dualism (*e.g.*, Ormuzd and Ahriman, God and World, World-Orderer and Chaos, Force and Matter, &c.), or any sort of plurality. There is no conception which the impressionable mystic mind more readily adopts than this—to apprehend the world as an indivisible Being, to feel oneself as part of this Being, but a part in which, at the same time, indwells the whole, and penetrated by this contrast to indulge the religious feeling of the sublimity of this vast Being and the sense of the ego's participation therein. Owing to Christianity this one existence has been called in the Teutonic languages God, and the view which asserts that this one existence is the all or the whole has been accordingly entitled Pantheism (in the widest sense of the term). Rightly understood, one may certainly let the word pass. I prefer, however, on account of the misunderstandings to which it is exposed, the synonymous term Monism, according to our explanation of Pantheism. Orthodox Catholicism and shallow rationalistic Protestantism, both of which thought to exalt God while they lowered him (attributing to him human passions), have undoubtedly always condemned and burnt as heretics the deeper minds in the Christian Church who perceived and declared the need of this Monism (*e.g.*, Eckhard, Giordano Bruno), but out of all such persecutions the tendency to the monistic purifying of Christianity has always emerged in greater strength, and has been ever gaining in influence over discerning minds. Schelling says: "That in God alone is being, and therefore *all* being is only the being of God; this thought neither reason nor feeling can take away. It is the thought to which alone all hearts beat" (Werke, Abth. ii. vol. ii. p. 39); and "That everything is from God has been at all times felt, as it were; nay, one may say: just this is the true primitive feeling of humanity" (Werke, Abth. ii. vol. iii. p. 280). This mystic primitive feeling of mankind in the form of a tendency to Monism often indeed only realised in an extremely defective manner, but with the exception of the sceptics always perceptible, runs like a red streak through all philosophy from the oldest Indian traditions down to the present day. Since a survey, however hurried, of the whole period would be impracticable with our space, I limit myself to sketching with a few strokes the most recent epoch in this respect.

The being which underlies the appearance of the object of perception was called by Kant the "thing of itself." It is remarkable that Kant never drew from his doctrine that space and time do not belong to the thing of itself, but only to its appearance, the rather obvious conclusion that there cannot be things of themselves, but only *thing of itself* in the singular, since all plurality only arises through space and time. On the other hand, he himself (Kant, Werke, ii. 288, 289, and 303) made the remark, that the thing of itself and the intelligible underlying the empirical ego could hardly be one and the same existence, since between the two there positively could be no further difference specified. This is one of the touches where the involuntary tendency of great minds towards Monism cannot be denied. That Kant, nevertheless, was so timid in his inferences lay in this, that he formed the *commencement* of the modern epoch of philosophy, an epoch in which the work formerly concentrated on one or two men of genius had to be distributed over the shoulders of several, because this work became the more difficult the more often the old problems re-emerged in novel and sharper form, and the more the circuit of knowledge and of experience expanded.

What Kant entertained as timid supposition, that the thing of itself and the active subject might be one and the same existence, Schopenhauer declared as catgorical assertion, in that he recognised the will as the positive character of this essence. (Comp. my "Gesammelte philos. Abhandlungen," No. iii.) It has already been mentioned above (i. 29, 30, and 120), that Schopenhauer's Will altogether comports itself as if it were united with perception, without Schopenhauer admitting it.

Fichte mistook the truth of the Kantian hint. He denies to the appearance of the thing all existence independent of the perceiving subject, and turns it into a phenomenon entirely posited by the perceiving subject. Thus the thing of itself loses its immediate essential being in the Ego. Only what exists in the form of an ego has with Fichte being, and dead Nature, so far as it does not enter into this form, remains a phenomenon purely subjective, *i.e.*, merely posited by the subject. But Fichte also was compelled to bend in his own fashion to Monism; the Ego is denuded of the accidental character of this or that limited empirical ego, being raised to the Absolute Ego. The Absolute Ego is the existence which alone *is* all the different, accidental, empirical limited egos, for the Being which is developed in the process of the Absolute Ego is the same which produces this process in its accidental empirical limitation; so that herewith the many egos also again became lowered only to phenomena of the One Absolute.

Schelling tries in his Transcendental Idealism to deduce the wealth of the external world, with its manifold determinations which had shrunk with Fichte into the bald abstraction of the non-ego, from the activity of the ego. But while he explains the agreement of the intuitions of the various limited egos from the equally strongly emphasised unity of the infinite intelligence or of the Absolute Ego in the finite intelligences or limited egos, the standpoint of transcendental idealism necessarily leads him to the Natural Philosophy, where, without reference to the limited ego's, he undertakes to directly deduce the extramundane determinations from the absolute ego or pure subject, and here, among other natural determinations, of course, also lights upon the mind and its products. In both systems he proceeds from the identity of subject and object; only this absolute subject-object makes its appearance at one time more from the subjective, at another time more from the objective side.

The method hereby employed of the pure subject gradually positing itself as object, which withdraws from all objectification into its gradually enhanced subjectivity, led Hegel to his dialectical method.

"The method is only the movement of the concept itself, but with the significance that the *concept* is *all*, and its movement the universal absolute activity."

Hegel perceived that the deduction of Schelling has

either no value at all, or a purely logical value as process in the realm of thought, but he claimed that his logic built upon this is at the same time ontology; that the *concept is all, i.e., sole substance* and *sole absolute subject*, and that the world-process is pure dialectical self-movement of the concept; that thus there remains no room for the existence of a strictly non-logical, *i.e.*, alogical (not anti-logical); for in his imposing compact system the world was exhausted with the concept raised to the absolute Idea, with the absolute Idea sundered in nature and returned to itself in the spirit. (Comp. my " Ges. phil. Abhandl," No. ii.)

Schelling in his *last* system (comp. " Schelling's Positive Philosophie als Einheit von Hegel und Schopenhauer," Berlin, O. Löwenstein, 1869, especially the second and third sections) maintained the negativity, *i.e.*, purely logical or purely rational constitution, of the Hegelian philosophy; he thus denied that it can say *what* and how it is, and only allowed that it can say, If somewhat is, it must be *thus*. He declared that, in the Hegelian and all the philosophies preceding it there can only be question of an *eternal* happening. "An eternal event is, however, no event. Consequently, the whole idea of that process and that movement is self-illusory; properly speaking, nothing has happened; everything has only taken place in thoughts, and this whole movement was only a movement of thought" (Werke, i. 10, pp. 124–125).

He declares *existence* to be the genuinely *super-rational*, which, as actuality, can now and never be in the reason, but only in *experience* (Werke, ii. 3, p. 69), and in this respect calls nature and experience that which is foreign to the reason (ibid., p. 70). If the absolute or highest Idea has no real value, if it is no longer anything more than bare Idea, if it is not the actually existing (ii. 3, p. 150), even this Idea could never be Thought if it were not thought of a thinking subject (i. 10, p. 132). One must then in a twofold respect go beyond the Idea as such to a being beyond and independent of thought, to something anticipating all thought (ii. 3, p. 164), to an *immemorial* existence. As long as we speak of the standpoint of the purely rational or negative philosophy of the existing, we properly speak of the same only according to its essence or its conception; more cannot be obtained *a priori;* the question, however, with which positive philosophy begins runs according to that: *what* (grammatical subject) *is the existing* (grammatical object)? Or, as Schelling also expresses himself, what *makes* the thing *be* or "becomes cause of being (αἰτία τοῦ εἶναι) to this which is not being (μὴ ὄν), mere all-potentiality?" "The One is known hereby or herein that it is the Universal Being, the πᾶν, the being according to content (not efficient being). It is therewith cognised and distinguished from other simple existences, as *the* single existence *which is all*" (ii. 3, p. 174).

If the passage from the Transcendental Idealism already cited in the Introduction (i. p. 25) be compared with this, it will be found that Schelling in his first system conceived under the name "eternally unconscious" essentially that which he raised in his third system to be the foundation of his Positive philosophy.

Thus we have seen in all philosophies of the modern epoch this tendency to Monism more or less perfectly realised in one fashion or another. What in the historic evolution is exhibited as the culminating point of the speculative work of modern times, the "individual which is all being" of Schelling, that we have evolved *a posteriori* by the inductive path, or rather involuntarily gained as it were, but now no longer as a speculative principle accessible only to few, but with the perfectly valid proof of its empirical authorization. By carefully separating the sphere of the Unconscious from that of consciousness, and recognising consciousness as a mere phenomenon of the Unconscious (C. Chap. iii.), the contradictions were resolved in which the natural consciousness was entangled and caught in its endeavour after a monistic view. But not merely consciousness, but also matter had proved to be a mere appearance of the Unconscious, and everything in the world which is not exhausted by the conceptions Matter and Consciousness, as organic formation, the instincts, &c., had been revealed (in Sections A. and B.) as the most immediately and easily cognisable effects of the Unconscious.

Herewith were (1) Matter, (2) Consciousness, and (3) Organic formation, Instinct, &c., comprehended as three modes of action or modes of appearance of the Unconscious, and the latter as the *essence* of the world. Lastly, after we had penetrated with the understanding the conception of individuality on the one hand, and the proper nature of the Unconscious on the other, so far as requisite, the ultimate reason for the assumption of a plurality of being in the Unconscious disappeared beneath our hands; all plurality henceforth only belonged to the phenomenon, not to the essence which posits the former, but this is the One Absolute Individual, the single existence, *which is All*, whereas the world with its glory is reduced to the bare phenomenon; but not to a subjectively posited phenomenon, as in Kant, Fichte, and Schopenhauer, but to an objectively (as Schelling, Werke, ii. 3, p. 280, says: "divinely") posited phenomenon, or, as Hegel expresses it (Werke, vi. p. 97), to the "mere phenomenon, not only *for us*, but *of itself*."[1] What appears to us as matter

[1] This objectively posited phenomenal world, or this world of the appearance in itself, is the indispensable causal link between the monistic essence on the one hand, and the subjective phenomenal mental-picture worlds of the many different consciousnesses on the other; whilst it is related to the sole Unconscious as the appearance to the substance, it is related to its subjective reflected images in the numerous conscious individuals as the thing of itself to its (subjective) phenomenon. Subjective Idealism commits the error of ignoring the indispensableness of this connecting link, and of trying to recede from the subjective phenomena of consciousness directly to the ultimate being, instead of acknowledging *one* objectively existing (in Kantian terminology, transcendent) world of things (according to Kant, things of themselves) as *archetype* of these *many* subjective worlds of perception, which certainly, referred to the sole existence, appears indeed only as "the living garment of Deity." As Kant in his old age and his school tried to repair this subjective error of his "Kritik d. r.

"is the mere expression of an equilibrium of opposite activities" (Schelling's Werke, i. 3, p. 400), what appears to us as consciousness is likewise a mere expression of a conflict of opposite activities. That piece of matter yonder is a conglomerate of atomic forces, *i.e.*, of fiats of the Unconscious, to attract from this point of space in this intensity, to repel from that point in that intensity. Let the Unconscious intermit these acts of will and annul them, at the same moment this piece of matter has ceased to exist; let the Unconscious will anew, and the matter is there again. Here the prodigy of

V.," so Schelling that of Fichte by setting up his Philosophy of Nature; so, finally, the aged Schopenhauer, and still more his disciples, through the recognition of a reality of the objectifications of the One Will, independent of the regarding conscious subject. (Comp what is said above, B. Chap. viii. vol. i. pp. 328-331.) On the side of the theory of Knowledge and of Metaphysics the stream of tendency is unmistakable towards the conception of the objective phenomenon; in it there is found the permanent kernel of the theistic conception of Creation and Preservation (comp. C. Chap. viii., also above, pp. 228 and 231), of the pantheistic conception of Emanation, the scientific conception of the "System of Dynamids" (comp. C. Chap. v.), of the Schelling-Schopenhauerian conception of the objectification of the Absolute Subject, *i.e.*, Will, of the Herbartian notion of the "Absolute Position," in contrast to the position merely relative to consciousness, *i.e.*, to the subjective position or phenomenon, in short everything is found in it that has ever been thought with regard to the relation of existence to its metaphysical ground. That the word "phenomenon" is here used in the *metaphysical* sense cannot be objected to on the score that the theory of Cognition has obtained possession of it since the rise of subjective Idealism; for the metaphysical signification was, till the time of Kant, the *prevailing one*, although it must be allowed that in the confusion between Metaphysics and theory of Cognition that special to the latter theory was likewise contained therein. After the complete separation of the problem of Metaphysics and theory of Knowledge, the word "phenomenon" also had to be differentiated (into "objective" and "subjective"), which is the more endurable, as different contrasts ("essence" and "thing of itself") are available for the two parts. It might be well, therefore, not to get rid of the word phenomenon also for the metaphysical relation, since much of that which Kant erroneously asserted of the subjective appearance actually holds good of the objective. This arises, however, from the circumstance, that with Kant Metaphysics was absorbed just as one-sidedly by the theory of Cognition, as before him for the most part the theory of Cognition was swallowed up by Metaphysics, or in other words, because he entirely carried over into subjectivity all the "what" of existence, and left nothing but the pure "that" for the *thing by itself*, so that it naturally became barer than the barest metaphysical *essence*, and a distinction between the two became an impossibility.

the creation of the material world is lost in the everyday marvel of its *preservation*, renewed every moment, which is a *continuous creation*. The world is only a continuous series of sums of peculiarly combined will-acts of the Unconscious, for it *is* only so long as it is *continuously posited ;* let the Unconscious cease to will the world, and this play of intersecting activities of the Unconscious ceases to be.

It is an illusion disappearing before thorough reflection, an illusion of the senses in the widest sense, when we think we have in the world, the NON-EGO, something directly real. It is an illusion of the egoistic instinct when we think we have in ourselves, in our ideal ego, something directly real. The WORLD consists only of a sum of activities or will-acts of the Unconscious, and the ego consists of another sum of activities or will-acts of the Unconscious. Only so far as the former activities intersect the latter does the world become *sensible* to me; only so far as the latter intersect the former do I become sensible to myself. In the sphere of the mental representation or pure Idea, the ideally opposed peacefully exist side by side, and for the most part form logical combinations calmly and without storms. Does, however, a will seize these ideal opposites and make them its content, then the will-acts filled with opposite content enter into opposition; they pass into real conflict (comp. above, p. 228), in which they mutually resist and threaten to destroy one another, when either the one succeeds entirely or both partially, so that they compel one another to a compromise. Only in this conflict, the mutually offered resistance of the individually parted will-acts of the All-One, arises and consists that which we call *reality*. Not an inactive passive substratum, like the matter criticised in C. Chap. v., is presented, but only an *active* actual function can claim the predicate of *actuality*. This table, *e.g.*, testifies its actuality to me through the forces of repulsion which the ether-atoms of its superficial molecules, when opposed to the superficial molecules of my body, exert in quickly increasing progression on approximation beyond a particular limit. This collision of the atomic wills constituting it with the atomic wills constituting my body is a part of the efficiency or actuality of the table, and the totality of its actuality consists in the sum of all the collisions which occur between the atomic wills constituting the table and all the other atoms of the world. If there were nothing in the world but this table, its reality would certainly be a far more limited one, but it would never be quite abolished, because the atomic wills constituting the table, if also no longer externally, yet always still among themselves, would come into active collision. If, however, one imagined all the atoms of the world save one suddenly annihilated, the actuality or reality of this one would be, in fact, thereby annihilated, since, owing to the want of an object of the manifestation of its force, it would be incapable of action, that is, of being actually manifested.

Let the Unconscious change the combination of activities or acts of will which constitute *me*, and I have become another; let the Unconscious intermit these activities, and I have ceased to be. *I* am a phenomenon, like the rainbow in the cloud. Like it, *I* am born of the coincidence of relations, become another in every second because these relations become other in every second, and shall dissolve when these relations are dissolved. What is *substance* in me is not *I*. In the same spot another rainbow may at some time or other stand, which perfectly resembles this one, but yet is not the same, for temporal continuity is wanting; so in my stead an ego perfectly resembling me may also at some time or other stand, but that will not be *me*. The *sun* alone is always shining, which is transiently reflected from yonder cloud; only the Unconscious for ever rules, which is also mirrored in my brain.

The results indicated here in broad outlines will find in

Chapters ix. to xi. a varied application and development, which it is hoped will contribute to make them appear less repellent to readers previously confined to the way of thinking of the practical sensuous instinct; but first we will try still further to elucidate the results hitherto reached by comparing the All-one Unconscious with that God-conception, which our educated classes are wont to obtain from the school-Metaphysic of the religions disseminated in Europe.

VIII.

THE UNCONSCIOUS AND THE GOD OF THEISM.

THE question may very probably be asked at the present stage of our inquiry—Admitting that the actions of the All-One displayed in the individual are unconscious so far as the individual is concerned, what is the proof that they are not conscious in the All-One Existence itself? The simplest answer to this query consists in transferring the *onus probandi* to its propounder. It is not for me to prove that the unconscious physical functions which, as such, are sufficient for explanation, may not on the other side be conscious in the All-One; but those, who desire to make this, so far as the explanation of the phenomena is concerned, entirely valueless and gratuitous addition to the hypothesis, have to adduce the proof of their assumption, which until then must be regarded as pure assertion, and accordingly to be scientifically ignored. Although this would suffice for setting aside the foregoing objection, I shall nevertheless enter more fully into the matter, because the consideration of this point will contribute to the more exact comprehension of the Unconscious.

If hitherto Theism has usually eagerly insisted on assigning to God a consciousness of his own in the sphere of his divinity, this has happened for two reasons, both of which had their justification, but from which an illegitimate conclusion was drawn, because the possibility of an unconscious intelligence had never been conceived. These two grounds are,—*Firstly*, As regards man, repugnance to the thought, in default of a conscious God, of being a *product of blind natural forces*, unintended, unwatched, purposeless and transient result of a fortuitous necessity. *Secondly,* As regards God, the fear of thinking this supreme existence, which, to honour to the utmost, it was deemed necessary in scholastic fashion to furnish with the sum of all conceivable perfections, to be destitute of that excellence which passes with the human mind for the highest, viz., clear consciousness and distinct self-consciousness. Both scruples, however, disappear before a correct estimation of the principles of the Unconscious, which hold the golden mean between a Theism constructed of the floating human ideal made absolute and a naturalism, in which the highest flowers of the mind and the eternal necessity of natural law, from which they have sprung, are mere result of a casual actuality, imposing to us on account of our impotence—the right mean between conscious teleology, which is conceived after the human prototype, and entire renunciation of final causes. This right mean just consists in the recognition of a final causality, which however is not represented according to the pattern of conscious human purposive activity by discursive reflection, but as immanent unconscious teleology of an intuitive unconscious intelligence is revealed in natural objects and individuals by means of the same activity which, in the last chapter, we described as continual creation or conservation, or as real phenomenon of the All-One Existence.

In our inability positively to apprehend the mode of perception of this intelligence (comp. above, p. 49), we are only able to indicate it through the contrast to our own form of perception (consciousness), thus only to characterise it by the *negative* predicate of *Unconsciousness*. But we know from the previous inquiries that the function of this unconscious intelligence is anything but blind, rather far-seeing, nay, even clairvoyant, although this seeing can never be aware of its own vision, but only of the world, and without the mirrors of the individual consciousnesses can also not see the seeing eye. Of this unconscious clairvoyant intelligence we have come to perceive that in its infallible purposive activity, embracing out of time all ends and means in one, and always including all necessary data within its ken, it infinitely transcends the halting, stilted gait of the discursive reflection of consciousness, ever limited to a single point, dependent on sense-perception, memory, and inspirations of the Unconscious. We shall thus be compelled to designate this intelligence, which is superior to all consciousness, at once unconscious and *super*-conscious. With this recognition, however, the two preceding scruples with regard to the unconsciousness of the All-One disappear. If the latter possesses a superconscious intelligence, all-knowing and all-wise, with all its unconsciousness, which teleologically determines the *content* of creation and of the world-process, *we* stand here neither as accidental product of the forces of Nature, nor is God dwarfed by denying Him *this* mode of consciousness.

Accordingly the dread on the part of Theism of degrading its God by denying him consciousness appears so unfounded, that the danger is rather the contrary of degrading him by the predication of consciousness, since his mode of thinking is, in truth, *above* consciousness. That which is really an unconditional pre-eminence is *rational intelligence*, which our Unconscious possesses just as truly as the God of Theism, but that which is just the limitation in our human intelligence, the form of consciousness depending on the division of subject and object, of that Theism must too of necessity denude its deity, if it will make it its "most perfect of all" existences. Beyond question *for us men*, consciousness and self-consciousness are marks of superiority, but yet not, like rational intelligence, absolute marks, but only relative and conditioned, *i.e.*, they pass with us as prerogatives only because we stand within the world of *individuation and its limits*, and need for the greatest possible furtherance of our individual aims, as sharp a severance as possible of our self from other persons and from the impersonal outer world,—considerations which, as a matter of course, fall away for the All-One Being, which has nothing outside itself. *In and by itself,* however, and *apart* from the special problems which arise through a position within the sphere of individuation for a limited intelligence, consciousness is *no excellence,* but in comparison with the unity of attributes in the Unconscious appears as a defect, as a disturbance in the absolute peace of the clairvoyant unreflecting intuition, as a rent in the harmony of the attributes of the All-One, which posits dissidence in the place of concord, and snatches out of their indifference and sunders subject and object, the moments reconciled and united in the absolute IDEA (comp. "Ges. phil. Abhandlg.," p. 64), through this disunion. The opposition of attributes for the genesis of consciousness, and the emergence of subject and object from indifference, is not at all possible within the self-sure and self-enclosed absolute Idea as such; it rather presupposes the splitting-up of the total function of the All-One into the plurality of individuation, and the crossing or the collision of the numerous tendencies of will which thus arise with their partially opposite content. Only by such conflict of the partial will with other partial wills, through the disagreement of the ideal content of the partial will with the compromise thrust upon it, does that shock become possible which causes the severance of subject and object in consciousness. (Comp. C. Chap. iii. 1.) This consciousness is based on a representation imposed on the mind by its body, *i.e.,* on *sense,* and attains a supersensible content only by discursive reflection through the medium of abstraction.

All these limitations must, as Theism itself acknowledges, be removed from its God; but thereby consciousness, which is dependent on these limitations, is itself abolished. If consciousness can only be described as limitation, the negation of this limitation can no longer be regarded as positive defect in the All-One, since freedom from limitation is rather a sign of superiority. Nevertheless, the positive superiority in point of content is formally a defect, just as the absence of poison-glands in the boa-constrictor, which it does not need on account of its greater strength, or the absence of sin in the orthodox picture of Christ is a formal defect.—Already when, in C. Chap. ii., we arrived inductively at the conclusion that there is no consciousness without a brain, ganglia, protoplasm, or other material substratum, the hypothesis of a transcendent and indivisible consciousness of the world-soul was set aside, since the search after a material substratum making possible this unity of consciousness would be hopeless. By the investigations of C. Chap. iii. this knowledge instinctively arrived at was at the same time proved by way of pure speculation, since the metaphysical ground of the impossibility of a consciousness without individuation and without separation of body and mind was made evident. If the limits of sensibility and finite individuality are set aside, as the notion of God of itself demands, and the limited representation be expanded to the Absolute IDEA, still the *pure matter of representation* remains, and by the removal of all finite opposition and collision we strip off also the form of consciousness. If one still, for one moment, tried to imagine the impossible demand satisfied, that consciousness should be, nevertheless, preserved as form of representation, yet this form also would have to be taken as infinitely elevated above the consciousness known to us, and it would then be at once apparent that the infinite form is equivalent to pure formlessness; that the *absolute consciousness* demanded for God must again prove to be identical with the *absolutely Unconscious;* so that thus even for this extreme standpoint, the phraseology being shown to be equivalent, every motive for opposing our absolutely Unconscious must perforce disappear. (Comp. Fichte's Collected Works, vol. i. pp. 100–253; vol. v. pp. 266 and 457).

Unquestionably, besides its value for the individual as such, consciousness has also in addition a universal significance for the redemption of the world, *i.e.*, for the conversion of the World-will and its return to the original condition before the commencement of the world-process (comp. below, C. Chap. xiv.); for this final purpose the All-One does in fact need consciousness, and accordingly it possesses the same,—namely, in the sum of individual consciousnesses, whose common subject it is.[1]

We have, namely, seen that the one Unconscious is, in fact, the support or subject of all individual consciousnesses, and that the individuals as such are only phenomenal combinations of an organism with the actions of the Unconscious directed to the same. He who accordingly *has, strictly speaking,* the consciousness of Peter and Paul, is not Peter and Paul, by which those phenomenal combinations are denoted, but the All-One Unconscious itself. Undoubtedly the consciousness which the Unconscious has in individuals is a more or less limited one, but any other is simply impossible. This consciousness always suffices to lead to the self-consciousness of the Absolute, namely, to the knowledge that the proper self of Peter and Paul is the All-One Existence.[2] That this self-consciousness

---

[1] With Spinoza, likewise, the infinite intellect of God (comp. Ethics, Part I. Proposition 31, Dem.), to be distinguished indeed from the attribute of the absolute thought, is only the sum of the infinitely numerous finite intellects, of which it is compounded as of its integral parts (Part V. Proposition 40, Obs.) Each of these infinitely numerous intellects is the Idea of a body or extended thing (2 Proposition 11 and 13), and by that not merely human intellects are to be understood, but the Ideas of all natural objects in general, which indeed are all more or less animated (2 Obs. 13), whose sum thus exhausts the ideal content of the universe.

[2] In Hegel also the Absolute Idea possesses no other self-consciousness than this. Much as Hegel insists that the Absolute is not merely substance, but also subject (of consciousness), yet it always becomes conscious, even according to his own doctrine, only in the limited individuals. From the erroneous presupposition that consciousness is a *necessary and eternal* moment in the Absolute, there logically follows for Hegel nothing more than the eternity of the process of Nature, thus the infinite duration of a world filled with things so highly organised that the self-consciousness of the Absolute never dies out; but there by no means follows from that false premiss the persistence of a transcendent consciousness in the Absolute in itself.

of the Absolute in the individuals is a reflex one, again lies in the nature of self-consciousness, which is impossible except on the basis of reflection. Thus it would be shown to those, whose minds are disquieted by the denial of consciousness and self-consciousness to the All-One, that it really does possess such consciousness and self-consciousness as is compatible with the character of these conceptions, namely, limited consciousness and reflex self-consciousness, which certainly must not be sought in the limitless and unreflective All-One as such, but in it as subject of the individual consciousnesses, since only the functions of the All-One directed to a particular organism form a limited part of its total activity, and attain to reflection in the organ of consciousness of the organism.—

If we for a moment assume what is unthinkable, that the Absolute still possesses over and above the consciousness and self-consciousness which it has in individuals another peculiar to itself, we immediately see insoluble difficulties to arise in respect of the relation of this absolute self-consciousness to those of individuals. We formerly assumed, namely, relying on the presumed unconsciousness of the All-One, agreeably to experience, that consciousnesses which arise at separate places, *i.e.*, not sufficiently connected by nervous communications, are *separate* consciousnesses. This could, however, scarcely be maintained on the supposition of an absolute self-consciousness. Does such an absolute consciousness once exist in the subject of two individual consciousnesses, the required nervous communication appears to play a right pitiable and superfluous part beside such a metaphysical bond of union, whilst on the contrary its significance is at once evident if there is only an *unconscious* identical subject of the individual consciousnesses. If the functions of the All-One which the latter determines to the particular organisms are *unconscious* functions, they are sufficiently separated by their different goals not to allow of any confluence of the consciousness arising in organisms by way of reflection. If, on the other hand, they are conscious functions of a self-conscious being, they are related and connected by this consciousness to the higher unity of that self-consciousness, so that it is no longer at all comprehensible how these functions, after their reflection or turning round in the organs of consciousness, should be able to part into *two* consciousnesses, instead of enriching the one absolute consciousness with modified content. It accordingly becomes not only incomprehensible how the consciousnesses of Peter and Paul are *separate* consciousnesses, but how *altogether* a limited individual consciousness can arise without its matter and its form being immediately swallowed up and digested, bones and all, by the absolute consciousness, *i.e.*, annulled as individual consciousness. But still, supposing a limited disparate individual consciousness to have arisen, the functions of the All-One exercised through the same, in case they were conscious, would allow the absolute consciousness to shine, as it were, in upon the individual consciousness; for one would not be able to see how these functions should denude themselves of the form of the absolute consciousness once adhering to them, and indeed essentially connected with them according to the assumption of the Theists, on their entrance into the individual, and on the formation of his special consciousness. The individual must in all directions be refulgent with the light of the absolute consciousness, and the absolute consciousness lie open to its view. All these consequences, contradicted by experience, fall away when we reject the impossible supposition of the absolute consciousness in the All-One.

Monism can by no means endure any absolute conscious world-substance, and only the declension from Monism to the Pluralism of one creating and many created substances makes possible the anthropopathic assumption of a conscious God; truly also only at the cost of comprehension of the possibility of inner relations between the creature and its transcendent Creator, which can then at the best only be conceived as the magical hocus-pocus of the possession of one personal mind by another.

A God whose reality only consists in his spirituality, and whose spirituality is manifested exclusively in the form of consciousness, undeniably becomes with distinct consciousness also a God *parted realiter from the world*, an external transcendent Creator. On the other hand, he who seeks and desires an *immanent* God, a God who descends into our breast and dwells therein, a God in whom we live and have our being, as every profounder religion must demand, and as Christianity and Judaism (Deut. vi. 4; xxx. 11; Isa. lxvi. 1) also actually demand, must make clear to himself that the All-One can only indwell in individuals if it is related to them as the essence to its phenomena, as the subject to its functions, without being parted therefrom by a consciousness of its own, or, in other words, that one and the same activity can only then be simultaneously and without collision of two consciousnesses activity of the individual and of the All-One, if the All-One diffuses itself as *impersonal* Will and *unconscious* Intelligence through the universe with its personal and conscious individuals. As God, by granting a personal consciousness, becomes parted from the world, with every action there inevitably arises the clear alternative, *either* activity of God *or* activity of the individual; a third, a combination of both activities without collision of the different conscious wills, would be only possible exceptionally and fortuitously, but not as a frequent occurrence or at all as general rule (comp. above, B. Chap. x. pp. 24–27).—

We have admitted that it is the Unconscious itself which attains consciousness in the organised individuals. It follows from this that the sufficient reason of its becoming conscious must be given in the Unconscious, or, more briefly, the Unconscious must be regarded as cause of consciousness. It would, however, be very vicious reasoning to try to draw the inference that Consciousness must already inhere in the said Unconscious, else otherwise it could not come out of it. This conclusion would be just as incorrect as the conclusion often, in fact, drawn by savages and the uncultured, that the fire must always lurk *as* fire in the steel and flint, since otherwise it could not leap forth as sparks on their impact. This much only is correct, that there must be contained in the cause the sum of all the indispensable and sufficient conditions in order that the effect may emerge or result from them; but the requirement that the effect be already contained as such in the cause, *i.e.*, already in the form in which it appears as effect, is by no means coincident with this, for then the occurrence of the effect would be no change at all, thus also no causality, but only the becoming visible of a something long existent. We saw above that the arising of *individual* consciousnesses from an *absolute* consciousness can never be rendered intelligible; from an Unconscious, on the contrary, it is quite comprehensible, if only the Unconscious contains in itself all the conditions, which are requisite and sufficient in order to allow of consciousness resulting as form of otherwise given and determined Presentation or Sensation. As these conditions, however, we have in C. Chap. iii. recognised the duality of the attributes and the possibility of an opposition of the functions compounded of them, and these conditions we must accordingly necessarily presuppose in the Unconscious. Whoever regards the stated conditions as incorrectly defined will be obliged to suppose others in their stead in the Unconscious, although he may leave them also quite indefinite if he only guards himself from the error of setting up consciousness itself as the indispensable condition of the origin of consciousness,—an assertion which must be characterised as entirely devoid of foundation,—whereas the most cogent reasons for the contrary have been already partly discussed above, partly will soon come before us for discussion.

The above-mentioned objection would only acquire a certain tinge of justification if it appealed to this, that according to the teleological conception of the Philosophy of the Unconscious (comp. below, C. Chap. xiv. 3), consciousness does not proceed from the Unconscious as an accidental or causally-necessary, thus, at all events, blind result, but that it is teleologically posited by the Unconscious, *i.e.*, *intended* for the sake of a higher end, in which certainly the ideal anticipation is contained. It might then be supposed that this ideal anticipation of consciousness or the teleological forethinking of consciousness must itself represent a consciousness, and, moreover, a higher stage of consciousness. Apart, however, from the implicit form in which in the Unconscious the thinking of the end includes the thinking of the means, and conversely, the following is yet to be considered.

The thinking of consciousness only necessarily presupposes a higher consciousness, if consciousness is thought *as* consciousness, *i.e.*, in the *subjective* mode, as the *subject* of consciousness feels itself affected by its consciousness. But thus it is quite certain the Unconscious does not think its consciousness, since its thinking is altogether absolutely opposed to our *subjective* thinking, so that it would have to be designated objective thinking if this designation were not just as one-sided and accordingly inappropriate. We have already seen in C. Chap. i. that, with regard to the mode of ideation of the Unconscious, we can only make the assertion that it does *not* perceive as *we* perceive. If we then would positively say *what* exactly the Unconscious thinks when it employs consciousness as an intermediate end of a further final end, since subjectivity is excluded, nothing can remain, but firstly, the *objective process*, whose subjective phenomenon is consciousness; and, secondly, the *effect* of the emancipation of the Idea from the Will which results from this process (comp. above, C. Chap. iii. 1). Hereby the two fixed points are gained, which alone are concerned in the teleological forethinking of consciousness, namely, means and end, whilst the subjective inner side of consciousness is accidental in a *teleological* reference, and is therefore not affected by the ideal anticipation of the event.

One might, however, put the objection in still more general form and say, *e.g.*, To posit ends means to provide for the future: how now can an Unconscious, *i.e.*, unconscious of itself as a present reality, be conscious of itself as future? Now I might of course appeal to this, that all this purposive activity is in respect to the merely negative ultimate end (the universal negation of the will) likewise only a negative one, thus only turns on this pivot, *to abolish* the *present* state (of the arisen world-Will), not to introduce a positive future one. However, the purposive activity on the one hand would always perceive the future state of privation as limitation of the present state which was to be annulled, and on the other hand the foregoing of the representation of the future state as goal of the process would little accord with the omniscient clairvoyance of the Unconscious, which we have everywhere found. This appeal, however, is not at all needed, since an error lurks in the inference of the objection.—In the sphere of individuation, namely, for the most part, only individual ends are pursued, individual states aimed at, *to the exclusion* of the participation of other individuals in the states aimed at; accordingly this exclusiveness of what is purposed naturally renders indispensable the sharp and clear discrimination of the substratum of the purposed state from other individuals. Otherwise is it in the sphere of the All-One Unconscious, where every distinction of different substrata of the purposed state, and likewise every exclusion of one in favour of another, ceases, because the phenomenal manifold does not reach into the sphere of the metaphysical existence (as we have seen in the preceding chapter). Here, one may say, state is *absolutely* state, *i.e.*, *all-embracing* state, beyond which at any time there is no state. If, then, in the sphere of the All-One Unconscious a future state is purposed, it is purposed as absolute, *i.e.*, all-embracing state, which has nothing beyond itself, and regarding which therefore the question as to the *support* of the state, as a perfectly meaningless one so far as the purposive process is concerned, cannot at all be proposed in a rational fashion. It follows from this, that it is absurd to transfer the reflection of consciousness on the substratum of the purposed state to which we are accustomed from the inertia of habit also to the purposive activity of the Unconscious. For we already see in individual instincts that the individual takes care for its own future, without therefore knowing that it is its own future well-being for which it cares, and we see even in the race instincts that the individual exerts itself for *general* ends, thus for alien subjects, without any idea for whom it torments and sacrifices itself.

Only thus much then remains tenable in the above objection, that the Unconscious must know the condition to be negated, and which it can only know in that it finds, feels it in itself, since the condition is indeed not spontaneously posited by the unconscious Imagination itself, as all later intuitions; *i.e.*, there in fact results here, from the need of explanation of the purposive activity of the Unconscious, *a posteriori* the necessity of the assumption of a transcendent extramundane consciousness, which feels its own content as a state to be negated, *i.e.*, as *unblessedness or torment*,— an assumption the necessity of which we shall subsequently, in C. Chap. xv. 2, *a priori* perceive to be founded in the nature of the will and the laws of the origination of consciousness. Observe, *this single transcendent consciousness* of the All-One which we have hitherto found occasion to assume has not for content an idea or representation, but it has for sole content *the absolutely indefinite transcendent pain or unblessedness* of the void infinite will, which vague metaphysical discomfort forms, as the state to be negated, the necessary *starting-point* of the unconscious teleological activity, as that which ought not to be the firm foundation of the world-process. The consciousness here allowed, which has arisen only through the mischievous elevation of the quiescent will into volition, and must again cease with the return of the will to its original state of self-enclosed peace (all this will be proved and elucidated in Chap. xv. C.), can obviously give Theism no occasion to triumph at the necessity of a consciousness in the Unconscious. The attempt, however, to deduce from the final purpose of the world-process a consciousness with richer content than that here specified turns out, at all events, a vain endeavour.

If we gather together once more our reflections on the question as to the consciousness of the All-One, there emerges the result that, besides the *notionless* consciousness of indefinite discomfort at the uplifted and unsatisfied world-will, the All-One only possesses a *limited* consciousness *in* conscious individuals, which, however, *suffices* it for the aims of the world-process, and that the peculiar mode or form of its all-knowing and all-wise intuition (absolute idea) is such of which, for lack of positive statements, we can only say this much, that it is elevated above that form which we know as consciousness, *i.e.*, that negatively defined it is unconscious, vaguely but positively defined superconscious. According to this we must declare the endeavour still to ascribe to the All-One an exclusively divine consciousness, conceived according to the analogy of the human, a not smaller anthropopathic error and degrading limitation of God than that of the biblical writings, when they ascribe to him anger, vengeance, and similar qualities measured by our own experiences. (Even pious Church Fathers like Augustine have been disquieted by such reflections on the consciousness of God.) If this holds good of consciousness in general, so much the more must we maintain it of the endeavour to posit in God as special content of such a consciousness *the idea of the All-One itself, i.e.,* to credit him with a *self-consciousness*. However, we shall have to examine this point a little more closely.—

The transcendent consciousness allowed by me has for its sole and only content absolutely indefinite pain, but no idea, least of all the idea of the All-One itself. The consciousness which the All-One has in its individuals has, it is true, for thousands of years been elevated by philosophic thinkers to the consciousness of the All-One itself, therefore to the self-consciousness of the All-One, but this is only an intra-mundane, not extra-mundane self-consciousness of the All-One, such as Theism requires. But we can at least negatively affirm this with confidence of the unconscious representation of the All-One or the Absolute Idea, that it has in the self-satisfaction of its own pure intuition just as little occasion for reflection in general as for a definite reflection on itself or on something else; not on anything else, since there exists nothing else besides itself; not on itself, since reflection on itself presupposes reflection on something else. But in the unity of the Absolute Idea the ground of the separation of subject and object is just that which is wanting, therefore also their appearance to one another, which constitutes consciousness, is also wanting, and in particular there is wanting the bending round of the ideational activity towards its origin, the turning back to the active subject as goal of representation, which retroversion of the activity of thought is precisely what is characteristic of the notion of self-consciousness as we have abstracted it from human self-consciousness. The Absolute Idea embraces all that is, for its ideal determinations become indeed as content of will those phenomena whose sum we call the world. The unconscious thought of substance accordingly exhausts the sum of all its modes, and so far as its whole proper nature is unfolded therein, itself as the sum of its unfolded moments (in its otherness),—but itself *only in this sense*, not in the proper acceptation of the notion of self-consciousness, as active centre of emanation.[1] To grasp the latter retroversion or reflection is required, which takes place in the brains of individuals, whereby the intuitive character of the presentation is lost, but instead thereof the self-consciousness of the All-One *in the strict sense* is really *gained*—only of course not as extramundane, transcendent—and at the same time as one which, beside the notion of the All-One as active world-centre, embraces only a very small part of its phenomena, not, as the unconscious idea, its whole plenitude. As the light-sphere, consisting of light rays, illuminates the whole space, but not the point from which it issues, unless a reflection of its own beams takes place at reflecting surfaces, and thereby a turning back of the direction of these rays, so the intuitive ideal total activity of the All-One may cognise the All, only not the point whence it issues, the active centre of the All, unless certain bundles of these rays are broken in the brain of an organism into consciousness, which then, however, must of necessity be a one-sided, limited, no all-embracing absolute consciousness.

The previous considerations, in combination with the argument stated below derived from the evil of the world, seem sufficient to render evident the perfect untenability of a specifically divine consciousness and self-consciousness in the All-One. In this way of thinking we find ourselves in perfect accord with the views of modern German philosophy. Here, too, neither in Fichte's earlier doctrine, where the Absolute is represented by the unreal unsubstantial abstract moral world-order (Fichte's Werke,

---

[1] Only in this sense does Spinoza speak of a self-knowledge of God. The idea, which in God is actual, is ever unique, all-embracing (Ethics, Part ii. Prop. 4), which includes in itself all individual intellects as the ideas of the modes of extension (comp. above p. 250 Obs.) and the ideas of all these intellects, or the ideas of these ideas (Ethics, ii. Props. 20 and 21), *i.e.*, the pure forms of these ideas without regard to their extended objects (2 Prop. 21 Obs.), and, moreover, includes as posited with logical necessity. God as subject or *natura naturans* therefore does not know himself as subject of the cognitive activity or of the attribute of thought, but as object of the same, *i.e.*, as *natura naturata* (comp. 1 Prop. 29 Obs.)

v. 186, 187, 264, 368), nor in his later doctrine, where it stands as the eternally unchangeable veiled Being behind our consciousness which reveals it (Werke, v. 441, 442), nor in Schelling (comp. his Werke, i. 1, p. 180; i. 3, p. 497; i. 4, p. 256; i. 7, p. 53, 54, and 67, 68), nor in Hegel (which, to be sure, is denied by the reactionary part of the Hegelian school), nor in Schopenhauer does the Absolute possess a consciousness outside of the individuals pervaded by it (comp. also vol. i. pp. 23–31; Introductory i. c., the remarks on the philosophers named).—

After these conclusions concerning the consciousness and self-consciousness of God, we shall hardly expect a more favourable result in regard to the notion of *personality*, to which Theism is wont to attach so much importance as predicate of its God, that it is precisely in order to save it that it still insists so urgently on the untenable predicates of consciousness and self-consciousness, even after former scruples (comp. above, p. 245 ff.) against setting aside these anthropopathic predicates of God have been removed by the recognition of the unconscious-superconscious reflectionless-intuitive intelligence in the All-One. Nothing would stand in the way of the application of the notion personality, if its definition were limited to an individuality combined with will and intelligence,[1] and it was certain that no inadequate anthropopathic accessory notions were interpolated. But unfortunately the guarantee of this is so small, that, on the contrary, the predicate of personality has almost always been employed only with the intention of thereby smuggling in unsuitable ideas, which, however, are perhaps consoling to the heart. *In a jural sense*, the notion of personality rests on the criteria of civil independence; this conception has, of course, no sense in reference to

---

[1] Only in this sense is Schelling willing in his later "Philosophy of Revelation" to understand Theism as doctrine of the One tri-personal God (comp. his definition of personality: Werke, ii. 7, p. 281, and my memoir, "Schelling's Positive Philosophie," pp. 42, 43, Obs.)

God. *Ethically* the notion of personality implies the capacity of judging one's own actions and the moral responsibility conditioned by the same, but this transference of a relation, which is highly important between separate and opposed individuals, to the absolute all-embracing Individual appears inadmissible, because there are no individuals *beside* itself, but only *in* itself, and because even these latter are only manifestations of itself, *phenomena*, not substances, therefore cannot be co-ordinated with the substance, through which alone they are, as the notion of the ethical relation would require.[1]

---

[1] Those readers who have been accustomed to think the conception of freedom inseparably united with the ethical conception of personality are reminded: (1.) That freedom may be temporarily abolished along with accountability, without personality being thereby abolished. (2.) That this concept of freedom only contains a relation to the concept of personality when it is opposed to the freedom of individual assertion on the part of other individuals, but that then, for the before-mentioned reason, it is not transferable to the All-One, since the latter has nothing whatever to oppose itself to. (3.) That the notion of the freedom of human *will* rests altogether on an illusion (comp. the commencement of Chap. xi., sect. B.), and accountability does not rest on a quality of the will, but of the intellect, and, moreover of the discursive *intellect*, cannot therefore be applied to the All-One. If there were a human freedom, it could not be analogically transferred to the All-One; if it were transferable it would still import no trace of a notion of personality into the All-One; but if it were purified from amalgamation with this alien concept, there would finally be nothing ascribed to the All-One by this transference which does not already appertain to our Unconscious as such. The contrast of a foreign compulsion, which is necessary to give the notion of freedom its special content, is wanting here, but the Unconscious is undoubtedly absolutely free inasmuch as it derives all its decisions from itself, and can be affected by nothing external. It further actually possesses, according to our investigations, the ability only erroneously ascribed to man, to intervene at any moment spontaneously as cause in the lawfully given phenomenal series, which adds a new factor determining the process to the existing ones, and continually exercises this faculty in its teleological interpositions. Lastly, it shows itself, as we shall see in Chap. xv. C., before the decision, by which it certainly ties its own hands until the reintroduction of the *status quo ante*, as free to comport itself rationally or irrationally, *i.e.*, to remain in the place of non-volition or to elevate itself to Volition, *i.e.*, to the world-creation; man, on the contrary, even then acts *according to* the absolutely rational plan of the world, *i.e.*, rationally, where he imagines he is acting *counter* to the same, *i.e.*, irrationally. The All-One Unconscious accordingly possesses all *possible* freedom, and can by no means acquire any not yet possessed freedom in addition to the same through the erroneous assumption of a human freedom.

Ideologically the concept of personality consists in the existence of a consciousness with respect to the identity of the conscious subjects underlying all the temporally distinct acts of self-consciousness in the same consciousness (comp. p. 79), is thus the result of a tolerably complex *reflection* on a number of *reflective* acts of self-apprehension comprehended by *memory*. Since God in his absolute intuition is raised far above all reflection (even above that of simple self-consciousness, to say nothing of the reflection of the identity of the subjects of those acts of reflection), and as, moreover, such a reflection, in the absence of any existence from which he could distinguish himself, would be for him perfectly superfluous and tautological, the ideological concept of personality also can have no application to God, any more than the jural or ethical. The attempt, from religious considerations, to save the ideological personality of God at any price, necessarily leads by its consequences to the fantastic assumption of an eternal nature in God elevated above material temporal Nature and different from it (Jacob Böhme and Franz von Baader), in order to render possible an eternal process in God with self-discrimination and reintegration as his actual temporal nature makes possibly the temporal world-process, with the resulting separation of subject and object in the finite consciousnesses, which are indeed collectively consciousnesses of the All-One Existence. One sees from this how weak an hypothesis must be when its most important advocates confess themselves compelled, in order to maintain it, to have recourse to such artificial, fantastic, and wholly imaginary auxiliary hypotheses.

According to these considerations, it seems most suitable not to give to the notion of personality so wide a sense as is given in the above definition, in order thereby to make it applicable to God. There are many *individuals* endowed with *will* and *intelligence*, which do not on that account admit of the concept of personality (animals, low savages, idiots, &c.), and to which we therefore refuse this designation. Why should we not exercise the same restraint with regard to an individual which no longer answers to that conception, because it is elevated above all the limitations which form the marks of the conception on its different sides? Here, too, the *degradation* of the Supreme Being does not lie on the side of those who refuse the predicate of personality, but on the part of those who *ascribe* it. Nay, looked at more closely, the lowering of God turns out to be *the secret purpose of the affair*, i.e., one seeks in God a person (according to the human standard), in order by this kind of co-ordination of God with the ego seeking consolation from him to bring it about, that one may place oneself on intimate footing, as it were, with God, as with a revered equal, in order, on pouring out the heart before him, to make more sure of a humanly sympathising understanding of one's own emotion. Even the Christian apostles, with the growing purification of the God-idea, began to have an inkling of the unsuitableness of this childish behaviour, at which the naïve anthropopathic imagination of the older Judaism had taken no offence; and the more sublimely the God-concept shaped itself with the progressive development of Christian Theism through the contact with Hellenic philosophy, the more the religious soul in its intellectual confusion saw itself impelled to take refuge in a mediating human personality (Christ, subsequently the Virgin Mary and the saints). As the Reformation found itself compelled, after the abolition of prayer to the saints, to lay more stress upon the human personality of Christ than in Catholicism, so in consequence of the now disappearing Christ-belief, Theism is trying again to bring God himself nearer to man from his abstract remoteness by imparting more human features, and this is the most important reason for the emphasising of the personality of God, although incompatible with the idea of the same. But when one considers that, from the philosophical point of view, the practical nerve of prayer is already paralysed by a purely subjective signification and activity being ascribed to it according to the modern view of the world, the value of the emotional postulate, contradicted by thought, appears also from this side more than doubtful. For when I have once perceived the illusory nature of belief in an objective meaning and efficacy of prayer, the nature of the object to which the prayer is conceived or addressed has become perfectly *indifferent*, since in truth we are here only dealing with a *monologue*, to which the possible jugglery of a conscious self-deception in respect of a feigned auditor can give no value. With this now-a-days unavoidable admission that the meaning of prayer is reduced to the value of a soliloquising soul-expectoration on self-rectitude (Schleiermacher,) *disappears*, even within the pale of Theism, *every practical motive of religion*, for hankering after the clothing of God with the predicate of personality in the proper sense of the term at the expense of good logic.

But with the renunciation of the predicate of *personality* disappears again, as remarked above, the practical religious interest in maintaining the personal divine *self-consciousness*, and with this the last interest in the assertion of an exclusive transcendent *consciousness* of the All-One. The practical religious interest being set aside which could not bring itself to abandon all these conceptions in spite of their long-proved untenability, the notional difficulties and philosophic proofs fully assert themselves, and *compel* that Theism, which endeavours to purify itself from the crude naturalness of an anthropopathic representation of God and to attain tenable metaphysical conceptions, to take the last necessary step in this process of purification and profounder thinking, from which it has hitherto recoiled from a mistaken religious motive. The result, however, which emerges in this last and now inevitable step of the self-purification of Theism, is the same as that which the Philosophy of the Unconscious on its own part from quite another side brings to Theism, and the old supports of the latter have gradually become one after the other so rotten and crumbling that it should rejoice when another new one is offered it.

That all the attributes of the divine intelligence (all-knowledge, all-wisdom, all-presentness) are also applicable to the clairvoyant unconscious intuition of our All-One, will be more precisely shown at the beginning of Chap. xii. C., and we have already admitted the omnipotence of the Unconscious Absolute Will. When we add, that we have in the last chapter recognised the Unconscious as the Individual in a pre-eminent sense (p. 223 ff., and 240–243), and that the former claims of Theism to personality, self-consciousness, and consciousness of God in their previous sense have become untenable, but that all that is tenable in the same is actually satisfied by our Unconscious, it is clear that on this side a *difference in principle* between a Theism that rightly understands itself and the Philosophy of the Unconscious *cannot be found.*—

This might appear still more plain in another direction, namely, in reference to the relation of the individual to the All-One; but here too we shall see that a well-understood Theism must necessarily move away some steps from the vulgar conception, and then likewise coincides with our point of view. Theism namely is originally *dualism*, in that it ascribes just as much substantiality to the world as to God. It is true this dualism is one only existing since the creation of the world (conceived as in time), thus no regressively eternal one, but it is intended to be a forwards eternal one, in that the substance of the higher creature is also conceived as eternal. The dualism is therefore indeed only the result of the act of creation, but it is now in operation, and moreover determined not to disappear again. Such a dualism is, however, philosophically untenable, and irresistibly tends to relapse into Monism. We have in the last chapter (pp. 230–234) seen that a seriously held dualism abolishes and reduces to Occasionalism or Pre-established Harmony—two equally untenable refuges from difficulty—the empirically given and *a priori* demanded causality of individuals among one another, and that causality as *influxus physicus* necessarily demands the taking up of individuals as phenomena into the one absolute substance. We can here reach the same result by a consideration of the notion of *creation*, which forms a distinguishing fundamental conception of Theism.— A consistent dualism must assume that the world fashioned as *substance* by the creative act would continue to subsist, even if the creator were suddenly annihilated; only on this condition would the world be a *permanent* residuum of a completed act of creation, only on this condition true and genuine substance. This consequence is, however, too strong even for Theism itself, and it therefore foregoes the regarding the world as a mere completed result of a single creative act; it lets its God permanently act the part of world-restorer or world-governor, as the world-architect of Greek dualism in presence of the chaos of the eternal uncreated matter. *For this matter*, however, and strictly taken also for the individual *immortal spirits* called into actuality, Theism tries to retain the notion of a *created substance*, a *caput mortuum* of a former long past creative act, which residuum, it is true, God has the power again to annihilate, if it seems good to him, but which *without* such a divine interposition would *of itself* be imperishable. However, Theism must soon perceive that it is here in presence of the same difficulty, of the same belittling of God, in that this residuum would then also continue to exist if God were *annihilated*, and that therewith an *independence* limiting God's absoluteness would have to be accorded it. This scruple could only be laid to rest if, on God's annihilation, continued subsistence were denied to the creature; the creature must collapse into nothingness, if the creator withdraws his hand from it even only for a moment; but this is only possible if continued existence is conditioned by a *continuously* active function of God, *by an act of will renewed every moment.*

Such a conserving activity of God, which prevents the constantly threatened falling back of the creature into nothingness, is now, however, in no way different from the first creative act, which summoned the creature out of nothing; for both substitute for the non-existence of the creature its existence; *i.e.*, however, the conservation of the creation by God is to be more precisely defined as *continuous creation.* Herewith is the untenable notion of the *caput mortuum* of a past act of creation stripped off, no matter whether this past is reckoned at thousands of years or seconds, and the existence of the creation is in every moment understood as creative act *of the same* moment. Creation out of nothing, which was emphasised by the Jewish-Christian Theism in contrast to Greek dualism, in order to render prominent the absence of an eternal matter existing before God, is then to be understood in this way, that that wherefrom God creates is his own creative energy, that the whole real existence of the creature consists purely in the divine creative power directed to the same, and its whole essence at every moment purely consists in the content which the divine creative act of this moment pours into it.

About thus far has Theism progressed in the philosophical purification of its conceptions; it is, however, easy to see that herewith the notion of *substance* has ceased to be applicable to the creature, since it no longer has *subsistence* at all, save through the absolute divine substance. Thus *only the latter* manifesting itself in a continuous creative act of will is the subsistent or self-existent, but the creature itself and its existence is only the *manifestation* or the *revelation* of the functions of the Absolute directed to its constant creation or preservation, or, in brief, an *appearance*[1] of

---

[1] By this expression we must, of course, not in the remotest manner think of the "subjective appearance" of the theory of knowledge, which is the correlate to the conception of the "thing of itself" of the

the All-One Being. The real existence and the essence of the creature is hereby not at all impugned, since we have indeed already seen that what we call its reality only consists of the sum of the acts of will which are functional in it (comp. above, pp. 242, 243). The notion of creation is, however, through the setting aside of the conception of the created substance, resolved into that of the continuous *manifestation* of the absolute will and the absolute idea, *i.e.*, into that of the Appearance of the absolute Being. The individual who has penetrated to this conception thereby attains for his religious feeling the desired conviction that he at every moment owes to God, and to him alone, his whole being and all he is; that he is nothing at all but in him and through him, and that the being in him is God's being itself. Thus also dualism has disappeared from Theism, and by dealing in earnestness with pure Monism has, at the same time, gained for the ardently devotional religious feeling the consciousness of an intimacy of relation between God and man, which is not even remotely to be reached as long as man by the perverse self-contradictory notion of a created substance is opposed as a foreign, independent, self-contained personal substance to God, who may now solve the puzzle how to enter into the man separated substantially from him. The purely monistic view of the world is also alone capable of laying the metaphysical foundation of an ethic exempt from the interference of all sovereign individual caprice (comp. Schopenhauer), which could only attain general validity on the ground of a pluralistic individualistic ethics, if the conception of the divine revelation of a universally obligatory moral canon were tenable. That profounder intimacy of the relation of the individual to the Absolute and this better foundation of ethics, which Monism affords as compared with dualistic Theism, and for

same theory, whilst we have here to do with the notion of the divinely or objectively posited, or objective phenomenon, which is the correlate to the metaphysical conception of the "essence" (comp. above, p. 241).

the sake of which the mystical theosophists and theologians of the West have always shown a strong and decided inclination to Pantheism, the purely Aryan religions of India possessed long before the origin of Christianity; whilst, on the contrary, Christianity from its Semitic origin retained the dualism between creator and creation, at any rate in the orthodox doctrines of the chief confessions. Whilst, however, the pantheistic religions of India, entangled in the error of the eternity of the phenomenon and not acknowledging the real existence of time, were unable to elevate themselves to an historical world-theory, and therefore allowed their believers to be lost in dreams and perish in unhistorical Quietism, the Jewish-Christian Theism, on the contrary, has in compensation for its other defects developed an historical world-view, in which the all-wise providence on the basis of natural process guides the historical process according to a teleologically predetermined plan to a rational goal; from this belief in a rational historical evolution which has found ever clearer expression have the European nations derived the strength of their devotion to the historical process.

At the present time, when the more special forms of the Christian religion are manifestly outlived, and the faith in the providentially guided historical evolution has besides passed into the flesh and blood of modern civilisation, the essential question is how to liberate from the deciduous shell and to unite with the real substance of the pantheistic Indian religions this remaining kernel of Theism, in order through these ideas, which have grown purely out of the spirit of our Aryan stock, to gain a religious profundity and enhancement of the intensity of religious and ethical feeling, which would be a vivifying renewal of our irreligious age clinging convulsively to the mere externals of religion. That the old creed is no longer tenable, and is still only artificially and violently preserved as a mummy, is generally felt and admitted. But that by mere critical negation nothing is directly gained, unless at the same time fresh elements of religious feeling are introduced, would be just as generally recognised if one did not frequently despair of discovering these new positive elements. If these are anywhere to be found, they lie in that genuine and imperishable core of pure Aryan Pantheism, which must be fused with the circuitously attained historical world-view of Judaism and Christianity, in order by this concrescence to reach a position that unites the advantages of both sides without their defects, and therefore stands higher than either of them singly. In this sense we may say: we stand directly before the time when the Jewish-Christian cosmic theory has only the choice *of dying entirely out or of becoming pantheistic.* The metaphysical foundation of this transformation, however, which was prepared by the pantheistic and mystical philosophies of the Middle Ages and the Reformation (Scotus Erigena, Martin Eckhart, Giordano Bruno, Jacob Böhme, Spinoza), has been philosophically laid and built on by the most recent German philosophers, whose partially authorised and valuable endeavours and tendencies have coalesced into a provisional unity in the principle of the Unconscious. Precisely in our own time, when the opposition between the unmediated extremes of a rigid *theistic dogmatism* and an *irreligious atheistic naturalism* is threatening to become more irreconcilable, the golden mean of a *spiritualistic Monism or Pantheism*, which supplies both parties with a bridge for mutual understanding and union on neutral soil, appears to be of the highest importance for the peaceful spiritual development of modern society.—

Having endeavoured to prove the evanescence of the main differences between the Unconscious and the God of Theism with the philosophical purification of Theism, a cardinal point must in conclusion not be left unmentioned. Theism, namely, asserts that the *existence* of the world is an *intended* consequence of God's goodness and omniscience, and sees itself therefore driven in presence of *evil* to the necessity of attempting a *theodicy*, the impossibility of which had already been convincingly proved by Kant in a special treatise. We do not deal here with the optimism of those who, like Jewish Theism, find the whole world and the life in it wonderfully glorious, and hold evil to be evanescent as compared with the happiness which exists beside it; we also do not insist on the necessity of a theodicy in regard to moral evil, which for the rest indeed were indifferent, if it did not contribute to the increase of suffering; we only ask an account of that Theism which, like the Christian, grants the preponderating woe and misery in this world (comp. C. Chap. xiii.), and yet regards the resolution to create the world as an efflux of the divine all-knowledge and all-wisdom. The consolation of immortality is no help here, for also in the other world the number of the blessed will be very small compared with that of the torment of the suffering damned (Matt. vii. 13–14; xxii. 14). The only partially accepted doctrine of the future restoration of every creature at the end of all things is in itself too problematical to deserve consideration, and leaves open the question why the world must be miserable until then. As now it would never do to make God the author of evil, Theism sees itself compelled to seek the origin of evil outside God, *i.e.*, since save God only his creature exists, in the creature. A moral guilt of the first (?) human pair is said to have had the deterioration of nature for its natural consequence, so that God must now look on while milliards suffer for the trespass of a couple of individuals dead thousands of years ago, *i.e.*, guiltlessly; since, however, notwithstanding the connection between human fall and deterioration of Nature, between moral guilt and natural world misery, appeared all too bold, a superhuman creature must be introduced, a devil, who ruined and brought into disorder the fair creation of God. For a more childish time this theodicy, by means of the two scapegoats, Lucifer and

Adam, might be well enough; we only smile now at such fancies. We repudiate, however, at the same time, in principle, every attempt to disburden God of the responsibility for the world-misery by shifting the same on to any of his creatures whatsoever, since, in the first place, such an independence of the creature crossing the intentions of God is, according to our foregoing discussion, not conceivable; and since, secondly, an all-knowing and all-wise God must, at the moment of creation, foresee and take account of the voluntary decisions of his creatures under all circumstances, and all the indirect consequences of their action as terms of the question, whether it would be wise to create a world with such a history.

It is to be noticed that it is quite immaterial, and does not at all affect the serious nature of the responsibility, whether the intelligence of God, which is active in this resolve to create a world, is assumed to be *conscious or unconscious.* Were the divine intelligence at all concerned in the decision whether a world should be created or not, the actual result of this decision in the case of affirmation would be an inexcusable cruelty towards the created substances on the assumption of dualistic Theism, but, on the assumption of Monism, the frenzy of a divine asceticism, a divine self-laceration. If an absolute intelligence (no matter whether conscious or unconscious) really be one of the attributes of God, as indeed we too assume, it is, in view of the misery of the world, *impossible* that it can have taken part in the decision in question, thus impossible that it was active and efficient during the exaltation of the will which decided on the " That " of the world. Only if the existence of the world was decided by the act of a *blind* will illuminated by no ray of rational intelligence, only then is this existence comprehensible; only then is God as such not to be made *responsible* for the same. Such a non-participation of intelligence in the world's origin, however, cannot be explained by Theism in any of its forms; it must maintain it to be simply impossible on the assumption of an eternal interior spiritual life of a self-conscious God. With our principles, however, it is perfectly comprehensible, nay, even not otherwise to be expected *a priori*, because, namely (according to C. Chap. i.), the Idea of itself has no interest in being, and can only be posited by the raising of the will out of non-being into being, thus neither before nor during the elevation of the will is existent, but only becomes so through the same. Suppose then the elevation of the blind will into actual volition (*i.e.*, the moment of the initiative preceding every actual intelligence in the All-One) sufficed, as we shall hereafter see, to posit the "That" of the world, it would thereby be explained how, despite the omniscience of God (*during* the world-process), the unfortunate *commencement* could have come to pass.

But now arises a *second* question: Why did not God in the first moment when he became *seeing*, *i.e.*, his all-wise intelligence entered into being, *repair* the error *blindly committed*, and turn his will against himself? Incomprehensible and unpardonable as the first commencement would be without the hypothesis of a blind action, no less incomprehensible and unpardonable would be the *laisser-aller* of this misery with open eyes if the possibility of an immediate recall remained open. Here we are again aided by the inseparability of the idea from the will in the Unconscious, the unfreedom and dependence of the idea on the will, in consequence of which the former has indeed to determine its "What," its goal and its content, but not its "That and whether." We shall see that the whole world-process only serves the one purpose of emancipating the Idea from the will by means of consciousness, in order by the opposition of the Idea to induce the peace of the will. Were now this end *attainable without consciousness*, or did such a consciousness in the sense of an emancipation of the Idea from the will exist at the beginning of the world-process in God, the whole cosmic process would be *foolish* and *aimless*, in that it would be struggling to attain somewhat that either is *not at all requisite* for the object, or that *existed long ago*. This consideration affords the last decisive reason against the assumption of a transcendent consciousness in God in the sense of an emancipation of the idea from the will, if the contrary reasons assigned above were not more than sufficient. This last argument, be it observed, is thoroughly *inductive*, drawn from the empirical fact of the misery of the world, and derives its force solely from this, that no hypothesis involving a conscious God is able to explain the fact without contradiction.

Although, since Spinoza's identification of God, Substance, and Nature, the God-idea has to a certain extent obtained a citizen's rights in philosophy, I still hold the origin of an idea to be so important for its comprehension, that it seems to me advisable to avoid as far as possible in philosophy an idea with an origin so exclusively religious as God. I shall therefore continue as a rule to employ the expression, "The Unconscious," although the previous discussion has shown that I should have more right to the use of the word "God" than Spinoza and many others. Although the formal negativity of my terminology for an out-and-out positive Being must for a length of time be inadequate, yet it will retain its proper prophylactic value as long as the anthropopathic error of the *consciousness* of the Absolute prevails to a considerable extent. When, however, the negative predicate of *unconsciousness* is *universally recognised* as a *self-evident* predicate of the Absolute no longer needing distinct enouncement, then undoubtedly this negative designation will, in the historical progress of philosophy, have long been replaced by one more appropriate and positive.

IX.

THE ESSENTIAL NOTION OF GENERATION FROM THE STANDPOINT OF THE UNIVERSALITY AND UNITY OF THE UNCONSCIOUS.

WE will now employ our recently obtained point of view to clear up a few questions, which either have occupied philosophers for thousands of years, or precisely at the present time have acquired special interest among the general public. It will be shown how the solutions which flow from the principles already obtained are in full accordance with what the facts to be explained require, and what an unlaboured criticism of possible explanations leaves over.

The first of these questions concerns the nature of Generation. Formerly two theories contended concerning generation, Creatianism and Traducianism. The former assumed a psychical new creation on every occasion of procreation; the latter, a transference of parts of the paternal souls to the child. The former accordingly affirms in every case of procreation a creation out of nothing, a new miracle; and is, therefore, unacceptable to the more sober thinking of modern times; the latter, however, contradicts the facts. For if a man with the requisite number of women could easily beget over a hundred children in the course of a year, during the time of his procreative power, accordingly, many thousands, and yet notoriously no diminution of his soul takes place; on each act of generation the part given off to the child must have been much less than the thousandth part of the minimum which could just be traced as the soul's loss. With such a tiny piece of soul manifestly the child could not for the length of time get along, still less his children and children's children, which, in decreasing progression, would soon acquire only the billionth part of a soul; accordingly, the transferred piece could only be regarded as a *germ*, which is capable of growth. Under a germ one understands, however, a *formal* power which is able to draw to itself and to *assimilate foreign material* elements, and thereby to grow. If, then, the infant soul were, at its engendering, only a germ, the question occurs, Where are the foreign elements to be sought by which it is augmented? The materialists answer very simply: The soul is only a result of material combinations; accordingly with the growth of the organism and its noble parts the soul also grows. This view we can of course not accept, but it is at least clear and self-consistent. But if we still ask where the elements to be drawn upon are to be sought, there remains nothing but the general spirituality, the impersonal psychical, in a word, the *Unconscious*. From this, accordingly, the piece given off from the parent-souls to the child-soul must draw its stock of increase.

But why, then, is a *soul*-germ wanted, as the *organic* germ can take the place of the same? Does the child in the womb need another kind of psychical activity than that of organic formation? And when by means of this unconscious psychical activity an organ is created in the brain for conscious mental activity, is there then needed yet another medium of attraction, in order that the Unconscious may turn its activity in this direction, than the presence of this organ itself? Why, then, this unnatural hypothesis of the given-off soul-germs, by which one must either think of *one-sided tendencies* of the parental souls, which are no aid to explanation, or diminutive souls, hatched and detached, as it were—a horrible idea?

And how, then, came these soul-buds first to get into the organic procreative germs, since both must be conceived as arising independently of one another? Is there on every seminal emission with each of the millions of spermatozoa a piece of soul carried away at random, or does the detached diminutive soul of the father travel into the particular spermatozoon, if the same has had the good fortune to light upon an ovum of its own species capable of fecundation? And how does the diminutive soul of the father, held in reserve, learn which spermatozoon, emitted during coitus hours or days before, causes the fertilisation of an ovum?

If the child's soul is drawn from the well of the universal world-spirit, represents as it were the psychical appurtenance crystallised round the newly arisen organic germ, this conveys an essentially different idea from that of Creatianism, where the soul in the moment of generation is created by God out of nothing. Further, this view does not, like Creatianism, render unintelligible the transmission of psychical qualities, in that the organic germ is conditioned by the qualities of the parents and the spirit crystallising, as it were, from the Unconscious, is again modified according to the qualities of the organic germ. In this sense, by transmission of the constitution of the brain spiritual qualities may just as well be transferred from parents to children as a finger in excess or a morbid diathesis. On the other hand, the addition of a *genius* to the infant soul, demanded by higher historical considerations, remains unrestricted; for if the Unconscious *needs* special organs for its revelation, it *prepares* them also in due time; it will create in an organism which offers itself as especially appropriate an organ of consciousness, which is capacitated for unusually lofty psychical achievements.

If in this way we escape the main inconvenience of Traducianism and Creatianism, it is still always not to be denied that as long as one regards the soul of the individual not merely in its activity, but also in its essence, its substance, as something self-enclosed and *limited*, both with respect to other individual souls and also with respect to the universal spirit, that so long the theory of generation has its great difficulties; for the rending of a new soul from the universal, and the attaching of the same to the new organic germ, is a very dubious proceeding, whether we regard this individualising of a new soul as a process of *gradual* crystallisation going hand-in-hand with the bodily development of the germ, or whether we regard it as a *single* momentary act, in which the new soul is engrafted ready made on the germ.

However, as soon as one remembers the results of our last chapter but one, the matter begins to grow clear, for now the soul both of each of the parents as well as of the child is only *the sum of the activities of the one Unconscious directed to the particular organism.*[1]

Now the souls of the parents are not separate, self-existing substances, can accordingly give off nothing of their substance, and the child *has no need* to acquire any special individualised soul, but its soul is likewise only the sum of the activities of the Unconscious directed at any moment on its organism. Could the parents really give off a portion of their souls to the child, they would still only draw from the great dish from which they, as all three, are fed.

Now there is also nothing wonderful in this, that the infant soul only grows *gradually* in proportion to the body, for the more developed becomes the organism, the more varied, rich, and noble becomes the sum of the activities of the Unconscious directed upon it. With our principle not only is the miraculous lost, but also that unique character that generation otherwise possesses; it becomes an act essentially similar to conservation and renovation even in spiritual reference, as it has long been

[1] We hardly need remind the reader that wherever the word "soul" occurs in the first two sections of this book, it must not, after the explanation of the last chapter, be understood otherwise than in the sense of the definition here given. If in the earlier sections the monistic view of the soul was less prominent, this only happened because, for the understanding of the matter there treated of, the current conception of the soul sufficed, and by premature insistance on the monistic point of view a proper understanding of the subject by the philosophically untrained reader would have been rendered needlessly difficult.

so acknowledged in material reference. Should the Unconscious cease to direct its activity (as sensation, ideation, will, organic formation, instinct, reflex action, &c.) at any moment whatsoever upon any existing organism, the latter would at the same moment be bereft of soul, *i.e.*, be dead, and would be unsparingly crushed by the laws of matter, just as the matter of this organism would cease to be as soon as the Unconscious intermitted the acts of will in which its atomic forces consist. Just as well, however, as the Unconscious at any moment animates every organism capable of animation, will it also animate the newly arising germ according to its capability of being animated. Add to this, that the moment is not at all to be determined when the germ becomes from a part of the maternal the independent organism, if one does not let the solution at birth pass for such. As long, however, as the organism of the child is a part of the maternal organism, and is nourished by it, so long we have still to do with a process which in essence is not distinguishable from any other organic formation. This will become more clear if we glance at the gradual progress from the lower kinds of propagation to sexual generation.

The simplest kind is *fission*, an ordinary case of the increase of cells, but also not rare in infusoria and other animals. That in a division of one animal into two there can be no talk of a division of the substance of the soul has been already repeatedly mentioned. There is a gradual transition from fission to *gemmation*, for the bud too is developed as part of the maternal organism, until, rendered capable of independent existence, it drops off (polyps, &c.)

A difference in principle in the process of formation cannot be asserted, whether the animal replaces lost parts or forms buds for multiplication. In the cases, however, where the buds are characteristically presented as such, and are no longer to be confused with simple fission, their development from a single cell deposited in the maternal tissue at any part of the body—*germ-cell*—is always to be recognised. Now it can manifestly make no essential difference at *what* part of the maternal organism the germ-cell is found from which the new organism is developed, whether this place lies at the side, or at an extremity, or on the arms, or in the abdominal cavity of the animal, or in a distinct ovarium. The two latter cases are distinguished from increase by gemmation as increase by germ-cells in the narrower sense. The germ-cells, which are developed in the abdominal cavity or in a special sac, mostly exhibit a marked external resemblance in form and size to the ova of the higher animals. Nay, one may even assert they are not to be distinguished morphologically from these.

In many animals (*e.g.*, plant-lice) multiplication by germ-cells already alternates with sexual propagation, or *one* generative act is sufficient to fertilise the germ-cells (or ova) for several successive broods. An insect belonging to the Diptera, *Cceidomyia*, by sexual propagation begets larvæ which, living under the bark of decaying apple-trees, develop without copulation in a species of ovary offspring so advanced, that they come into the world in a form resembling that of the mother. In some butterflies also the remarkable phenomenon of virgin generation or parthenogesis takes place, likewise in a whole series of lower crustacea; in both the offspring born without fertilisation are exclusively *females;* in the black humblebees, wasps, and bees, on the other hand, conversely, the males come forth from unfertilised, the females from fertilised eggs. Whilst among the bees only the queen lays eggs, which it can at will bring into contact with spermatozoa reserved from a former copulation or not, in the humblebees and wasps the bearers of the male and female offspring are separate individuals; the females, namely, that have survived the winter, which had copulated in the autumn, bring forth female young; these females born in spring, however, now produce without being fecundated the males for the autumn coupling.—The germ-cell or the unfertilised ovum develops in a manner perfectly analogous to the fertilised ovum, only that the former does not need the appulse of fertilisation; yet there are accredited examples of the ova of animals that only increase sexually, which were notoriously unfertilised, entering into the process of yolk-furrowing, as if they were fertilised. (Such cases were, *e.g.*, observed years ago in the ova of pigs by the anatomist Bischof in Munich.) It is true their energy did not reach very far, and they remained at the first stages of embryonic development. Under certain circumstances, however, even here the process of growth of the egg can proceed to a tolerably advanced stage; thus, *e.g.*, it has long been known that hens without contact with a cock sometimes lay unfertilised eggs, which have accordingly traversed a tolerably long course of development from their microscopic origin.

The seminal corpuscle penetrating into the yolk-membrane with the point of its head, and there probably exchanging by endosmosis its substance with the yolk, does, therefore, nothing else in the first instance but give to the yolk-mass a powerful impulse towards entering upon the furrowing process,—an impulse which is indispensable under favourable circumstances for ova, under all circumstances for germ-cells. The transmission of qualities also on the father's side, on the other hand, proves that the union of procreative materials with the higher development of sexual generation certainly acquires a still profounder significance, in that through the mingling of the matter of generation there is produced a real blending of the parental qualities. The copulation of certain zoospores naturally occurs to the mind as prototype of this process, in which nothing but the united force of two cells appears to be decisive as long as no difference of the combining elements is to be made out, either in their own nature or in their origin.

According to the foregoing, we can see nothing further in the formation of new organisms through a female animal, whether with or without the aid of a male organism, than an organic formation, which is distinguished from other organic formation, *e.g.*, the fresh development of certain previously non-existent organs at certain periods of life, not in the essence of the process, but only by the end which the newly formed object subserves, in that this end lies in all other organic formation (with the exception of the lacteal secretion in mammals) *within*, and only in generation *without*, the forming individual. If, now, the new formation, no matter from what beginnings, has attained a degree which renders it capable of existence as an independent organism, there follows the liberation from the maternal organism, an act to which we can hardly be inclined to ascribe any psychical importance, which goes beyond the reflectorial-instinctive accommodation to the changed life-conditions (*e.g.*, in mammals, occurrence of respiration).

Thus it is also empirically confirmed that the organism of the embryo, of the fœtus, and of the child, just as much as any other part of a finished organism, has at every stage and every moment of its life *precisely as much soul* as it needs for its own bodily preservation and continued development, and as its organs of consciousness are able to grasp. That, however, the Unconscious *lays hold of life wherever it can*, and that in this respect, too, quite apart from its connection with the maternal organism, the animation of the new germ relatively to its capability of animation is only the special case of a universal natural phenomenon, will become still more evident from a few examples.

In Autenrieth's "Views of the Life of Nature and of the Soul," we find on pp. 265–266 the following notes: "Thus also Lister (Kirby and Spence, 'Introduction to Entomology'), Bonnet and Stickney, saw caterpillars and pupæ of butterflies, and larvæ of the *Tipula oleracea* freeze into lumps of ice, and on being thawed revive.—According to the more exact observations of Spallanzani ("Opuscoli di Fisica Animale e Vegetabile," Modena, vol. ii. p. 236), the tiny rotifers, *Furcularia rediviva Lamarck*, which are found in boggy water and in the sand from gutters, if they are not exposed to the open air, but covered in a little sand-heap, and left to dry along with it, after the lapse of three or even four years (during which time the dried sand has been preserved in a glass or a chip-box), sometimes revive as soon as the dry sand is moistened afresh with water, except that the longer they are kept in the dried state, the smaller is the number which again become living and perform all the ordinary life-functions. They revived, however, although by the process of drying they had become so indurated (and they usually possess merely a gelatinous body), that, if one pricked them with the point of a needle, the body burst like a particle of salt into several pieces. Thus these animalcules may be alternately dried and rendered lifeless eleven times, and yet when mollified in water again return to life. They also do not lose their capability of becoming reanimated if they *freeze* along with the water, and then are exposed even to a cold of 19° R. below freezing-point; just as in their dried-up state they may be exposed even to 54° above freezing-point without losing the capability of reviving by the aid of water, whilst, if they are in the living condition, they perish utterly in warm water of even 26°."

Ibid., p. 20:—"John Franklin ('First Voyage to the Shores of the Polar Sea'), in the winter of 1820–1821, on his first voyage to the North American coasts of the Arctic Ocean, saw fishes freeze immediately on emerging from the water, and become so solid an icy mass that they could be cloven by the axe into pieces—even their viscera presenting a mere solid frozen lump. Nevertheless, some of these fishes when warmed at the fire, without previous injury, recovered their vitality. A carp, notwithstanding that it had been for six-and-thirty hours completely frozen, recovered so completely that it was able to throw itself about with considerable energy."

When Ellis ("Voyage to Hudson's Bay") was wintering on the River Nelson at Hudson's Bay, a perfectly frozen lump of black autumn-flies was found; on being brought near the fire they revived. He reported that frogs are often found there on the shores of the lakes as firmly frozen as the ice itself, which yet, thawed by a moderate temperature, recovered to such a degree that they crept from one place to another.

Thoroughly frozen trees, too, can, after being slowly thawed, revive and put forth fresh leaves.[1]

Hunter found, however, from his experiments, that when a fish perished *rather slowly* in the intense cold, and then was frozen, it became incapable of being recalled to life by thawing, on which account the attempt is unsuccessful to freeze an entirely warm-blooded animal and to try to revive it by thawing; and we must renounce the hope of ever again beholding in life, even under favourable circumstances, say an elephant or rhinoceros of the primeval world, preserved quite whole in the polar ice, as one has found toads in rocks in which they must have been enclosed for centuries, perhaps thousands of years, and which when liberated hopped about quite briskly.

When modern authorities declare the reanimation of frozen warm-blooded animals to be impossible on account of a decomposition of the blood induced by the frost, they are met by the most recent investigations of Schenk, according to which a temperature of $-3°$, sometimes even a briefer refrigeration to $-7°$, is borne quite well by blood corpuscles, salivary corpuscles, spermatozoa, and even by

---

[1] *Helleborus niger* and *Bellis perennis* freeze on the occurrence of cold in all stages of florescence, and continue to grow after being thawed, a circumstance which occurs more than once in winters of variable temperature. Göppert saw expanded flowers for weeks in this state. Of course there is for each species of plant, even for those which bear cold best, a definite limit, the overstepping of which occasions death. According to Cohn's direct microscopical observations, e.g., cells of *Nitella synearpa* perish on being cooled below $-3°$ C., whilst the protoplasmic contents of the primordial sac are disorganised by the freezing of the water. Other plants, on the contrary, die even some degrees above freezing-point.

fertilised ova, notwithstanding their more advanced state of life, motion, and development. (Pox lymph, even after prolonged cooling to $-78°$, loses none of its force.) If the proceedings on the questions appertaining to this subject are not yet closed, yet the instances quoted are in general sufficient to render plausible the *a priori* belief that every trace of life can disappear from an organism, and that notwithstanding the *ability* to begin a new life-career, under favourable circumstances, can remain intact, if only none of those changes have taken place in the same which render anatomically or physiologically impossible the resumption of the life-functions after the restoration of the normal circumstances. For this it is necessary that both during the lifeless condition (induced by dying or freezing, or by hermetically sealing), as well as in the passage from the normally vital to the lifeless condition (*e.g.*, through the *rapidity* of the freezing), a chemical or histological change detrimental to future vital activity be prevented. On the other hand, such changes are indifferent as regards resuscitation which only destroy the normal character of the future vital functions, and cause the organism to awake to a merely pathological life, which is, however, soon again extinguished of itself.

In Rotifers one might assume that the drying up never goes so far as to allow of any interchange of matter, so that, strictly speaking, one would not have to do with an absolute stoppage of the vital functions, but with their reduction to a minimum (as in winter sleep). But even this assumption fails when it is a question of frozen bodies, as hard as stone, in the winter cold of the polar regions, or of toads which have been enclosed in rocks for centuries, or even still longer. For the latter, a minimum of exchange of matter, which one may conceive to be brought about by the water percolating the rock, must have sufficed in the enormous stretch of time for the animal's consumption. In the case of frozen organisms, however, only a slight superficial evaporation can have taken place. Vital function, however, is rendered impossible both by the absence of the most general physical conditions of the organic change of matter, endosmosis, as also by the indispensableness of a fluid state for every chemical reaction.

Now, if it be granted that in the utterly frozen body every organic function, *i.e.*, all vital activity, is impossible, the body is deprived of every trace of life, *i.e.*, it is *absolutely lifeless;* its condition is then *specifically and totally different* from all states of depressed vital function, like sleep, hibernation, swoon, tetanus, apparent death; the body in this condition bears the same relation to life as an inorganic body.

It is of course intrinsically unimportant whether one applies the epithet *dead* to the body, for that concerns only the definition of the notion dead. If one absolutely identifies *lifeless* and *dead*, as is natural, one will do so; if one, however, makes a distinction between the two conceptions, and calls only that lifeless object which cannot become again living dead, one will not do so. The latter view could, however, result only from the prejudice that what is dead cannot again become alive,—a proposition, of course, not to be proved *a priori*, but only to be induced from experience, and which for a long time might pass for true. But now, when facts come to light showing that something dead can under certain circumstances become alive again, one should rather recognise the exception to the induction hitherto assumed as a universally valid axiom, than arbitrarily restrict the conception "dead" for the sake of the old prejudice. This remark would certainly be idle, if that prejudiced limitation of the concept *dead* did not also entail the further prejudice, that the absolutely lifeless need not also be void of soul, which one would rather have thought self-evident; for the soul of a body is indeed only the sum of the functions or *activities of the Unconscious* referring to it, which for the sake of brevity are called *its* vital functions.

From the circumstance that an organism, so long as it

is frozen, possesses neither life nor soul, it follows that if after a certain time life and soul return to it, this soul can no longer be regarded as *one and the same* with that inherent in it before the passing into the frozen state, since for the sameness of two temporally divided souls the temporal *continuity* of the activities of the former with the activities of the latter is requisite; but by no means can the sameness of the *organism* in question and the *similar nature* of the souls depending upon it be deemed sufficient. If, to speak with the vulgar, on the cessation of life the old soul has gone away, with the reappearance of life *another* soul might just as well as the former one have taken up its abode in the organism. The absurdity of this way of regarding the subject is, however, immediately evident, if one reflects that the Unconscious is all in all, and remembers that old and new soul are activities of the same essence of the All-One directed to the same organism that sends life again immediately into the organisms, so far as is *possible*, according to the laws of matter.

One sees from these examples that it makes no difference to Nature whether, as ordinarily, the vital organisms enjoy a continuity of their vital functions, or whether a body hitherto incapable of life becomes at this moment vital; *as the possibility* of life is given, the Unconscious *animates* it, in that it directs upon it the psychical functions adapted to its constitution. If we then assume the case, that the germ of a young organism, which we commonly have seen arise as an integral element in the life-course of the maternal organism, that such a germ, liberated from all dependence on an already existing life, suddenly begins to be, it must just as infallibly as the thawed fish or the mollified rotifer in the first moment of its organic *capacity* for life be animated by the Unconscious, and such a phenomenon should now no longer be regarded as an isolated exception.

To this view I refer any one who should assert that the unfertilised ovum is not yet animated, and only receives its soul at the moment of fertilisation, which, indeed, in lower animals, for the most part, takes place outside the maternal organism; although this conception not only runs counter to our view of the animation of *every cell*, but also fails to explain the evolution of the *germ-cell* without fertilisation. But at any rate our doctrine finds a sufficient application in the instance of spontaneous generation, or the arising of organic beings from inorganic matter without a maternal organism. Such an original generation *must have taken place*, for geology shows that the earth has gradually cooled down from a molten mass to our present temperature; but now, as no organisms can exist at a temperature higher than that required for the coagulation of albumen, the earth must, for the longest part of its existence, have been uninhabited; and as it is now actually peopled by organisms, there must of necessity have been a point of time when the first being or beings came into existence,[1] whereas before this time there only existed inorganic matter. Here the conception of spontaneous generation is satisfied.

I do not say that at that point of time no organic, but only that no *organised* matter was in existence; on the contrary, I believe we must assume that, under the influence of a humid atmosphere, very rich in carbonic acid, of greater heat, of light, and strong electrical influences, even by the inorganic path highly complex combinations of carbon, hydrogen, oxygen, and nitrogen were formed, which the chemists of to-day, on account of their especial occurrence in organic beings, have designated by the improper name of organic substances.

Very recent chemical investigations have succeeded in refuting the earlier assumption, that organic substances could not be obtained by an inorganic path, by facts so

[1] When Thomson (speech at the British Association for the Advancement of Science at Edinburgh, 1871) suggests a transferring to our earth of germs elsewhere developed by means of meteoric stones, he has to meet the difficulty that such germs must always be destroyed by the heat produced in cleaving the atmosphere before reaching the earth's surface, if they had not been previously killed by cold in the mundane space.

striking, that it now only seems a question of time when man shall obtain complete mastery over the province of organic chemistry likewise. Synthetic chemistry is already in the organic department on a level with analytic chemistry. A number of the most talented investigators (*e.g.*, Berthelot) devote their energies to it, and well-nigh every month it has new and striking triumphs to report. The problem of producing the acids, aldehydes, and alcohols belonging to the so-called fat series from inorganic elements is to be regarded as solved in principle, and the discoveries in the so-called aromatic series (to which most liquid combustibles, organic colouring matters, essences, and perfumes belong) take place with such rapidity and with such certainty, that we now hardly need to ascertain more than the organic-chemical constitution of such bodies in order to be sure of their synthesis in advance. But the keen eye of the chemist gazes still farther; the resinous and saccharine substances are beginning to reveal their true nature, and to awaken unbounded hopes for the future of organic synthesis.

If thus the boundary-line between inorganic and organic *matter* has long fallen away, that between inorganic and organic *form* begins more and more to waver. Undoubtedly the compound organic types exhibit forms for which (with the exception of the radiated type) no analogy is found in inorganic nature; but we must not forget that life dwells also even in the great kingdom of unicellular organisms, and the cell finds, in fact, its analogue in inorganic nature. In the first place, most fluids possess at their surface a considerably greater density and tenacity than in their interior, a difference which appears nowhere more plainly than in albumen and its solutions. If in every drop an analogy here presents itself with the often infinitely delicate cellular membrane, the resemblance becomes a surprising morphological identity with starch-granules in the microscopic corpuscles of carbonate of lime, which Famintzin precipitated by bringing together saturated solutions of chloride of calcium and carbonate of lime. Here is exhibited the same nucleus, the same stratification, the same concrescence of several granules, the same augmented capacity of resistance of the internal layer to acetic acid as in the starch granules. It follows from this, in the first place, that starch granules are not *living* cells, but lifeless secretions of other living elements, a magazine of material destined for future reconsumption. But it also follows that the *cell-form*, with nucleus and membrane, of itself proves nothing at all with respect to the existence of organic *life*, not even when it has organic matter for its contents, but that for life something *quite other* is required than organic matter and organic form, something *ideal*, which manifests itself in the preservation and *elaboration* of the form *by the interchange of matter*, whilst every conservation of the form by passive conservation of the matter is related to life as a mummy, which at the most deludes the naked eye with the *semblance* of life.

I said, therefore, it is probable that before the coming into existence of the simplest organisms, so-called organic combinations of a lower stage were already in existence, which rendered the building up of an organism from them essentially easier, as water, carbonic acid, and ammonia, by which complete organisms are nourished. For the formation of the primitive germ these organic substances would then have, at least, played the part of *manure*, which now arises from the process of decomposition of organisms. The probability that these first organisms lived in water is generally recognised; that they must have been very simple beings, simple cells standing at the indifference-point between plant and animal, has been already shown in Sect. C. Chap. iv. Now, however the process itself may be conceived in detail, this must be firmly held, that the Unconscious *apprehended* and realised the *first* possibility of organic life that occurred. When previously, in discussing sexual generation, we conceived the "moment" of the animation of the germ, as if the Unconscious approaches a *formed* germ in order to animate it, this was only admissible because, in harmony with the traditional mode of apprehension, we tacitly supposed the unconscious-psychical activities requisite *for the formation* of the germ to proceed from the parental organisms; but now, as such a distinction has no place from the point of view of the All and Only Unconscious, we must call to mind that the *animation* of the germ does not follow, but *precedes* the *origin* of the germ, *i.e.*, that the germ can only come into existence by the Unconscious causing a special activity to effect its origination, which *predestines* its typical form in accordance with the possibilities given by the existing conditions, precisely as in the plastic energy of the *vis medicatrix* the typical form of the leg growing again on the salamander is predestined by the activity of the Unconscious. Here, as there, no inorganic laws of Nature are contradicted, none assumed to be inactive even for a moment, but they are only employed for a higher purpose; something is formed which could not have come to pass solely by the co-operation of the laws of inorganic Nature, and which only becomes possible through the will of the Unconscious stepping in and inducing a state of affairs in which now, by the normal action of the inorganic laws of Nature, a new form capable of new performances is fashioned.

As the Unconscious hourly seeks to realise and to retain life in millions of germs, which indeed are soon again, often even at their origin, dashed to pieces, owing to unfavourable circumstances, through the pitiless necessity of inorganic laws, so when first life seethed on the earth's surface millions of primitive germs may have been nipped in the bud before life succeeded in taking firm footing, as it were, on the earth. But when once it had succeeded in producing one or a few organisms, the Unconscious had freer play from this conquered basis of operations; it could now secure the aid of *parental procreation*, and by its help maintain and extend the conquered ground with proportionately less effort. For it is manifestly very much easier to draw together the organic substances diffused and distributed in the water about an existing organism than around an ideal point; it is very much more easy to effect the requisite chemical transformations and modifications by assimilation aided by the contact action of a given organism than without such; and it is very much easier to produce the typical form of the cell, with its ever-richer inner articulation, through the simple artifice of cell-division with the help of furrowing, than from amorphous matter.

It needs, then, at all events, an infinitely far less effort [1] of the will, to form organisms by the aid of those already existent, than *without* the same, just as in the case of a higher animal it needs a far less effort to act on tissue with the help of nerves than without. We may then

[1] It might appear to superficial observation as if the resistance which the Unconscious finds in inorganic matter to its organising activity were an instance against the all-unity of the Unconscious. This is, however, by no means the case. We have seen above that the strife and struggle of the individualised natural forces or formations of the Unconscious is a necessary condition for the coming to pass of the objective phenomenal world and for the origin of consciousness in particular (comp. pp. 227, 228); here occurs only a special case of this general truth. As little as an organisation could proceed from mere inorganic matter without an organising principle, so little could the organising principle realise itself in organisms, if it did not find matter pre-existent. The Unconscious must, therefore, previously create a matter in order to be able to create organisms, the substrata of consciousness, and, moreover, a matter subjected to exceptionless laws, because only in such is the setting up of accessory mechanisms possible, which always perform the same tasks. That, however, such a matter, comporting itself according to its own laws, which of itself does not tend to the formation of organisms, opposes a certain resistance to the activity of the Unconscious, which constrains it to the formation of organisms, is self-evident, and it is no wonder that this resistance, varying in amount according to the accidental configuration of the natural forces active at any spot, can under certain circumstances assume such proportions that the Unconscious, interested only in the universal, not in the single case, forbears to master the difficulties that present themselves, since it more easily attains by another path, or attains indeed at other places, often enough for the purposes of the whole process, the same end. (This explains, *e.g.*, abortions in consequence of material disturbances of embryonic development.)—According to these observations, the expression "effort," if one only keeps aloof from every anthropopathic suggestion, need no longer appear unsuitable for the designation of the degree of the intensity of the will, the application of which is requisite in behalf of the organisation for the overcoming of occasional material resistance.

assume that the same application of force or will, whereby a cell comes to be by means of spontaneous generation, is sufficient to form many *millions* of cells by cell-division.

But now we have found that Nature altogether is bent upon attaining her ends with the least possible application of force; that she everywhere prefers the setting up of mechanical contrivances for utilizing the inorganic molecular forces actually present to direct intervention; at any rate, however, she tries to limit these interpositions, since in the last resort they are not quite to be done away with, to a minimum of expended force.

Thus we saw (Sect. A. Chap. i. a) that the nervous system of animals is nothing else than such a force-saving machine, which by means of the slight triggers and levers of the brain overcomes hundredweights attached to the limbs. We saw (Sect. A. Chap. iii. v. vi. viii. and C. iv.) a number of contrivances in animals and plants so arranged that the facilitation of stimuli by these provisions, or even their purely mechanical mode of action, rendered special instincts superfluous. Conversely we saw instincts employed to render needless extensive efforts in organic formation, *e.g.* (B. Chap. ii. and v.), the instinct of sexual selection to achieve an improvement of the race in respect of beauty and otherwise; the next chapter will furnish us with more examples of a like kind, which prove with what delicacy the Unconscious everywhere endeavours to attain its ends in the most mechanical, *i.e.*, least troublesome manner.

From this point of view now likewise sexual generation appears as a *mechanism* replacing spontaneous generation by an immense saving of energy.

As a rational man does not ride across country when there is at hand a turnpike road, neither does the Unconscious after establishing a nervous system in an animal still effect muscular contraction by direct action of the will on the muscular fibres, nor continue to make use of spontaneous generation when sexual generation is open to it.

This law derived from the nature of spontaneous generation has very recently attained its complete empirical confirmation, in that the microscope has uniformly revealed, where one had formerly supposed spontaneous generation, sexual generation, and at the present day *no single case* of actual spontaneous generation has been observed, notwithstanding that the microscope has very carefully swept the province of minute life in all directions.

I do not at all dispute that the possibility is at any moment open of establishing spontaneous generation at the present time ; I even concede that the negative proof, that now there *can* be no spontaneous generation, must always remain for experientialism an *impossibility;* but nevertheless we may well assume that an assertion, in which theory and empirical observation *agree*, has a considerable probability in its favour.

For the reader not conversant with the interesting facts relating to this subject I add a short notice of the same.

Aristotle believed that most of the lower animals arose by spontaneous generation. A few centuries ago spontaneous generation was assumed for intestinal worms and infusoria, although for a long time voices were heard suggesting the possible overlooking of parental germs. First the modes of immigration and different states of the intestinal worms were scientifically established; then it was shown that infusions boiled *for more than five hours*, which came in contact only with heated air, gave rise to no organisms. The advocates of spontaneous generation, however, justly replied that the heating of the air must also destroy the capability of the production of organisms.

Schröder and Dusch first showed that a plug of cotton twenty inches in length filtrates the air in such a way that it allows no organisms to arise.—Pasteur examined the germs floating in the air by catching them in gun-cotton and dissolving the latter in ether and alcohol.

He found the same to answer in all respects to the otherwise familiar germs of the lowest animals. He also positively proved, that they are the cause of the development of organisms in the infusions, by introducing along with the heated air a small plug of cotton containing germs, and the organisms always appeared, as if the air had had free access. Pasteur even compared by an ingenious method the relative quantities of the germs contained in the air at different localities. Recently Crace-Calvert ascertained by his exact investigations that temperatures of 100° C. do not essentially affect the minute organisms in question;[1] that at 149° C. only those which develop in solution of gelatine become incapable of germination, but that for the destruction of the germinal power of the organisms which develop in the other experimental solutions a temperature of 204° C. is requisite. Accordingly the assumption of a spontaneous generation in infusions has been scientifically set at rest once for all.

I will mention one more case, the origination of *Monas amyli*. A swarm of unicellular infusoria was seen to arise in starch granules, and it was thought that spontaneous generation was being witnessed. But when the history of these creatures was traced farther, one saw them become liberated on the final disruption of the starch granule, each seek a fresh starch granule and completely cover it, expanding after the fashion of the Amœbæ. This thin little skin on the surface of the grain, the animal, which had swallowed the corn, as it were, and now slowly digested it in layers, had previously escaped observation. Now, of course, the origin of the brood was recognised as endogenous increase.

The law of reproduction is so universal in Nature, that not only no case of the parentless origin of an animal or a plant is known to us, but even *not a case of the parentless origin of a cell in an existing organism*.

---

[1] Those capable of resisting higher temperatures are, according to Ferd. Cohn, the germs of Penicillium, whilst according to the same investigator the germs of Bacterium are killed already at 80° C.

If spontaneous generation could occur anywhere, one would certainly expect to find it in a spontaneous arising of cells in the juices of an existing organism, where both the temperature and the chemical composition of organic matter affords the most favourable suppositions conceivable; but in vain. *Even within the organism cell only arises from cell.*

All sober-minded naturalists allow that, from the negative results of the most careful investigations with our present perfect instruments, there results a high probability for the supposition that spontaneous generation does not take place at the present day. From the probability of this assumption one must however regressively conclude that the spontaneous generation even of the simplest Protozoa must be none so easy and simple an affair, and that for the re-establishment of the same quite other conditions are required than a mere mechanical individuation of existing protein substances. Were it not so, the spontaneous generation of Protozoa from protein-containing fluids must be observable under the microscope with the proper temperature, illumination, ozone-containing air, &c.; but even supposing a case of successful experiment, it would still never appear credible that such a Moner, which always belongs to a well-defined species in virtue of its mode of nutrition and propagation, could arise and functionally persist by the mere play of inorganic atomic forces (comp. also pp. 212, 213 and 291–293), without psychical influences from the Unconscious ideally regulating the mode of this activity.

X.

THE ASCENDING EVOLUTION OF ORGANIC LIFE ON THE EARTH.

We have in the last chapter shown the probability of the assertion that the Unconscious expended its energy in spontaneous generation only as long as was necessary, *i.e.*, until reproduction could be substituted for it. From the same first principle of Nature of the greatest possible saving of energy directly follows also the other proposition, presupposed as self-evident in the preceding considerations, that spontaneous generation, *i.e.*, a direct production from unorganised matter, can only have reference to the very simplest forms of organic life; that, on the contrary, for the genesis of higher life-forms the Unconscious will by no means choose the course of direct production, so difficult for the simplest beings, but a mode of origination effected by gradual stages. Not that I would maintain the *absolute* impossibility of the direct original creation of a higher animal; on the contrary, I have always maintained the Will can do what it will, if it only wills with sufficient intensity to overcome the opposing acts of will. Not that I would deny the theoretic possibility that even *within the range of the inorganic laws of Nature*, at certain moments of terrestrial development, the Unconscious could have set up a direct spontaneous generation of higher animals; to presume to decide the point were folly. Only this much I assert, that a direct spontaneous generation of higher organisms would have required an enormous application of force, an expenditure of energy which would have infinitely exceeded that requisite for the original creation of the simplest cell; that therefore the infallibly logical in the Unconscious, agreeably to the principle of the attainment of all ends with the least possible expenditure of energy, could not but prefer to the spontaneous generation of higher organisms a mode of production effected by many transitional stages, each of which, besides paving the way for higher beings, *served in addition other and independent ends*, and at the same time was attainable with a relatively trifling expenditure of force by means of a plastic principle of descent.

If we ask plainly, what would be needed for the spontaneous generation of a higher organism? the answer is: in the first instance, organic substances of not too low chemical composition in sufficient quantity and sufficient concentration. Where, however, are these more easily to be found than *in an already existing inferior organism?* In any case, therefore, the direct transformation of an already existing inferior organism into a higher one (*e.g.*, of a worm into a fish) would offer fewer difficulties than the spontaneous generation of the latter without the assistance of an existing organism. But here too the difficulties would always be still so great, that an enormous application of the energy of the Unconscious would be required to surmount them; for the already established forms and elaborated organs of the lower organism must for the most part be first *annihilated*, in order to give place to the corresponding forms and organs of the higher being. This not inconsiderable negative work, of previously annihilating what had been *created in the embryonic development* of the lower organism, is manifestly altogether avoided if the metamorphosis begins at stages of development so early that these specific forms and organs of the lower stage are never brought to perfection, but in lieu thereof at once those of the higher grade. Strictly then one can only speak in an *ideal* sense of a metamorphosis, for only the ideal type, which proceeded according to the ordinary course of development from the germ of the lower organism, has yielded to the realisation of a different ideal type, but in reality no transformation, but only an embryonic development has taken place. Even Agassiz, a leading upholder of the distinct creation of species, admits that this creation could only have taken place in the form of *ova*, and that for the development of these asexually created ova there must at the same time have been created similar conditions to those under which the sexually produced ova now develop, which indeed comes to this, that *foster parents*, of course from *other* species, must have been provided for the ova needing parental care.

But now I ask, which conception is the more monstrous, this, that an individual of a higher species is evolved from the ovum of a lower species, or this, that the ovum of the higher species was made at a stroke by spontaneous generation, an ovum, indeed, from which absolutely nothing but this higher species could proceed, and in which consequently all the characters of the higher species were already implicitly contained? It is, moreover, to be remarked that the ova of the highest and those of the lowest animals are morphologically and chemically so similar, and the first stages of development—of embryonic development—are so uniform, that they are not at all or scarcely, and even then for the most part only by accidental signs, to be distinguished. It is of no avail to rely on this, that usually all the characters of the genus are actually implicitly contained in the fertilised ovum of a species. However correct this (for the rest indemonstrable) view may be, yet an ovum must always have already passed through a number of stages of development before it can possess independent existence, and the young be hatched by the action of solar heat, or the animal heat of the foster parents, or the temperature of the earth for the time being, not to mention that the ova of the animals which bring forth living young never attain this independence. Where now shall this development of the ovum before self-dependence have taken place; whence is it supposed to have got its stock of albumen, unless from a female animal; whence came the first focus for the primitive yolk-sac, unless it lay in an ovary? Albumen is in truth not so common in inorganic nature that the spontaneous generation of a yolk-sac were something easy. At all events, it would have cost the Unconscious infinitely more difficulty to produce by spontaneous generation such an egg, possessed of all the characters of the higher species to be newly created, than either to evolve an individual of the new higher species from an ovum containing the characters of another inferior kind, by obliterating these characters always merely foreshadowed in the germ, and adding new ones, or however to develop the ovum containing entire the characters of the new higher species in the ovary of an individual of a lower species, or, lastly, to make use of *both expedients at the same time*, i.e., to develop an ovum particularly favourably constituted in view of the new species, *both* in the ovary of the inferior individual, as well as *after* quitting the same with the modifications necessary for attaining the higher species. Where is the natural origin of the individual unless in the ovum? Where is the natural origin of the ovum unless in the ovary of a female animal? How inconsiderable appear the difficulties, which the Unconscious has to overcome in the evolution of a higher organism from the womb of a lower, to the colossal difficulties which would oppose it in the original creation of the higher organism. When we have thus only a choice between these two assumptions, we shall unhesitatingly decide for the former, that the higher species proceeds by reproduction from the lower, but by a reproduction with modified development of the ovum, as Kölliker (Siebold and Kölliker, Zeitschrift für wissenschaftl. Zoolog. and Medic., 1865, Heft 3), who adopts this point of view, calls it, "*heterogeneous generation.*"

We have hereby gained a fixed support for the intermediate stages presupposed from the very first for the production of higher animals; it is a scale of ever higher and higher species by which the organising Unconscious realises the highest organisms. Certain, however, as is this general result, no less certain, however, is it that we cannot stop there.

Although we have proved in Sect. A. Chap. viii. that the Unconscious is active at every moment of organic formation at every part of the organism, and makes its influence felt quite specially in the relatively impetuous embryonic development, yet, on the other hand, it is not to be denied that, as everywhere where it is possible, so also for the evolution of the ovum the Unconscious has, as far as possible, facilitated its intervention and reduced the material actions to a minimum by previously established mechanisms. Accordingly, in all probability, there exists in the male and female reproductive materials an energy intentionally implanted by it itself at earlier stages, which enables these substances to develop under the requisite psychical guidance *more easily* in the direction predesignated in the parental organism than in any other. Now since the Unconscious always follows the line of development previously indicated, as the direction corresponding in general to its predetermined ends, and offering the least resistance to realisation, if it has no particular reason for deviation for a particular purpose; and since such a reason is wanting in ordinary generation, *where the sole end is the preservation of the species*, it usually takes, in the psychical guidance of embryonic development, the course indicated as the easiest by the qualities previously imparted by itself to the materials of generation, *i.e., the begotten resembles the begetters*, and this phenomenon is called the "transmission or inheritance of qualities."

From such a universal teleological rule the Unconscious is the less inclined to deviate the more general is its scope, *e.g.*, from the inorganic laws of Nature not at all. Since now the difficulties are already sufficiently great, which arise through the transcending of old species and the adding on of new characters, the Unconscious will seek to withdraw itself as far as possible from those difficulties, which it would have to overcome in the annihilation of such characters of the old species as could or should not be taken over into the new species, and will for this purpose seek to create the new higher species from *those* species in which *only* new characters are *to be added*, but the fewest possible or no extant positive characters are to be *destroyed, i.e.*, from *relatively imperfect* species, provided with few specific characters, affording much scope for further development, but not from species already highly developed, *strongly differentiated*, and endowed with many and definite characters.

This is fully confirmed by the palæontological history of the animal kingdom. Every important order of the animal kingdom resembles the branch of a huge tree, and at a particular geological period is developed from lowly beginnings into higher forms. It is not these latter, however, that resemble the extremities of the branch, whence, under the changed circumstances of a later geological period, a new animal order arises,—for they have by abundance of decided characters strayed, as it were, into a *cul de sac*,—but those imperfect primitive stocks of the order, that have maintained themselves in the struggle for existence with trouble and difficulty all through the earlier period against their far superior descendants, the shy offshoots of the branch, as it were, standing nearest to the trunk, from which, by addition of new and hitherto non-existing characters, the new order subsequently arises. This is a general law of Nature, the special application of which to the development of humanity has long been familiar to every student of history. If the races or stocks, which at a certain time represent the summit of the human evolution, have fallen into stagnation (or temporary depravity), there appear less developed virgin races or stocks, as it were on the theatre of history, to develop speedily to a height which decidedly exceeds the bloom of the previous most advanced races (pp. 11–13). It is the same in the development of the animal kingdom, only that the advance in organisation always going hand in hand with growing intelligence is there more obvious than in the case of man, who, with the exception of the increased development of brain, forms and fashions the organs of his growing culture into external instruments (instead of like the animal into bodily organs).—Defective as is our knowledge of the transitional stages, derived from the forms preserved in the existing fauna and the palæontological remains hitherto found, it yet perfectly suffices to sustain the above assertion.

After the Crustacea have attained their maximum development in the crabs, the Arachnida make their appearance with the very imperfect mites; after these have reached their limits in the spider, there follows in the insects a retrogression to the inferior lice. The highest forms of the Mollusca are the Sepiæ, of the Articulata the Hymenoptera; both are far more highly organised than the lowest known fishes, both possessed a form as perfect as that met with to-day, before the Vertebrata existed at all. But they were too one-sidedly and too completely differentiated for a class to spring from them requiring quite other fundamental structural conditions. Fishes rather developed from Ascidians, Worms, and Crustaceans. For reasons easy to understand, the oldest *fossil* fishes belong only to the transitional forms of the Crustacea, because the other two classes were too soft to leave fossil remains; on the other hand, the transitional forms of the latter have remained as two species down to the present day. The almost transparent little lancelot, two inches long, living on the coasts of the North Sea and Mediterranean, *Amphioxus lanceolatus Pall*, possesses no skull and no vertebral column, but only a simple massive cartilaginous cord as support of the nervous axis, no brain separated from the spinal cord, no heart no spleen, only a cœcum in lieu of a liver, no coloured blood, no proper fins, but merely a narrow membranous border expanded at the caudal extremity. Just as Linnæus had regarded another fish (*Myxine*) as a worm, so had Pallas taken the Amphioxus for a slug (*Limax*); but recent anatomical investigations have proved that it is constructed on the type of the Vertebrata, represents the lowest known stage of fishes, and altogether must pass for the *prototype* or primitive form *of the whole vertebrate kingdom*, as the immediate descendant of the oldest Vertebrata of the primæval world, whose relatives undoubtedly peopled the primitive seas in innumerable quantities. The Amphioxus is most related to the Ascidians (a kind of mollusc), in which not only in embryonic development[1] (as in certain lower worms) the peculiar formation of the so-called germinal membrane, hitherto regarded as characteristic of the vertebrate type, presents a similar appearance to that of Amphioxus, but which even at a certain stage of their development possess the cartilaginous groundwork of the vertebral column, although, to be sure, they afterwards lose it again.

Passing from the fishes to the Amphibia, a transition is again presented only in imperfect and lowly forms, whilst the two classes part company from one another the more they are developed in their characteristic one-sidedness. The scaly salamander living in the Amazon, or *Lepidosiren paradoxa Natt.*, is an animal three feet long with a fish-like form, with gills and a scaly covering, which altogether answers to that of the osseous fishes. Two fins on the head

[1] Embryology is now one of the most important aids and sources of inquiry for the theory of descent, since we may say generally that every animal in its embryonic development briefly repeats the stages of organisation of all its direct ancestors. Forms which do not lie in the direct line of descent, but only in side-lines, are never met with; but the development-series even of the direct ancestors, especially of the more remote ones, may be indicated in a form so abbreviated, nay, even proceed by such leaps, that the eye of the investigator only perceives the likeness to the remote ancestors, when he comprehends them by the light of the study of the embryology of intermediate stages of organisation (*e.g.*, Mammal and Ascidian through Amphioxus).

and two on the belly indicate the anterior and posterior limbs. Besides the gills, however, the animal has also a pair of lungs, which open by an air-passage into the œsophagus; accordingly an organisation such as never occurs in the true fishes, but, indeed, in the fish-like Saurians, *e.g.*, *Proteus*. Respiration and circulation accordingly assign the scaly salamander to the higher class of the Amphibia, whereas all the rest of the organisation is that of a fish. If we now consider the stage of development of the animal simply as vertebrate, it stands as low in the scale as possible. Its skeleton is only imperfectly ossified, the vertebral column consists of an undivided cartilaginous cord, to which the ossified vertebral arches are fitted. Similar to *Lepidosiren* is constructed the *Protopterus* living in Western Africa, which in the flooded marshes only needs gills, in the dried-up marshes, however, lungs. Huxley, fifteen years ago, found these marks sufficient to fix the derivation of the double-breathing scaly salamander from the circular-scaled cartilaginous fishes, a determination no longer doubtful since the discovery of an animal (*Ceratodus*) by Krefft in the river Burnett (Queensland), which is exactly intermediate between the cartilaginous fishes and scaly salamanders (figured and described in the "Ergänzungsbl.," vi. p. 227). It may accordingly be regarded as proved that the Amphibia (and along with these also the higher animals) spring from the *cartilaginous* fishes, and that the *osseous* fishes now mostly peopling the waters form a side-branch in the pedigree of the animal kingdom, in which they rank decidedly higher than the cartilaginous fishes.—These examples may suffice to verify and to illustrate our assertion.

These facts, which Darwin admits, cannot be explained by his assertion that the strict *constancy* of the transmission of qualities is in every case determined by the duration of their persistency, and that every species is the less inclined to deviate from its specific character the older it is. There lies in this assertion the truth that young species stand nearer to the original stock than older ones, which, unmindful of their origin, as it were, have become arrested in their limited idiosyncrasies, and that therefore young species of common descent show, even among one another, more affinity and capability of mixture than older ones. Such young species which give rise in crossing to hybrid races, are called *fluent* species, in contrast to the self-contained fixed species, in which each hybrid race again speedily perishes by reversion to the stock. Such fluent species are, *e.g.*, the species of dogs, finches, mice, whilst the races of man are in the stage of transition from fluid to fixed species; at that stage, indeed, when between the more remote forms of the series no permanent hybrid race is any longer to be obtained.—Decidedly *incorrect*, on the contrary, is the above assertion of Darwin, so far as he asserts that universally and uniformly the capability of varying decreases with the length of persistence; rather the artificial breeding of plants and animals has hitherto revealed no difference in the capacity for variation of old and young species. But suppose the assertion were correct, we should in consequence expect just the *contrary* of what it is said to explain; for as the more perfect and highly differentiated species are always of more recent existence, accordingly are *younger* than their less perfect stem forms, the latter, as the *older*, would be *less* adapted for commencing a new-development series, whereas the facts teach the contrary. We must therefore maintain that more perfect species do in fact vary just as easily and just as much as the more imperfect, if they are caused so to do by change of circumstances; only the former have not the tendency to be so easily converted *into higher orders* as the latter; and why this is not the case, and why this conversion into a new order only takes place when within the previous order the abundance of the more perfect forms is exhausted, can never be proved from the assumptions of the Darwinian theory.—

Having become acquainted in heterogeneous generation with the one expedient employed by the Unconscious to facilitate the formation of new species, let us observe its operation a little more closely. Hitherto we have not at all taken into consideration how far in heterogeneous generation the offspring may differ from the parents. It is, however, clear that the Unconscious, in the formation of higher species, will make no unnecessary leaps, but draw the boundaries as close as possible to one another. A *leap* there certainly always is, for otherwise *indefinitely numerous* generations must fill up the gap between one species and the next, which in the limited period of development of organisation on the earth is impossible. But at any rate, the actual step will *overleap* no species lying directly in the line of development, but at the most pass at once to the *next* higher species.

Here we approach the question *how far* a species may lie from the nearest related one, or how the notion of a species may exclude, on the one hand, differences that are greater than specific, on the other hand, those that are less than specific; or, in a word, the question with regard to the *definition of the term Species.* But now every unprejudiced naturalist admits that such limitations of the idea of species are not at all found in Nature, but that it passes by very fine degrees on the one side into the notion of the variety or of the race, and on the other hand into that of the family, or however one calls the nearest higher class; that accordingly, as in all quantitatively limited notions, it is a matter of subjective caprice and of mutual agreement how far one shall extend the notion of species; that, indeed, *on the whole* there is agreement as to those anatomical and outward marks which appertain to a difference of species, but that naturally at the boundaries differences of opinion will always remain as to the application of this notion. Some have thought to settle the dispute by setting up as a criterion of the specific difference of two animals the impossibility of begetting *fertile* offspring. But, in the first place, two animals are not necessarily very different because they can beget no fertile offspring, but they are unable to engender fertile offspring because they exceed a certain limit of difference, and this mark would accordingly not concern the *essential notion*, but only a *corollary* of the specific difference. Secondly, however, the limit of the generation of fertile offspring is just as *fluent* as the idea of a species, since only the *relative number* of procreative acts giving rise to fertile offspring becomes less, the more diverse are the animals; but no one can assert before the trial of *infinitely numerous* experiments that a procreation of fertile offspring is *impossible* between these two animals. Thirdly and lastly, this mark is, in fact, in not a few cases, in contradiction with the established use of the idea of species, for from animals universally recognised as specifically distinct fertile offspring have been obtained by crossing, *e.g.*, from horse and ass (in Spain), from sheep and goat, from goldfinch and siskin, from *Mathiola maderensis* and *incana*, from *Calceolaria plantaginea* and *integrifolia*, and many more; nay, even voluntary crossings, without the intervention of man, have been found to take place between wild or half-wild animals (between dog and she-wolf, fox and bitch, steinboc and goat, dog and jackal, &c.); and there are numerous mongrel breeds which yield fertile offspring indefinitely, *e.g.*, hybrids of hare and rabbit, of wolf and dog, goat and sheep, camel and dromedary, lama and alpaca, vicuna and alpaca, steinboc and goat, &c. On the other hand, the state of the case varies much with *races*. Some can, others will not at all intermingle; with others, again, fertility is actually very much limited in the course of generations. As little as the fertility of hybrids for species in general, so little can the incapability of yielding persistent hybrid races with other species be regarded as an absolute mark of *fixity* of species (in contrast to fluent). This contrast, too, is only to be limited quantitatively; for, in the first place, the question always is with *which* other species the hybridism is attempted; and, secondly, even in the now most fixed species, sometimes, if very rarely, surprising reversions to an ancestral form make their appearance (atavism).

Accordingly if we are compelled to maintain the fluent and conventional character of the idea of species, if we must grant that there is in nature only less and greater differences, but in such abundant gradations that from the least noticeable individual shade of difference to the extreme difference between the higher and the lower organisms there takes place a transition by small stages unnoticeable by us (comp. Wallace's "Contributions to Natural Selection"), then neither in the idea of Species nor in a similar narrower or wider notion can there exist a compulsion for the Unconscious, regulating the minimum interval of its steps in the progressive development of the organisation, but the *smallest* extent of the leaps of heterogeneous generation will still only have to be sought in the magnitude of the modifying resistances and the ends pursued by the Unconscious (*e.g.*, attainment of certain stages of organisation in certain *intervals of time*). But now, as we know, not *perfect similarity*, but only *general resemblance*, is found between parents and children, for the various material circumstances bring about in generation individual variations from the ideal normal type, which *perfectly* to level would require an altogether *useless* expenditure of force on the part of the Unconscious, since these individual variations usually and in the main are neutralised *of themselves* by the inter-mixture of families. Accordingly one has not to *wonder* at the unlikeness, but rather at the likeness of parents and child; for if the Unconscious should behave in all generation within the same species in the same way, and save itself the labour of a continually neutralising interposition, the differences between begetters and begotten which would arise through the diversity of the material circumstances would be still far greater than experience now shows us. Nevertheless, we see cases occur in which the Unconscious prefers to send monsters into the world to endeavouring to overcome the existing material difficulties.—The remaining individual differences are undoubtedly great enough to lead quickly to an essential alteration of the type, and the Unconscious need only hinder the neutralising of these differences by crossing in those cases in which the variations answer to its progressive plan, either by directly retaining them or by an external mechanism; thus, again, a large part of the expenditure of energy is in this manner saved.

That such origins of species by the summation of individual variations have actually occurred, numerous animal classes in our geological collections prove, when the collectors do not discard the inconvenient intermediate stages, which will not fit into any artificial division. "Numberless are the species of ammonites that have been described; annually new ones are added to the old, and whole cases are filled with books on ammonites. If we arrange them in a series, the differences between any two specimens are in fact so inconsiderable that everybody must undoubtedly regard them as individual peculiarities. In a dozen, however, the small differences amount to something considerable, and in two dozen the amount of the differences has become so large that no resemblance at all can any longer be observed between the first and the last. Here no specific difference any longer holds water, as soon as one has only specimens enough to illustrate the transitions" (Fraas, "Vor der Sündfluth," p. 269). Very much the same may be said of the Trilobites, and many other classes. One other quotation concerning snails. "At Steinheim (Würtemberg) there is a hill of tertiary date, which more than half consists of snow-white shells of *Valvata multiformis*. One end of this snail is extremely turreted, like a Paludina (twice as high as thick), the other has a quite flat umbilicus (discoid, its length one-fourth of its thickness). Even the most cautious savant, who employs all sorts of distinctions for establishing a species, stands puzzled before the Klosterberg of Steinheim, and must confess that all the million forms on which his foot treads pass so easily and imperceptibly into one another, that he can only speak of one species" (Fraas, p. 30). At the lower part of the hill lie the flattest, at the upper part the most turreted forms. In the thousands of years that this hill was in process of formation the species has in this manner changed. In the same calcareous sand of Steinheim one may quite distinctly trace in the superposed strata the gradual severance of one stem-form into diverging, subsequently sharply separated species (comp. Hilgendorf's Communication in the Monthly Report of the Berl. Acad. of Sc., July 1866).

If, therefore, we may look upon it as established that the Unconscious will frequently be able to employ for the production of a new species a sum of accidental individual variations, that by no means implies that these are always offered to the Unconscious in all those directions which it intends to adopt; there always remains the possibility, that just the most important advance of all can *not* be comprehended as accidental variations, but only as *systematically varying formative processes*. I think we must even assume that *all* the elevations to *essentially higher* stages, which presuppose the formation of organs not previously in existence, cannot be explained by accidental individual variations, although the latter may have performed the main work in the thorough *elaboration of an existing type* in all directions.

How can a change *simultaneously* occurring *at different parts of the body*, which exhibits a systematic correlation in its different parts, be sufficiently understood by *accidental* variations, *e.g.*, the formation of the udder in the first marsupial, which must necessarily go hand in hand with bearing alive if the young are not to perish miserably after birth, or the correlated change of the male and female sexual parts if copulation is to remain possible? Just as little can the principle of accidental variation be regarded as sufficient where certain animal forms exhibit peculiarities of anatomical structure, which, *valueless* for themselves, have a significance only as *intermediate transitional forms* for more highly developed stages, where accordingly one clearly sees the existence anticipated for the sake of the future purpose, *e.g.*, the first formation of a cartilaginous spinal cord in those primitive fish-forms, which by their exo-skeleton possessed perfect solidity like the Crustacea, whence they are derived, so that the primitive endo-skeleton had an importance not for themselves, but only for their later descendants, which converted the shell-cuirass into a scaly coat; or, *e.g.*, the brain of the lowest savages and primitive men, which is five-sixths as large as the brain of the most advanced races, whilst for the functions it subserves the brain of the anthropoid apes would quite well suffice, that only amounts to one-third of that of civilised man. Even Wallace literally says: "Natural selection could endow the savage only with a brain which surpasses slightly that of the ape, whilst he actually possesses one which stands a little below that of a philosopher." This circumstance, combined with the fact that hair is absent from the back of man; that hand and foot seem needlessly perfect organs for the savage, and that the human vocal organs, especially the soft palate, contain such wonderful, and, for the savage, useless latent capabilities, which only find application with higher civilisation, —all these circumstances cause Wallace to draw the conclusion "that a superior intelligence guided the development of man in a particular direction and to a definite end, precisely as man guides the evolution of many animal and vegetable forms."

The Darwinian theory has the merit of having pointed to the *summation of individual variations* in a particular direction, and the change of a type thereby rendered possible into that of another species, and of having proved the same by copious examples. It is very pardonable for a new and meritorious view when it *exaggerates its range* and thinks to explain *everything*, when in reality it explains only *some*, perhaps even most facts, and the more interesting is the above testimony of Darwin's rival Wallace, which openly confesses the insufficiency of this theory for the explanation of the origin of *Man*.—

Let us now consider what expedients the Unconscious employs in the cases to which its sole remaining task is limited—*to retain* the accidentally arisen individual variations, and *to prevent* their normal neutralisation and obliteration by *crossing*.

The sole expedient already familiar to us is the *instinct of individual selection* in the gratification of the sexual impulse. In Chap. v. B. we saw how beauty is increased and enhanced in the animal kingdom by this means; in Chap. ii. B. we perceived the value of the same for the improvement of the human race in every respect, and cast a side glance at the possibility of similar processes in the higher classes of the animal kingdom. If this aid is almost without significance in the lower classes of animals, it increases in importance with the progress of development, acts, however, certainly always more for the *fixing and improvement* of a species in itself *than for the passage into another*. Frequently, in place of the active selection of the male, occurs a passive selection of the female, in that the inflamed males, animated by a special *fighting instinct*, contend for the possession of the female, when of course the most powerful and most active carry off the victory.

Much more thoroughly operates for the change of a species another circumstance, the which to have made good is the most signal merit of the Darwinian theory—*natural selection in the struggle for existence.*

Every plant, every animal, has in two respects to carry on a struggle for existence: first, negatively to defend itself against the enemies threatening to destroy it, as, *e.g.*, the elements, and the robbers and parasites, who would prey upon it; and, secondly, positively to compete in acquiring or retaining what is necessary for the continuance of life, as food, air, light, soil, &c. The fleetest animals, those which know best how to conceal themselves, or least attract notice by their colour and form, will most easily be able to elude the persecutions of their enemies. Of animals and plants, those will least fall a sacrifice to the injuries of the weather, storm, frost, heat, wet, dryness, &c., which are most capable of resistance to these circumstances by their external or internal organisation. Of beasts of prey, only the most active, quickest, most powerful and craftiest will be able to escape hunger when there is dearth of food; of plants, those which maintain themselves most vigorously under like circumstances will become more luxuriant in growth than others, and, as regards the enjoyment of light, air, and rain, will attain so decided an advantage as to stifle those lagging behind. We see this struggle for existence most frequently entered upon between different species, and end with the perfect annihilation of one, *e.g.*, the domestic rat by the migratory rat. Less noticed but far more general is that among different individuals of the same species. The latter naturally causes an improvement of the species, for it is in all cases the feeblest individuals which are excluded by premature annihilation from the office of propagation, which is accordingly exercised by the cleverest and most powerful individuals for the longest period. Besides improvement, however, such a variation of the species can also take place that varieties and races, and finally new species, arise. This case can of course only occur if the external relations of life become *different;* then will natural selection favour in reproduction those individual characters which especially in the new circumstances show special vital force. The consequence will thus always be an accommodation to the external conditions of life. As now the Unconscious likewise wills this accommodation, so has it only to leave natural selection in the struggle for existence perfectly unchecked in order to see this end attained without trouble, without any special interposition.

Such changes of the outward conditions of life may take place in very different ways. In the first place, the plant or the animal may seek the same by wandering, and thus by local separation or formation of colonies protect the variety about to be formed from the threatened reversion to the ancient stock; secondly, their own homes may be sought out by strange plants and species of animals on their wanderings, and they may be compelled to test and strengthen their powers in contest with these; in the third place, by elevations or depressions the situation of the ground and height above the sea may be altered, mountains may become a table-land, plains mountain-ridges, sea-bottoms plains, coasts continents, severed lands be united, united lands be separated, &c.; in the fourth place, changes of climate, even apart from the already mentioned causes, may occur; and finally, in the fifth place, changes in the vegetable kingdom are altered conditions of life for the animal kingdom, and conversely. These relations offer a rich variety, and in most geographical districts such changes in the course of the geological development of the earth's surface have not taken place once but innumerable times.

If a plant migrates to a more uniformly moist soil, its leaves generally become less divided, more glabrous and grass-green, the flowers smaller and darker. Conversely, if a plant settles on a more porous and dry soil, its leaves become bluer, more procumbent, more divided or separated into fibres, the flowers larger and brighter, and it is enveloped in a thick hairy covering. Thus on a dry calcareous soil *Hutchinsia brevicaulis* passes into *H. alpina*, *Arabis cœrulea* into *bellidifolia*, *Alchemilla fissa* into *vulgaris*, *Betula pubescens* into *alba;* on a damp soil devoid of lime *Dianthus alpinus* is transformed into *deltoides* (according to A. Kerner in the Austr. Bot. Journal). In the animal kingdom, where the altered outward circumstances do not lie so close together as the different soils for the plant, owing to the present average constancy of the geographical and climatic relations, specific variation by natural selection has not yet been observed, but certainly formation of strongly marked varieties, especially under the unintentional influence of man, *e.g.*, origination of very different races of domestic animals (dogs, cattle, sheep, horses); and bearing in mind the above-mentioned facility of the transition from the race to the variety, it may justly be assumed that in former times, when not seldom a more rapid transformation of the external circumstances may have occurred than the human race has historically recorded, that in these earlier times many formations of new species may have come about by natural selection in the struggle for existence.—In opposition to this it is maintained that then the infinitely many intermediate forms through which one species passes into the other must be capable of demonstration in the strata, whilst yet the fossil species for the most part are just as sharply, and still more sharply, distinguishable from one another than the living. This proves nothing at all; for it lies in the nature of the case that that form must be the final form which is more capable of life than all the preceding phases, which therefore conquers, *i.e.*, eradicates, all these in the struggle for existence; but if they are soon thrust on one side by the final form, they have only had a brief existence as compared with the final form, which now, as the best adapted to the circumstances, persists at least as long as these circumstances; acordingly one cannot wonder if hitherto so few transitional forms have been found between different species. That none of these have ever been found is not true; on the contrary, both among higher, and quite specially among lower animals, an astonishing number of transitional forms are found.

In addition to the examples mentioned above (pp. 304–307) the following may be instanced. Passing from the radiate to the bilateral type, we are acquainted with two series. (1) Star-fish, sea-urchins, holothuriæ; in the latter, what was upper and under has become back and front, and as by the arrangement of the so-called ambulacra a new upper and under side has been formed, at the same time a right and left side has arisen. (2) Corals, Rugosa, slipper-shells; in the palæozoic Rugosa, the dividing walls of the calcareous shell answering to the septa of the bodily cavity are no longer arranged regularly as in the other corals, but at least in the interposed after-growth always at the side of a primary dividing-wall, so that in respect of the latter a bilateral type arises. When the Rugosa develop an operculum in addition, there arises the slipper-shell, hitherto reckoned to the Conchifera.

As the Australian and New Zealand fauna is in general to be regarded as an arrested representative of an older geological period, it has recently furnished us in the New Zealand bridge-lizard with an animal which, in certain characters (biconcave vertebral axis after the fashion of the Saurians, sexual apparatus without male organ), has remained at the stage of the fish-salamanders, but in other respects has developed into the external form of a lizard, which, in a remarkable manner, unites the normal characters of the tortoises (absence of teeth), crocodiles (immobility of the four legs), and snakes (movable rami of the lower jaw united by a ligament, and participation of the ribs in locomotion).

Huxley traces back the pedigree of the horse of the modern period step by step through the horses of older times, through Hipparion and Hipparitherium to Plagiolophus, which latter is already a species of the genus Palæotherium (the common ancestor of the hoof-horses and pachyderms), and in a similar manner the musk animals of the present day through the Cainotherium of the Miocene to Dichobune from the Eocene as primitive form. Gaudry has found in the Miocene strata of Pikermi in Greece "the group of the *Limocyonidæ*, which is intermediate between bears and wolves; the genus *Hyænictis*, which unites the hyenas with the civet cats; the

Ancylotherium, which is related both to the extinct mastodon and to the living pangolin or scaly ant-eater, and the Helladotherium, which unites the now isolated giraffe with the stag and the antelope" (Wallace).—A rich world of forms reveals itself to us in the contemplation of the genus Crocodile. The crocodiles of the cretaceous period are different from those of the older tertiary period, and these again are just as different from the crocodiles of the younger tertiary strata as from those of the present day. Nevertheless, the differences between one form of the series and another are so slight that they are only discernible by the eye of the connoisseur.—Reptiles and birds seem to be two of the most widely separated orders, and yet the Soolenhofen slates have, on the one hand, yielded a bird (*Archæopteryx*) which by its elongated form, unfused bones between the hands, and strong claws on the wing-fingers, far more closely approaches the reptiles than the ostrich-like birds of the present day; and, on the other hand, laid bare a reptile (*Compsognathus longipes*), that not only (as probably most Dinosauria did) went exclusively on its hind-legs, but also in the parts found is remarkably similar to the Archæopteryx. The footprints of reptiles and birds of that time, interconnected through all conceivable shades, lead us to expect that we shall yet find more remains of intermediate forms, which will bridge over the hitherto existing differences.

When one considers that almost every year brings to light new and surprising intermediate forms, and that already the old zoological classification has become absolutely untenable, the appeal of the opponents of Darwin to the want of intermediate forms may, in fact, be looked upon as a lost battle. One may at length regard it as an established fact that, if one traces backwards the pedigree of the now living kinds, not the species, but the genera have their corresponding representatives in former geological periods, and that these representatives of different genera and orders are distinguished in still remoter epochs only as now different species of a genus or order. Thus Owen in his "Palæontology" assures us "that he never let slip a good opportunity of communicating the results of observations, which prove the *more generalised* structures of extinct animals, compared with the *specialised* forms of more recent animals." (Comp., as supplement to this and the last chapter, Ernest Häckel's excellent popular work, "The Natural History of Creation.")

As the transition from water to land animals, so also that from water to land *plants* takes place through amphibious organisms. The anatomical structure of a stalk and leaf living in water must, to be capable of life, be at least as different from one living in the air as gills from lungs. Thus *Utricularia vulgaris* consists of two different organisms as it were, one of which is represented by the part of a plant living under water, the other by the branches bearing the blossoms rising into the air. In each of the three great divisions of the vegetable kingdom (Cryptogams, Monocotyledons, Dicotyledons) there are atmospheric plants (*e.g., Marsilia, Sagittaria, Polygonum*) which prove their origin from aquatic plants by the circumstance that when one puts them under water their young shoots send forth stalks and leaves with the anatomical structure of aquatic plants, which more aërial plants, that have, as it were, forgotten their more remote ancestors, do not do.

Although we have thus recognised natural selection in the struggle for existence as an important contributory to the origin of new species, yet I can by no means grant that with this principle the history of the origin of the organic world is at all exhausted. Not because this hypothesis would not be quite compatible with our presumptions concerning the essence of the Unconscious,—for if this at all facilitated matters, it would be quite natural for it to concern itself only with the individual, and leave the progress of species to go on quite mechanically by itself,—

but only, because the facts to be explained are far *more numerous* than the range of the principle of explanation, can I not deem the same sufficient.

In the present general interest in the Darwinian theory and the frequent over-estimate of its reach, it may reward us to spend a few moments in considering to what extent it appears to be insufficient (comp. also vol. i. pp. 287–289).

If we assume that by the struggle for existence alone organisation has developed from the primitive original cell to its present pitch, that thus every more highly developed species has only proceeded from the proximate lower one owing to its having possessed a higher degree of vitality, the consequence necessarily follows that *every* higher species on its own ground surpasses *every* lower species in vitality, and surpasses it indeed in a so much higher degree, the greater the interval of their stages of organisation, since indeed with every new advance in development a new accession of vitality results, and these increments mount up. This direct consequence is now, however, in complete contradiction with the facts of the case, which yield the result that *every stage of organisation*, taken as a whole, *possesses the same vitality*, and that only *within* the same stage of organisation *the different species or varieties* are distinguished by a greater or less vitality; which harmonises also with the circumstance that the struggle for existence in the competition for the conditions of life occurs *the more frequently, is the more embittered*, and the more certainly terminates in the complete *annihilation* of the one side, *the more related* are the competing species or varieties, whilst the species dwell beside one another *the more peacefully*, and *render more assistance* in the preservation of life, the farther they stand from one another in the pedigree of organisation. In *every* locality, if we disregard the difference of land and sea, *all* the stages of organisation are found represented, and all thrive excellently well beside one another; whereas, according to the Darwinian theory, taken strictly, *at every locality at least only one species*, and that the *highest*, must remain, because this surpasses all others in capacity of living under those circumstances. That is, however, just what is remarkable and grand in Nature, that every final type of a class is *so perfect in itself*, that one may indeed go beyond it, yet only by adding new anatomical-morphological structural details, but not by enhancement of the physiological functions or of its accommodation to the conditions of life, for both are *finished*. Had not really all stages of organisation on the average the *same* vitality, in the struggle for existence waged for millions of years all lower species must have long ago been completely superseded by the higher ones, whereas the fossil relics show that, under the most diverse circumstances, there have been relatively few classes of animals and plants which at the present time have not their perfectly life-capable representatives.

The capacity of accommodation of a class, and even of a species, *within its own limits*, is, in general, far greater than one thinks. This follows partly from the continued existence of not a few species from their origin to the present time, where, in truth, the environment has sufficiently changed, partly from the great *circles of distribution* of the classes and species of the present day. Several classes people the whole earth or all seas; many species have a distribution over twenty to thirty degrees of latitude. Lastly, it is proved by the *capacity of acclimatisation* of species, which often borders on the miraculous, if the instances only range over sufficient periods of time. Thus the common peach-tree, which is probably an Indian plant, would not thrive in Greece in the time of Aristotle, whereas we get good peaches at the present day in North Germany. Accordingly, the capacity of accommodation of species within their specific limits, partly by internal physiological changes that are withdrawn from observation, partly by the formation of varieties, is so great, that they are quite well able to adapt themselves to a very considerable alteration of the climate, &c., *without* degenerating. Extremely numerous are the examples in which closely related species dwell beside one another in a locality without noticeable change of their relative number, and yet the struggle for existence is most violent precisely within the specific limits between varieties and still slighter differences. Should, however, this struggle occur or be absent in a particular case, yet in no one of the cases here considered will a transgression of the limits of the species show itself. Lastly, there will not easily happen so great a change of external circumstances, nor a species pass under such different circumstances, that the capacity for accommodation and acclimatisation within the limits of the species recognised by us as so considerable would not suffice for these claims. But if subsequently a second change of the conditions essential to life occurs at the same place, it will mostly be a *return* to the formerly existing circumstances; then the species will simply adapt itself to this change by repeating the former stages in a reverse direction (as is observable in the before-mentioned experiments with transplantation of plants to different descriptions of soil), and there is again no occasion for the passage into a *new* or a more remote species. If, on the other hand, the second change of the conditions essential to life is in the same direction, the species will more easily become extinct at this place (*e.g.*, the fauna of the European glacial epoch), than pass into a new species, which is more remote from its stock than its previously attained standpoint.

How could the commencement of a new path of development, after an exhaustive working through of the last attained stage of organisation, and perhaps a pause of thousands of years, be intelligible from the struggle for existence? We have seen that it is precisely the more imperfect forms of the preceding stage from which proceeds the development of the higher stage. Apart from the already mentioned circumstance that these more imperfect forms of all the species of the lower stage remain *longest* unchanged, thus, according to Darwin's view, must be the most stable and the least capable of an individual variation and further advance; apart also from this, that, if *only* the struggle for existence had created the later forms of the lower stage, these primitive forms must have *all already changed for the same reason and by the same process* into more developed forms of *the same* grade, or indeed must long ago have been *annihilated* by the more capable forms in the immeasurable intervals; apart from all this, one would think that, if from some unknown cause these primitive forms that have maintained themselves had actually received an impulse to further development, that then through the struggle for existence always only a *repetition* of the development *lying far nearer* to them into the already existing higher forms of the *same* stage must have been called forth, rather than a transition to the morphologically diverging higher stage, since notoriously the higher forms of the lower stage show themselves *also* under the new circumstances mostly *just as capable of life* as the species of the higher stage. This consideration obtains the more weight the more geology attains to the knowledge, that the climates and vital conditions of earlier geological periods (with the exception of the first times after the cooling of the earth's surface) always far more closely resembled those of any localities whatsoever of the present surface than the older geology, dreaming of catastrophes and vast revolutions, assumed.—Most unintelligible on Darwinian presuppositions is the passage from the unicellular to the multicellular organisms, since it is just the incredible indifference of the unicellular plants to their environment, *i.e.*, their capacity of accommodating themselves even to the most varied circumstances by relatively slight modifications, that makes the want of a motive for the conversion into compound types so very conspicuous.

Lastly, if one asks positively of what kind are the

useful adaptations that arise through the struggle for existence, the answer is: They are *exclusively of a physiological* nature. Here lies the proper limit of the Darwinian principle clearly before our eyes; it is sufficient so long as it has to do with *the elaboration and transformation* of an existing organ for a *physiological* function *required by the circumstances;* it leaves us in the lurch when a *morphological* change is to be explained. That morphological changes are also possible by the addition of individual variations is not to be doubted, and Darwin proves it by many examples, especially by the skeleton of pigeons; but in all the cited cases an *artificial* breeding takes place. A couple of teeth, of vertebræ, or a toe more or less, a vertebra formed thus or thus, are for the struggle for existence perfectly *indifferent,* and yet these are the marks by which zoology *most surely* distinguishes species; the struggle for existence, on the contrary, can obviously only produce a change in such elements of the organism as have some importance for the same, and will so much more energetically work for their transformation the greater their significance for the struggle for existence. The struggle for existence brings it about that one and the same organ (in morphological reference) undertakes the most diverse physiological functions, whereas in species, placed under similar vital conditions but of different origin, often the same performance is carried on by organs morphologically quite different. (Thus, *e.g.,* the parasitic mites living on animal hairs have an organ for clinging to the hair, on which they roam; this is, however, represented in Listrophorus by the transformed lip, in Myobia by the more advanced pair of feet, in Mycoptes by the third, or also at the same time the fourth pair of feet.) With all these changes, however, the morphological fundamental type remains unaltered and untouched.

In the animal kingdom the thorough-going acknowledgment of the assertion that only the physiological but not the morphological changes are decisive for the degree of vitality, is encumbered with difficulties, because the occurrence of *sympathetic* changes frequently causes morphological changes to go also hand in hand with the physiological change of an organ, often at quite other parts of the body, which phenomenon, springing from special laws of organic plastic activity of the Unconscious, is altogether calculated to confuse the judgment. Our assertion, however, appears quite clearly justified in the vegetable kingdom. The competent judgment of Nägeli ("Origin and Conception of the Species of Natural History," Munich, 1865, p. 26) on this point runs: "The highest organisation manifests itself in two moments, in the most varied morphological articulation, and in the most thorough division of labour. Both moments usually concide in the animal kingdom, since the male organ also possesses the same function. In plants, however, they are independent of one another; the same function can be undertaken by quite different organs; even in closely allied plants the same organ can carry on all possible physiological functions. Now it is remarkable that the useful adaptations which Darwin instances as regards animals, and which one can discover in quantities for the vegetable kingdom, are exclusively of a physiological nature; that they always show the improvement and transformation of an organ for a particular function. A morphological modification in the vegetable kingdom which could be explained by the Darwinian theory is *unknown* to me, and I do not even see how it could take place, since *the general processes of formation are so indifferent as regards physiological performances*. The Darwinian theory requires the assumption, confessed by itself, that *indifferent characters* should be *variable;* the useful, on the contrary, *constant.* The purely *morphological* peculiarities of plants must accordingly most *easily*, the relations of organisation conditioned by a definite *function* with the greatest *difficulty* be capable of alteration. Experience shows the *contrary.* The relative positions and the co-ordination of the cells and organs are both in nature and under cultivation the most constant and persistent marks. In a plant that has opposite leaves and quaternary corollas it will be far easier to produce all possible functional variations in the leaves than a spiral arrangement of the same, although these, as altogether indifferent for the struggle of existence, could have attained no constancy through natural selection." Had Darwin borrowed his examples more from plants than from animals, he would perhaps himself have perceived the limitation of the action of the struggle for existence. It is clear that the latter can only alter the behaviour of organisms to the external conditions of life, *i.e.*, their functions, and the organs only so far as the functions are dependent upon them, but that it can have no influence on those qualities of organisms, whose alteration as regards the relations between the organisms and the external world brings to the former neither advantage nor disadvantage. To the latter attributes belong, however, in plants, and even in animals, most of the *fundamental principles of the morphological type, e.g.*, the *numerical proportions* selected for the same.

We have here found a confirmation of our preceding assertion, that natural selection in the struggle for existence is an extremely valuable aid for the exhaustive *elaboration* of an existing type within the same organisation, but cannot serve for the explanation of the *passage* from a lower to a higher stage of organisation, since a raising of the morphological type is always connected with such. In his most recent researches (Botan. Mittheilungen, 1868) on the behaviour of individuals of one and the same species of plants, on the one hand under the same, on the other hand under different external circumstances, Nägeli comes to the conclusion that the formation of unlike varieties occurs just as much under like, as the formation of like varieties under unlike circumstances; whence we may conclude as follows:—(1.) The external circumstances do *not* suffice as *sole* cause of the formation of varieties, but presuppose as second favourable condition a quality inherent in the plant, a "tendency to vary" (and that, too, in definite directions). (2.) But without a doubt this inner quality of the plant can *by itself* suffice to introduce, even under *similar* external circumstances, a formation of *different* varieties. This confirms our preceding assumptions. Among zoologists, quite recently Kölliker has declared for the hypothesis of Nägeli, that the transformation of existing organisms by the accidental change of external circumstances yields in importance and range to the tendency inherent in the organic world of development from internal causes according to preordained laws, no matter by what name this creative principle, this productive activity is called; in this sense he desires his former announcement of "heterogeneous generation" (comp. above, p. 301) to be interpreted.[1]

Before quitting the subject, a special expedient may be mentioned, the *actual* use of which indeed has not hitherto been proved, whose possible application is, however, so interesting, that I will not withhold from the reader a short indication of the same.—Until fifteen years ago, it passed as a scientific axiom that, of all animals that undergo a metamorphosis, only the most perfect state is transmissible. Now, however, we already know three exceptions. The young of *Leptodera appendiculata*, a parasitic tape-worm living in the foot of the common slug, represent the larva form of their parents; with abundant food and moisture they do not, however, undergo the chrysalis change, but propagate among one another any number of times without diminution of fertility. A second example is that of Cecidomyia,

---

[1] Morphologie und Entwickelungsgeschichte des Pennatulidenstammes nebst allgemeinen Betrachtungen zur Descendenzlehre, von A. Kölliker. Frankfurt a M. bei Winter, 1872, pp. 26-27, and 30 ff. The whole general introduction to this memoir is a very interesting contribution to the theory of Descent and to the criticism of the theory of natural selection.

already mentioned in the last chapter (p. 281). A third, the Mexican Axolotl, whose identity with the likewise long-known Amblystoma was established through the circumstance, that in aquaria the metamorphosis of the Axolotl into Amblystoma was directly observed in certain cases. The larva form of this animal has external gills like the Proteus, which undergoes no metamorphosis, whereas the perfect form is without gills. Now here manifestly the larva form is the older and original, and one must assume that, under favourable circumstances, one of these salamander-like animals underwent a metamorphosis for the first time, a change which was facilitated in its descendants by inheritance. The Axolotl now has not attained the next stage of development, where the metamorphosis, as in most Amphibia, is a regular phase of the life-history. As, however, the progress from the fish-salamanders to the higher Amphibia takes place by the capacity for metamorphosis becoming by transmission normal, one may imagine the further progress from the Amphibia to the reptiles brought about by this, that under favourable circumstances an Amphibian acquires the power of bringing forth young in the final form, or, in other words, of transferring the metamorphosis to the embryonic life. The preceding reflections on *metamorphosis* may be extended to the *alternation of generations* (comp. Häckel), but hitherto data are too much wanting for the attainment of certain results on this subject.—

If we briefly epitomise the conclusions of this chapter, there results from the principle of always attaining the proposed end with the least possible expenditure of energy the following :—

(1.) The Unconscious in the production of higher phases of organisation *foregoes spontaneous generation*, and prefers to employ already *existing* forms of organisation.

(2.) It does *not directly* transform the lower form into

the higher, but shapes the latter from a favourably constituted *germ* of the lower kind.

(3.) It takes as small steps as possible, and forms the larger differences by *adding together* a number of *small* individual differences.

(4.) It makes use of the individual variations *casually* arising in generation, *so far as such are present, in those directions which answer to its own end.*

(5.) For maintaining the variations arising, no matter how, it makes use of *natural selection* in the struggle for existence, *so far as they are of greater service to the organism.*

(6.) The Unconscious must (apart from its continuous interposition in every organic formation, thus also in all generation) display a direct activity in the progressive development of the organisation: on the one hand, in order with new germs *to call forth* the variations that do *not accidentally* arise; and, on the other hand, to *preserve* from being *again obliterated* by crossing the variations that have arisen, which belong to its plan, but *do not aid the competition* of the organism *in the struggle for existence.*—

Lastly, it may be remarked that, for the same reason that no spontaneous generation takes place after sexual reproduction has been rendered possible, the development of a new species from a lower one *only* takes place if the species *does not yet*, or at least not at this locality, *exist.* The development of a new species would thus have to be conceived as a process occurring only *once*, or at least only *a few* times, at different localities, under similar circumstances, which is empirically confirmed by the favourable results of the most recent investigations concerning the places of origin or centres of diffusion of the species of plants and animals; whilst, on the other hand, after a new species has once arisen, the similar, or but slightly modified reproduction of the same, is the normal and ever-repeated process, till the possible destruction of the species. (According to Darwin, the process of formation of certain higher species from their lower primitive forms must be repeated as long or as often as the external conditions which called it forth the first time last or occur afresh; but this requirement can hardly be brought into harmony with the facts of experience, since it must have recourse for the purpose to the further improbable single appearance of shortly enduring and never recurring circumstances.) However long, then, one may imagine the process of developing a new species to take (hundreds or thousands of years), it will still be an *inconsiderably small* part of the space of the *essentially similar* continuation of the formed species (some hundreds of thousands to ten millions of years).

This is a *second* reason, in addition to those already mentioned above, why so many more similar fossil specimens with distinct specific characters are found than those, which exhibit the transitional stages between closely allied species.

XI.

INDIVIDUATION.

1. *Possibility and Manner of Effecting Individuation.*—
If the Essential Being that manifests itself in the world
is sole and indivisible, whence comes the plurality of
appearing individuals? whence the singularity of each of
the same? what is its object? how is it possible?

The answer to these questions has always been a cardinal difficulty for every explicitly monistic philosophy.
It was, in particular, the rejection or insufficient answering
of the same that always paved the way to the relapse
of Monism into a realistic polyism or pluralism (*e.g.*,
Leibnitz after Spinoza, Herbart after Schelling and Hegel,
Bahnsen after Schopenhauer). Spinoza ignores the above
questions as much as the ancients; he dogmatically
declares individuals to be *modi* of the One substance, but
the development of the *modus* from substance, or the
demonstration why each *modus* is distinguished from
another and forms a unique existence, he altogether fails
to supply. Subjective idealism (Kant, Fichte, Schopenhauer) imagines it has done enough when it declares
plurality in the world to be *subjective* appearance, arising
through the forms of subjective intuition—space and time
—unconcerned that, in the first place, the difficulty is
only transferred from the objective to the subjective
sphere, but remains just as unsolved here as it was there;
and that, secondly, the question remains unanswered how
this unique percipient individual, which discriminates
itself from every similar individual, is possible according

to monistic principles, since either, if it is conceived as one among many, the incomprehensible real plurality is again inconsistently introduced, or however in the other case, on the hypothesis of Solipism, again the *limitation* of this whole and sole perceiving subject remains incomprehensible.

The latter side of the question was certainly seen by Schelling (Werke, i. 3, p. 683): "But now the problem is just this, How from an action of the absolute Ego the absolute Intelligence, and how again from an action of the absolute Intelligence the whole system of limitation, which constitutes every individuality, may be explained." The answer follows on the next page: "If now the intelligence remained one with the absolute synthesis, there would indeed be a universe, but there would be no intelligence. If there is to be an intelligence, it must emerge from that synthesis in order to produce it again *with consciousness;* but this again is impossible without the addition of a special or second to that first limitation, which now no longer can consist in this, that the intelligence in general perceives a universe, but that it perceives the universe precisely from this fixed point."

I confess that I should envy that man who was able to pick out the truth from this passage and its connections, if he did not already possess it.

As for the Hegelian system, our question unmasks one of its weakest points. According to Hegel, the concept is the sole substance; it is nothing but the concept, and the process of Nature is an objective notional dialectic. On the other side, he himself confesses that the Notion just as little as the word is able to grasp the simple This in its singleness—*this* individual, which as such one can only show, but not describe. Individual singleness stands outside the range of the concept, and therewith outside that of the Hegelian system, if this will be consistent with itself. Plurality as real phenomenon cannot explain the same, for one can see no reason why, on the dismission of the absolute Idea into Nature, every phase of development of the logical process should have more than a corresponding phase of development of the process of Nature. The dialectical self-splitting of the one into the many yields indeed plurality as pure concept, but not plurality as accident of real phenomena; for Hegel would never have maintained the self-disintegration of a half-crown into many half-crowns or sixpences, and as little as in this real instance would the self-division of the one be applicable to a self-splitting of a world-soul into many real individuals. Real plurality is *more* than the idea of plurality; it is a sum of individuals, none of which resembles the others, each of which is a This, nameless, sole (as I am nameless, sole), each of which is attainable by no conception, but only by perception.

Whoever has not felt the need and the difficulty of comprehending individuation from the point of view of Monism may securely pass over the first half of this chapter; he would find no interest in it. For him, on the other hand, who hitherto has kept aloof from Monism precisely on account of this more or less distinctly conscious difficulty, and has put up with the pluralism of the real phenomenal world as an ultimate, for him lies in this chapter, taken in conjunction with Chap. vii. C., the centre of gravity of the present book. In fact, pluralism and individualism have a warrant which cannot be under-estimated with impunity; as every improperly neglected moment always revenges itself by a reaction exceeding a justifiable limit. With Fichte the conscious individual still occupies the foreground, but its significance is not that of a characteristic *sui generis*, but that of the *type* of a limited absolute intelligence, which is revealed still more distinctly in Schelling; whilst with Hegel even this type is volatilised into the abstract category of the subjective spirit. As concerns the other side of individuality as separate natural existence, with Fichte there is no mention of it at all, since Nature is to him only subjective illusion; with Schelling and Hegel, however, there is plenty of reflection and speculation about abstract natural potencies and their dialectical play, but the significance and the right of the natural individual as such is perfectly ignored, when it is not expressly denied. In the reaction against this one-sidedness of abstract idealism and in the re-erecting of the standard of a realism recognising the plurality of things-in-themselves lies the historical authorisation of the Herbartian pluralism; its *truth* lies in the assertion *that the right of plurality and individuality reaches just as far as reality of existence in general;* its *untruth* lies in *failing to perceive the phenomenality of all reality and all existence.* Subjective idealism had had the right inkling that reality is only phenomenality, but it had distorted and disfigured this thought by recognising no other than subjective phenomenality, so that plurality sank to only subjective illusion. When, however, one has perceived the existing to be objective appearance or manifestation of the super-existent (*i.e.*, independent of the apprehending conscious subject), or existence of the subsisting, then are reality and (objective) phenomenality perceived to be identical notions; then one, however, also knows that the plurality, whose right reaches as far as the reality of the existing world, has just as this only a phenomenal, not transcendent-metaphysical validity. Schopenhauer obviously steers towards this standpoint, but his adhesion to subjective idealism prevents him from clearing up his notion of the individual objectification of the Will and developing it into that of objective phenomenality; and the want of this latter notion leads him again, in contradiction with his own principles, to allow plurality and individuality to reach *also* into the transcendent-metaphysical (intelligible individual character and individual negation of the will). From this point it was possible for Bahnsen to set up a system of ethological individualism or metaphysical will-pluralism and to reject Schopenhauer's Monism, because he saw through the contradictions of Schopenhauer's system, and yet did not see how otherwise to save the right of individuality. The notion of objective phenomenality introduced by Schelling and Hegel into philosophy, and emphasised especially by Frauenstädt amongst the adherents of Schopenhauer, explains, however, everything that has to be explained in a more satisfactory and less one-sided fashion. Whilst I defend and uphold the uniqueness of the individual and its right within the real world as against abstract Idealism and Monism as energetically as Herbart, I just as decidedly dispute every claim of the individual to a transcendent-metaphysical validity extending beyond the world of objective appearance as unfounded, unwarranted, and presumptuous, and deem even that Pluralism which *flatly denies* all transcendent-metaphysic behind the real world to be *more endurable* and *philosophical* than that which inflates the individual to an eternal transcendent essentiality or substance; for the former merely *foregoes* all metaphysic in favour of physics, but the latter has a *false* metaphysic, and that is far worse. As certainly, however, as the former Pluralism satisfies all the justifiable claims of individuality, so certainly does the philosophy of the Unconscious also do this, which accords to the individual precisely *the same* authority as that unmetaphysical Pluralism, only that it adds to this theory of the real world and its plurality a metaphysic (and indeed, what is here indifferent, monistic metaphysic). The philosophy of the Unconscious is thus *the genuine reconciliation of monism and pluralistic individualism,* in that it recognises each of the two aspects as authorised, assigns each the sphere appertaining to it (metaphysical or physical-real), and *unites both in itself as sublated moments.*—

From the previous results of the foregoing chapters the solution of the question placed at the head of this chapter follows without difficulty. We will, however, leave the question, Why is there individuation? for the present undiscussed, and consider only the other, *How is it possible on monistic principles?*

Stated in general terms the answer runs: "Individuals are objectively posited phenomena, *i.e.*, they are willed thoughts of the Unconscious or particular will-acts of the same; the unity of the essence remains unaffected by the plurality of individuals, which are only *activities* (or combinations of certain activities) of the one Essential Being." But to render this very general answer plausible, we must enter into details, and once more picture to ourselves by what combination of what activities an individual arises, and how far each individual must necessarily be different from every other, or unique.

The individuals of higher order arise, as we saw (C. Chap. vi.), by composition from individuals of lower order, with the addition of new activities of the Unconscious directed upon the resulting compound; one must therefore begin with understanding individuation in the individuals of lowest order, *i.e.*, the atoms. Here, according to the present state of the scientific hypotheses, only two different kinds of individuals, repulsive, and attractive forces, are to be distinguished; within each of these groups there obtains perfect resemblance between the individuals, with the sole exception of their *place*.

Only because the atomic forces A and B act differently on the same atoms are they different, and because the lines of action of A and the lines of action of B have distinct foci, this difference is shortly expressed as A and B occupy different places, whilst in strictness force occupies no place at all, but only its effects are locally discriminated. But if one imagined two equal atoms united in a mathematical point, they would not only cease to be *distinguishable*, but even to be *different*, for they would cease to be *two forces*, and would be *one* force with double the strength.

Here then the application of the answer given above in general terms is in itself clear and intelligible: the Unconscious has at the same time different will-acts, which are distinguished by their content so far as the space relations of their effects are differently represented. But when the will realises its content, these many will-acts enter into objective reality as so many force-individuals; they are the first primitive manifestation of Essential Being. Since every effect of atomic force is represented by the Unconscious as different from every other, thus single, its realisation is of course different from that of every other atomic force, thus likewise single, without prejudice to the circumstance that it is in its nature indistinguishable; the intuitive imagination of the Unconscious distinguishes it, however, without thought in its space relations, as well as one recognises by perception the right glove as right, which no notion and no combination of concepts is ever able to do.

Here we may also remember what was said (C. Chap. i. 3 and 4) on the way in which the Unconscious forms representations. The concept is a result of a process of separation or abstraction, but the Unconscious always apprehends the totality of its matter of representation without condescending to a separation of parts within the same. The concept is a product of discursive thought, a sorry make-shift due to its weakness; but the Unconscious thinks not discursively but intuitively; it thinks concepts only so far as they are contained in intuition as integral and undifferentiated elements, consequently it cannot be surprising if among the intuitions of the Unconscious there are such from which, even for discursive thinking, no concepts can be abstracted; as, *e.g.*, the perception that the actions of the atomic force A must be so directed that their lines of direction should intersect *in this point here*, those of the atom B, *in that point there*. Consequently, in the case of atoms, the difference and singleness of the individuals is, in fact, reduced in the most direct manner to the difference and singleness of the ideas which form the content of the acts of will of which the individuals consist, in such wise that to each individual there corresponds a single act of will.

Unfortunately Matter has never been comprehended as a combination of will-acts of the Unconscious, so that the sole example where the comprehension of individuation is really simple was not available. In all other cases, however, where we have to do with individuals of higher order, the comprehension of individuation is rendered difficult by a complicated combination of will-acts, changing every moment, forming the individual.

If we dwell a moment more upon the atomic forces of matter, and inquire respecting the medium whereby individuation in this sphere becomes possible, respecting the so-called "*principium individuationis*," undoubtedly the combination of space and time can alone be so characterised; for we saw that the atomic forces A and B, equal in thought, are only distinguished by the different *space* relations of their effects, improperly and briefly expressed by their *places*, and only omitted at the time to add to "their effects:" "at the same point of time." This addendum is, however, necessary, for completeness' sake, because indeed *with the time* the place of an atom may change. The phrase *principium individuationis* is not, however, well chosen. It should be *medium individuationis;* for the *authorship* or *origin* of individuation, just as that of space and time, belongs solely to the Unconscious, namely, the *ideal* difference and singleness of the atoms to the idea, their *reality* however to the will.

It might now appear, on superficial consideration, that here only the same thing is said as by Schopenhauer, who also claims space and time as the *principium individuationis*. However, between his and my conception there exists the fundamental difference, that with Schopenhauer space and time are only forms of *subjective cerebral perception*, with which the (speculative) transcendent reality has nothing at all to do; that for him, therefore, all individuation is a *mere* subjective appearance, to which corresponds no reality outside the cerebral consciousness.

According to my conception, on the other hand, space

and time are just as much forms of *outward reality* as of the subjective cerebral perception; certainly not forms of the (metaphysical-) transcendent SUBSTANTIAL BEING, but only of its activity, so that individuation has not merely an apparent reality for consciousness, but a reality *apart* from all consciousness, without thereby curtailing plurality of substance.

Here is the salient point for understanding the conception of objective appearance in opposition to the mere subjective appearance of Kant, Fichte, and Schopenhauer. The possibility of a plurality and individuation independent of the conscious subject perceiving it depends on the condition, that the *principium* or *medium individuationis* is a datum independent of the perception of the conscious subject, *i.e.*, that space and time are not merely forms of intuition, but also forms of existence of the *of itself* existing (*i.e.*, independent of the representation of the conscious subject). Whoever denies this must necessarily also deny that another plurality and individuation than that posited by the conscious idea exist—must then deny that his wife and himself are *two individuals*, independent of his mental picture. But now the essence of matter is only will and idea, and moreover one as the essence of all being; plurality only lies in action, and is real plurality only so far as at the same time a collision of will-acts takes place (one atom would be no atom). It is herewith, however, at the same time implied that plurality and individuation (thus also reality, presence, and existence) reside only in the *manifestation* of metaphysical force (comp. above, pp. 242–243), only in the action of substance, only in the *manifestation* of the hidden ground, only in the *objectification* of the will, only in the *appearance* of the one Essential Being. Plurality is therefore, on the one hand, not mere *subjective* appearance (of being in the abstract); on the other hand, however, still mere appearance of the one essence, therefore we call it *objective* appearance. In like manner we call space and time as principle of individuation of the plurality of the objective appearances, objective forms of phenomena.

Had not Schopenhauer unfortunately leant too much on Kant, he must of necessity have enounced the true view; whereas, as it is, he persists in the statement that the whole diversity of the world only acquires existence *through* the first animal consciousness and *in* its perception. Only thus much truth lies in this, that objective manifestation also, in order to be real, *i.e.*, to emerge from the unconsciously ideal composure into external reality, needed an opposition between *different* acts of will; error creeps in only when the union of one of the affected will-acts with a *conscious* subject is required as condition. If we eliminate this unwarranted requirement, the simple truth remains that the objective phenomenon which *rests on* the individuation of the one into the many, is also only possible *in* this plurality without self-contradiction.

Moreover, there lies in Schopenhauer's assertion that the world of individuation comes into existence only with the first conscious subject perceiving it an incorrect assumption, as if the subjective appearance which the intellect spontaneously constructs out of the material processes in the objective appearance of its brain were the immediate and true appearance of the Essential Being, whilst it is, in fact, very unlike, nay, in many points perfectly heterogeneous to, the objective phenomenon (*i.e.*, the sum of natural individuals as they are, independently of being perceived). Only the objective phenomenon is the true and direct manifestation of the Essential Being; the subjective phenomenon, however, is a subjectively coloured and distorted copy of the objective phenomenon. To gain an *adequate* thought-picture of the objective appearance by eliminating that which merely appertains to subjectivity, and by the scientific investigation of the objective causes of the particular given affection of the subject, is the endeavour and problem of Natural Science (*Physics* in the widest sense), whilst *Metaphysics* endeavours to cognise the Essential Being according to its attributes and its mode of revelation, which underlies the objective appearance (natural things). Thus, *e.g.*, matter as subjective phenomenon is matter with its palpable sense-qualities; as objective phenomenon, a definitely extended complex of punctual atoms; as essence, that which underlies this phenomenon, the All-one Unconscious with the attributes will and idea. The first is the sensuous, the second the physical, the third the metaphysical definition of matter.

The second point wherein I depart from Schopenhauer is this, that he knows no atoms at all, wherefore, properly speaking, he cannot think anything by "individuation of matter," because he cannot say what are individuals of mere inorganic matter. The third is, lastly, that he naïvely regards organic individuals as just as much direct objectifications of the will as I the atomic forces, whilst I, following physical science, suppose the same to arise by the composition of atomic individuals.

With Schopenhauer, therefore, space and time are for organic individuals *principium individuationis* in the same sense as for atoms, whilst for the individuals of higher order I can only admit as direct *principium individuationis* those individuals of lower order of which the former are compounded, if also space and time, of course in the last resort, always remain indirect *principium individuationis*, since indeed the whole material world is built up out of atomic forces. Only his subjective idealism, to which matter, as also the organic body, must be a merely subjective appearance without corresponding reality beyond consciousness, could lead Schopenhauer to explain the body as a *direct* objectification of the individual will—an assertion which, in presence of the facts of the extremely defective control of the will over the body and of the change of matter, which is the first condition of all organic life, can by no means be upheld. Experience teaches us, in the first place, that the matter which constitutes our body is something foreign and indifferent to us; that it is being continually thrown off and replaced by other matter; secondly, that the matter of our body, in contrast with the mind, forms in the same way as the will of other persons a quite real power, with which one must reckon in order to be able to control it so far as is practically necessary, to which one, however, immediately succumbs as soon as one either thinks to be able to neglect it, or makes demands upon it to the enforcement of which the psychical power is unequal. Experience, in a word, teaches that matter behaves as an already pre-existing, to a certain extent indifferent, crude building material, which the plastic individual soul attracts to and repels from itself according to its needs, whose laws it must, however, respect, and dare not attempt to infringe with impunity.

Bearing in mind the results of Chap. ix. C., according to which the Unconscious realises life wherever the possibility of life offers itself, and considering that organic life is only conceivable under the organic form and requires matter for its realisation, it is evident that these are the conditions determining the individuation of organic life; for it must for its realisation make use of a complex of atoms enclosed within certain limits of extension, and put these into their appropriate situations and groups, so as to render possible the organic interchange of matter; the atoms employed, however, are individuals, *i.e.*, each of them is *single*, consequently the organically constituted complex of these atoms, and the activity of the Unconscious exclusively directed to it, which together make up the higher individual, must be *single*.

Thus, as already above suggested, the lower order of individuals turns out to be *medium individuationis* for the higher.—There would be no special gain for the purpose of this inquiry in going deeper into evolution, and showing in detail how, for the many-celled individuals, the cells are just as much a power whose laws must be respected as the matter for the cells, for in the body a change of *cells* just as much takes place as a change of *matter*, if also much more slowly, &c. The essential thing is, that the individuation of organic life takes place only in and through matter, but the individuation of the atoms in and through space and time. In all higher individuals the general form requires a content or matter in order to become concrete; what was *matter* for the individuals of higher order becomes for those of the lower order *form*. Only with pure matter is the last term of this series reached; *only here* does the typical form become of itself concrete,—become as it were *itself matter* through the simple artifice of fixation at the extended point, through the device that here the directions of force all intersect at one and the same point. Since the atomic forces have no matter lying outside them whereby they may be individualised, but only their place, they are also discriminated (apart from the difference between body and ether atoms) *only* by their place, which is just their sole *medium individuationis;* higher individuals, on the other hand, which have matter for their *medium individuationis*, find also, *besides* the difference of the occupied place, in the matter taken into possession by them, a rich field for individual differences.

With this is first given in the case of individuals of lower order the possibility of an *individual character*, and to this we must pay some attention, for it meets us at all stages of organic life, from the individual character of the simplest cell to that of the foundations of the human mind, as a phenomenon at first perplexing for monistic principles.

2. *Individual Character.*—Concerning human character there are two extreme opinions. The one (Rousseau, Helvetius, &c.) asserts that all men are at birth equal, *i.e.*, devoid of an individual character; that their mind is just as much a *tabula rasa* as regards character as regards ideas, and that it only acquires the one as the other by external impressions, and the character in particular by education and circumstances.

The other view (Schopenhauer) asserts that character is *unalterable;* that it manifests itself indeed, as is natural, differently through different external opportunities, *e.g.*, at different periods of life, but in its essence it is at once the man's inalienable and unchangeable nature and foundation, consequently remains the same from birth to death.

Each of these two views explains a part of the facts very well, is closed, however, to another part of the facts. If we ask, which of the two views appears metaphysically more acceptable, the remarkable case occurs that nothing can be objected to the view of the French naturalists on the metaphysical side, while, on the other hand, that of the metaphysician Schopenhauer, who assumes the establishment of character by a resolution taken once for all out of time, can hardly stand the test of criticism derived from his own principles.

Schopenhauer himself wishes to be an absolute monist; if, then, the will of the world is in its essence one; if, further, the character likewise, according to his own assertion, is nothing but the peculiarity of the individual will, the *individuality* of the character can manifestly only be conceived as possible in an individualised *activity* of the universal will, but not as directly based on the *essential nature* of the universal will, since this always remains *universal.* How, however, the *activity* of the will which produces character is to be thought as extra-temporal, of that I can form no idea. I can only imagine a being, but not its activity, as out of time, since activity at once supposes time, unless one also assumes as possible an activity in zero-time, in which case it is in the moment also again *extinguished.* The character, however, that is to live through the life-period of the individual manifestly requires also an activity of the universal will, which lasts just as long. Otherwise expressed, the doctrine of the *intelligible individual character* is a contradiction to the monistic principle a contradiction also to the transcendent ideality of space and time. For in the intelligible the *principium individuationis* is wanting, consequently also plurality and individuality, consequently also the *many* individual characters. The individual character *pre*-supposes the individual, or rather individuals, thus plurality, individuality; in short, the world of appearances: like this, it only becomes possible through *time*, through the temporal activity of the Universal Intelligible Being.

If this is now the state of the case, it is, in the first place, not at once obvious why, if the characters are in fact so different among one another, each individual should during the duration of life, *i.e.*, the whole time in which this particular activity of the individual will exists, remain the same, and not rather continually change.

Much more plausible, metaphysically, is the hypothesis of the French rationalists, that only typical generic characters, but not individual characters, are innate; that, however, through alteration of the character in different ways, the individual characters are gradually fashioned. On this assumption we come to terms much more easily with the all-unity of the Universal Being, for the individual variation of the originally similar generic character might then be referred to different brain impressions, each of which leaves behind a permanent change in the brain, which brings it about that thenceforward a molecular movement in the same sense as that called forth by those impressions more easily arises than one of a totally different kind (vol. i. pp. 33-34). This is the way in which altogether *habit* becomes a *power* in special application to character. The first action of a particular kind is purely decided by motives, on the assumption of a still undetermined character; in what mode and strength these come to the man depends on external circumstances. If, however, the first action turns out in a particular way, for the next similar case the motives which act in the direction of the same decision as before have attained a certain imperceptible advantage over the opposite motives, which is heightened in every decision resulting in the same way.

In this way it comes about that in the case of any particular individual certain motives exert a greater, others a less effect, than on the average typical generic character, and the *sum* of all these *tendencies* is the individual character.

According to this view, consequently, the individual character arises especially by an individual constitution of the brain, which is produced by former impressions conditioned by external circumstances; for habit can exercise a direct influence only on the organ of consciousness, not on the Unconscious. Nevertheless, with the constitution of the brain the kind of activity also changes which the Unconscious directs upon the same; for this changes with every change of the organism, and the brain is one of the most important parts of it. The Unconscious usually always calls forth as a motive in the brain *the reaction which is the easiest;* only where particularly important, especially general interests are at stake in an action, may we suppose that it takes upon itself the trouble of answering with another than this easiest reaction on the stimulus of the motive, a case which occurs in all action according to unconscious purposes, when the reaction which otherwise would directly respond to the motive fails to take place, or is outbidden by another, exclusively conditioned by unconscious intermediate terms.

In all cases, however, where the Unconscious has no such considerable interest that it would reward it to replace the reaction most easily occurring by another, will also a customary change of this easiest cerebral reaction have as its consequence a change of the activity of the Unconscious. The mode of this activity is, however, the character itself,—as we said before (B. Chap. iv.), man's inmost being. It is no contradiction that this character lies in the *Unconscious*, and yet its nature is conditioned by the brain, the special organ of *consciousness;* for the organ of consciousness, together with all its molecular relations, which must be regarded as *latent dispositions* to certain vibrations of this or that kind, lies itself so much beyond all consciousness, that between its material function and the conscious idea the whole complex of those unconscious psychical functions is interposed with which we have been hitherto occupied. At the same time, however, we must here call attention to the circumstance that the latent dispositions of the brain are by no means the sole and sufficient cause, but only one of the co-operating conditions for the determination of the idea entering into consciousness, or of the will to act; for they alone would never attain any psychical effect, but the spontaneity of the Unconscious borrows only from them a determining direction for the manner of the unfolding of its activity, to which it is not so far bound as not spontaneously to modify it for higher purposes.

From this consideration it follows that a man, *even if he were born without individual character,* would have *acquired* as adult an individual character deviating more or less from the typical generic character. If this man now, however, begets children, we know that, according to the law of inheritance, the peculiar dispositions of his brain, deviating from the typical human brain, pass on to some of his children more or less completely. Then is such child born with these latent dispositions, which condition the individual character, and as soon as it comes into circumstances where these dispositions are active, its innate character comes to the front. The phenomena of reversion in the paternal and the maternal line, and the blending of such qualities handed on from different sides, make the inquiry very difficult in the individual case *whence* the different qualities of an innate character arise; yet is the undeniable fact of the innate character *only* thus to be explained. Whether the *first* man had an individual character is an altogether idle question; his *general* character was indeed his *individual* character, since as the first individual of his species he completely represented the same. According to the theory of descent expounded in the last chapter, where the conception of kind was found to be a somewhat fluent one, every organic individual (accordingly also the first man) occupies a place in a series of organic developments, within which it receives from its immediate ancestors a whole treasury of ethological peculiarities as its inheritance, which on its part it again bequeaths, modified by the impressions of its life (before procreation), to its descendants.

Every human being accordingly brings the *main part* of his character with him into the world; how large in proportion to this is the part which he acquires in addition, depends on the uncommonness and abnormal nature of the circumstances in which he moves. In most cases the habits of *one* man's life do *not* suffice to produce far-reaching changes in the inherited character. Usually the acquired part of character is confined to fresh unimportant qualities, or the strengthening of existing ones, or the weakening of others by disuse. The latter takes place relatively in least degree, for as in all learning the most difficult is the forgetting of what has been learnt, so of all changes of character the most difficult is the suppression and weakening of existing qualities. It is this in particular that caused Schopenhauer to maintain the *unalterableness* of character.[1]

Whoever is disposed to doubt the fact of inheritance of *acquired* qualities of character, I refer to examples of the transmission of distinctly acquired qualities. Nobody will doubt that the tendencies to disease hereditary in families must, if one retraces the pedigree, be found in an ancestor who did not inherit but acquired them.

[1] For the fuller discussion of this theory, as well as on the relation of will and motive, I may refer to my essay on Julius Bahnsen's writings ("Beiträge zur Charakterologie," and "Zum Verhältniss zwischen Wille und Motiv") in the Philos. Monatshefte, Bd. iv. Hft. 5.

That amputated arms and legs and such-like mutilations are commonly not inherited proves nothing against our assertion, for they are too rough and palpable infractions of the typical idea of the species for us to expect their realisation in the child, and yet even here there are remarkable exceptions. According to Häckel, a bull whose tail had accidentally been wrenched off engendered nothing but tailless calves, and by continuous cropping of the tail for several generations a tailless breed of oxen has been obtained. Guinea-pigs, who had been made epileptic by artificial injuries of the spinal cord, transmitted this disease to their descendants. In general acquired qualities are more easily transmitted; the less they derange the type of the species, the more minute are the organic changes in which they consist. The latter is, however, in high degree the case with all cerebral dispositions to certain nervous vibrations. It is a well-known experience that the young of tame animals become tamer than the captured young of savage animals; that of domestic animals, again, those young promise to be most tame, most tractable, most teachable, &c., that spring from the tamest, most tractable, most teachable parents. Any taming of an animal in a particular direction affords so much the more prospect of success the further the taming of the parents has gone in the same direction. Young untamed hunting-dogs from superior parents act in the chase, almost of their own accord, tolerably correctly, whilst with dogs derived from parents who have never been employed for hunting training for the chase is a fearful work. Sons of generations of horsemen attain a good seat and balance at the very first trial. All these are examples of acquired qualities which are nevertheless inherited. They belong entirely to the subject of our inquiry, individual character in the wider sense, *i.e.*, to the sum of bodily and mental marks which distinguish an individual of a higher order (apart, too, from his spatial distinction through the occupation of place and the possession of a material body) from all other individuals.

If, in contemplating human individual character, we have hitherto kept in view the narrower sense of character, this happened only because the controversy specially turns upon the latter, not as if the difference in mental tendencies, faculties, and talents were not just as essential in the establishment of individual distinctions. But whoever has followed with approval our explanation of character in the narrower sense will at once see that the latter distinction can far less be conceived as arising in some other way, and a repetition of the explanation would be quite superfluous. How little character in the narrower sense is separable from mental endowment follows from this: that, on the one hand, the possession of an intellectual disposition or capacity is always accompanied by the *impulse* to use it; and, on the other hand, that character in the narrower sense always includes mental endowment, since it is the source of the modes of reaction of the will on different descriptions of motives, and every mode of reaction becomes a special one only because the volition following on a given motive possesses a special *ideal content* diverging from that of other individuals. If, then, the character is innate (*i.e.*, inherited), so also is the special matter of thought innate, the willing of which on a given motive makes up the special character of the innate mode of reaction. A mental representation can, however, only be innate as (inherited) slumbering idea of memory, *i.e.*, as molecular cerebral disposition to certain kinds of vibration (comp. vol. i. pp. 33-34). In this way, *e.g.*, the behaviour of the untrained young hunting-dog (its attention to game, the pricking up of its ears, its tendency to fetch and carry thrown objects), is to be explained by a memory inherited from its ancestors, in such a way, however, that the ideas (of memory) arising on suitable occasion from inherited cerebral dispositions do not become conscious *as* memories, but only make their appearance as the content of the acts of will called forth by those occasions (motives). (Here appears a special confirmation of Plato's explanation of learning and reminiscence from a former life, except that the validity of this explanation is a very limited one, and the earlier life did not belong to the same individual.) In man, too, a large part of the external manners and peculiarities of deportment of movement and of behaviour is composed of inherited cerebral dispositions of ancestors affected with the same peculiarities. That certain mental talents are hereditary for several generations in a family is proved by numerous examples (painters, mathematicians, astronomers, actors, generals, &c.) All such inherited predispositions contribute their quota, however, to the constitution of the total individuality of the man in his *uniqueness*.

I only add, that, whilst the character in the narrower sense is always again equalised by cross-breeding, and in the main remains at about the same level in the human race—although the contrasts within the same become ever *more abundantly* worked out and more *sharply drawn*—that the mental endowments and faculties in the human race are liable to a progressive enhancement. This is owing to the circumstance that the various characters, provided they are not eccentric, get through life about equally well; but the man endowed with higher mental capacities has always the advantage in the struggle for existence. Still more than in individuals does the truth of this contrast appear in nations; the character of the latter has for their struggle for existence but very small importance in proportion to their mental fitness and education. Now the open, upright, and brave, now the cunning, treacherous, and cowardly, now the slow and enduring, now the ready and quickly recovering, now the morally strict, now the corrupt, but always for the length of time the *intellectually higher* nation comes off conqueror in the struggle for existence, which accordingly in this sphere also acts on the individual differences, confirming and enhancing them, whether these have first arisen fortuitously or unconsciously in generation, or through the outward circumstances of life or personal conscious industry (comp. Chap. x. pp. 10–13).

If, on the other hand, we throw our glance backward beyond the commencement of human history on the history of development of organic life, of which humanity only forms the ripest fruit, there appears an advance of character and intelligence preserving a perfectly equal pace. We must ascend tolerably high in the animal kingdom before we find manifestations of an intelligence which are more than the immediate content of an act of will that takes its direction from the present motive. Hence the innate modes of reaction or inherited slumbering ideas of memory have in those lower mental spheres a relatively far higher importance (vol. i. pp. 88–89). But as the Unconscious creates for itself in these cerebral or ganglionic dispositions mechanisms for the easier performance of certain voluntary reactions (*e.g.*, the tendency of bees to construct hexagonal cells), so very well may something similar take place also with abstract human ideas, which frequently recur, and are of special importance for the organisation of thought (*e.g.*, mathematical notions, logical categories, forms of language, &c.) Should we have recourse for describing such latent dispositions of brain to the term "innate ideas," this would be just as improper a designation as the other, "slumbering ideas of memory" (comp. i. 301 note), since the idea or presentation is something added to the material function through the ideal reaction of the Unconscious, and is not dispensed with, but only facilitated by, the predisposition. It is also never to be forgotten that even if the hitherto quite unproved supposition of cerebral dispositions answering to the concepts in question is correct, yet the unconscious psychical function must always be the *prius* of the first formation of a mode of vibration, from which the corresponding disposition originally arose, and that further, in the case of other formal elements of thought, special reasons oppose the above supposition (comp. i. 343-344). But at all events, one may regard this much as settled, that the enhancing of conscious intellect in the history of development of organisation and of humanity depends not only on an increase of the intensive and extensive capacity and faculty of combination, but also on an enhancement of the inherited cerebral dispositions for all practically useful intellectual directions of activity. We must not be puzzled by the circumstance that in man (and even in the anthropoid apes) the embryonic evolution of the brain goes on for a tolerably long time after birth (comp. also i. 352–353).

The same results, which we preferred to obtain here by another path, we might of course have also got if we had directly built upon the results of the last two chapters, and had kept in view the different causes of the individual variations from the origin of the cell. The agreement of the goal to which both roads lead may serve for corroboration. The difference which would still have to be adjusted is the following:—

In lower organisms, where the variations are found essentially in the bodily structure and the organic functions, we sought the origin of the individual variations more especially in that period of life which opposes the least resistance to modifications; in Man, however, where the variations of the mental qualities are far more interesting than those of the bodily, we must of course seek the origin of these variations in that period of life when the mental functions are already active, thus *after birth*, and indeed *some little time* after that; but yet *not in the later* periods of life, when the development is, as it were, indurated, but in the receptive age of *childhood* and *youth*.

Essentially, however, the source of individual differences is the same in the whole domain of organisation: external circumstances condition a varying structure of the organism, and the varying structure of the organism conditions a variation of the activity of the All-One Unconscious directed to it. These differences are added to that already conditioned by the diversity of the material substratum, and together form that total of differences which secures to every individual his *peculiar oneness.*

XII.

THE SUPREME WISDOM OF THE UNCONSCIOUS AND THE PERFECTION OF THE WORLD.

At all times, and among all peoples, the wisdom of the Creator, World-orderer, or World-governor has been the theme of admiration and of praise. None of all the peoples who in the course of history have attained even a moderate degree of civilisation, whatever may have been their other opinions in religion and philosophy, has been so barbarous as not to have attained this perception, and to have given it more or less rapturous expression. Although this expression must, in part, be laid to the account of a flattery of the gods with self-interested objects, yet at all events the greater part of it remains the announcement of a genuine conviction. This conviction thrusts itself already on the mind of the child as soon as it begins to comprehend the remarkable combination of means and ends in Nature. He only who denies natural ends can close his mind against this conviction; such a view can, however, only be evolved from systematically ordered philosophical abstractions, since it runs counter to the first natural apprehension of the phenomena of Nature. Before men form abstractions, they are most strongly moved by the power of the concrete case, and the deeper heads of a childlike nation may be lost in astonishment and reverence at the perception of a striking natural purpose even in a single case. Thus it is related of an ancient Brahmin that he was so affected with astonishment at the sight of an insect-capturing plant, that, forgetful of meat and drink, he remained seated before it till the end of his life.—Then when man arrives at inductions from the concrete instances, it is such propositions as "Nature does nothing in vain," "Nature does everything for the best," "Nature employs for its ends the simplest means and ways," in which he already early acknowledges the wisdom ruling in Nature. This conviction finds its strongest rational expression in the period of Leibniz and Wolf. Although Leibniz, in his denial of evil in the world, overshot the mark, although a great part of the extravagant laudations of the iterators of the "best world" was only hollow bombastic declamation, which merely injured their case in the eyes of posterity, yet a core of truth still remains.

If we consider the matter in connection with our former conclusions, it will take somewhat the following shape:— According to C. Chap. i., the Unconscious can never *err*, nay, not even *doubt* or *hesitate*, but when the entrance of an unconscious idea is *wanted*, it follows *instantaneously*, implicity enclosing the process of reflection occupying time in consciousness in the one moment of its occurrence, and undoubtedly correctly, since all the data that can in any way be taken account of stand at the command of the Unconscious in virtue of its absolute *clairvoyance*, and indeed *always* and momentarily stand at command, not as the data in conscious reflection that have first to be dragged out by severe meditation from memory one after the other, and still oftener are entirely wanting. All future ends, the nearest as the most distant, and all considerations of the possibility of intervention in this or that wise, act together in this manner at the moment of origin of the required idea, and thus it happens that every interposition of the Unconscious occurs precisely at the *most suitable* moment, when the whole purpose-frame of the world requires it, and that the unconscious idea which determines the manner of the interposition is the *most suitable of all possible ones* for this whole machinery of ends. Such an interposition of the Unconscious in a manner adapted to the peculiarity of the case according to our investigations takes place at *every* moment in the department of organic life; both the *preservation* consisting in a replacement of the used-up material by nutrition and in a ceaseless struggle against invading disturbances, as well as the *plastic energy* manifesting itself partly in a re-creation of accidentally destroyed parts, partly in an enhancement of the individual form of life, and also the plastic energy becoming *reproduction* through the setting-up of fresh individuals; they all three are only conceivable as a ceaseless ever-renewed interposition of the Unconscious at every single point of the organism at once; each of these interpositions being modified according to the particular circumstances to which it refers, and each uniformly keeping in view the important ends which they all subserve in common.

Every natural cause shows itself accordingly as means for the great ends of Providence; every natural cause in the organic realm presents itself as including a direct participation of the Unconscious. But these continual interpositions of Providence are themselves *natural, i.e.,* not *arbitrary,* but *according to law,* namely, determined with *logical necessity* by the main design fixed once for all, and the circumstances of the moment in which the interposition takes places.

When the Christian theory emphatically declares that God's action is not merely a guidance on the large scale, but that his immeasurable greatness is most remarkably displayed in this, that it is everywhere active in the smallest detail, this view is only confirmed by our researches in regard to organic life.

The fitness of the activity of the Unconscious is not however herewith exhausted, but as the cleverness of a person is much more to be commended, who relieves himself of an ever-recurring work by the construction of an ingenious machine, than that of one who himself performs the same in each single case with the utmost skill, so must we also far more admire the wisdom of the Unconscious, when it saves itself a part of its interposition by mechanical arrangements contrived for the purpose or even by a clever use of external circumstances (*e.g.*, of the struggle for existence, or of the existing atomic forces), than when it solves its problems by continuous direct interposition in the most excellent fashion. Examples of this we have already found in such numbers in the course of our inquiries that I consider a special reference, to say nothing of enumeration, to be scarcely necessary here. The most comprehensive and important of all these mechanisms, however, is the system of the physico-chemical laws of Nature.

But however many mechanical contrivances the Unconscious may employ to facilitate its labour, these can never dispense with the continual direct interposition, for they fall according to their very nature into a class of *homogeneous* cases, whilst in reality each case is distinct from the other; the best-contrived mechanism thus always leaves over a remnant of work, which falls afterwards as before to the direct activity of the Unconscious, and which consists in the complete adaptation to the peculiar nature of the case. As soon as the expenditure of force needed for the setting-up of a machine would become greater than the saving of force attained by the mechanism (which is the case in all combinations of circumstances which by their nature occur but seldom, or where for other reasons a mechanism can only be constructed with difficulty), there of course the direct activity of the Unconscious must display itself without hesitation. Of such a kind are, *e.g.*, the incursions of the Unconscious in human brains, which determine and guide the course of history in all departments of civilisation in the direction of the goal intended by the Unconscious.

If, now, according to all this, we cannot avoid ascribing to the Unconscious, first, absolute clairvoyance (which answers to the theological notion of omniscience); secondly, an infallible and indubitable logical concatenation of the included data, and the most appropriate action at the most suitable moment (in theological language, omniscience united with supreme wisdom); and, thirdly, a ceaseless intervention at every moment and at every place (theologically omnipresence; one must add omnipresence at all times); if we further consider that at the first moment when the Unconscious became active, thus at the moment of the first positing and disposing of this world, just the same ideal world of *all possible* conceptions, thus also of all possible worlds and world-goals and world-ends and their possible means rested in the omniscient Unconscious,—if, lastly, we take notice that the chain of final causality cannot from its very nature be conceived interminable like that of bare causality, but must terminate in a final end, because every preceding link of the chain in final causation must be conditioned by the *following;* thus a *completed infinity* of ends would have to be included in the idea, and yet all the infinitely numerous final terms would hover as impossible in the air, because they wait in vain for the true end which is to determine them,—we may with justice confide *that the world is contrived and guided as wisely and well as is possible; that if, among all possible ideas, that of a better world could have lain in the omniscient Unconscious, certainly the better one would have come to pass instead of the present one;* that the *unerring* Unconscious neither could have been *deceived* in positing this world as to its value, nor that in the omni-temporal omnipresence of the Unconscious a *pause* in its action could ever have been possible, since by such a remissness in the government of the world the better-founded world would have of itself *deteriorated.* Consequently, we can only regard the assertion of Leibniz as perfectly justified, "that the existing world is the best of all possible ones." To be sure, the path by which we arrive at the preponderating probability of this assumption is an *indirect* one. To aim at it by a direct path is indeed a manifest impossibility, for how could we comprehend the infinitely many *possible* worlds, how sufficiently know the existing ones, to compare it exhaustively with these? It was certainly, however, possible for us to prove the existence of those qualities in the Unconscious in consequence of which it must overlook the possible worlds with a glance as it were, and of these worlds realise that one which attains the most rational end in the most efficient manner.

But now, although in this respect we agree with Leibniz, we can yet by no means approve of his conception of *evil*, which he has adopted from Athanasius and Augustine, and which consists in explaining it as something purely privative, or a *less degree of the good*. Were it declared to be something *negative* in the true sense of the word, rightly understood, one could only approve this, for pleasure and pain, good and evil are in fact related as positive and negative, *i.e.*, as thesis and antithesis; only it is to be remarked that the negative has *exactly as much* reality as the positive; that it is purely a matter of the subjective point of view, consequently, as this is self-chosen, an arbitrary affair, which of two opposites is termed positive, which negative.

But Leibniz had also too fine and too mathematical a head to attempt, from the negativity of evil, to show its unreality. Since, however, he is only concerned to prove this *in majorem Dei gloriam*, he does violence to the facts, and ascribes to evil not a negative, but a merely *privative*, and indeed *relatively privative* character, *i.e.*, he asserts: "Evil is not the contrary, but the defect of the good, and indeed only absolute evil could be the absolute defect of the good; every relative evil, however, is only a relative defect, *i.e.*, a *less degree* of the good."

This is an actual untruth, for from the proposition it would at once follow that I must prefer the union of the evil *a* with the good *A* to the possession *of the latter alone*, since indeed the evil *a* is not by a long way absolute evil, *i.e.*, zero-evil, but only a less degree of good, thus increases the degree of good contained in A by its own good. The *non plus ultra* of madness would be, however, according to this view, when somebody to avoid a great evil foregoes a good, and the man who at the same time suffers in the extremest degree all conceivable bodily and mental torments would have to be called happy even at this moment compared with the insensitive state of one under chloroform, to say nothing of the peaceful sleep of death. To such unnatural perversions does a false hypothesis lead, that is invented for the sake of certain foregone conclusions.

If we inquire, however, concerning the motive in whose interest it was set up, it is remarkable that this proves to be mistaken, and therefore the whole hypothesis superfluous.

It used to be thought that there lay in the existence of a real evil a contradiction to the perfect world. Much mischief has at all times been wrought by the word "perfect." Already Plato (Timæus, 7) and Aristotle regarded the world as a sphere, and the astronomical movements as circular, *because* the sphere is the most perfect form, and circular movement the most perfect movement; and in old manuals of artillery, too, one may read that balls are used for shot because the ball is the most perfect shape.

If "perfect" has any sense at all, it can only be "the best of its kind," for nothing *can* of course be better than possible; and only in *this* sense would one have grounds for regarding the world as possible. But now another notion was substituted unperceived for that of perfect, the *immaculate* or faultless, representing an absolute value, filling the possessor with untroubled blessedness. For such a perfection of the world, however, not the very least particle of evidence was offered; it was a baseless supposition, the result of confusion of ideas. It was supposed the best possible must also be *good*, and it was not at all considered that the *best possibility* of a thing does *not* say anything whatever as to its goodness; that it therefore may be as bad as one can imagine, nay, that in certain cases the extreme of goodness and the extreme of badness is precisely identical, namely, when only one case is possible, or even when all possible cases equal one another in goodness. Thus, then, because this world is the best possible, it may still be thoroughly bad, and since the best possibility says nothing at all as to its goodness, the strongest *proof of its badness can never become an objection to its being the best possible*, and consequently the refutation of these objections never can become *a support* to the assertion of its being the best possible, are therefore in *this* respect quite superfluous.

Only if the defects and worthlessness exhibited prove either the pursuing of a reprehensible purpose or an application of *unsuitable* means to *demonstrably* good ends, only then would they establish a doubt of the all-wisdom of the Unconscious, and thereby indirectly, but only indirectly, also of the best possible character of the world. This is, however, the case neither as regards evil, nor as regards the morally bad, nor as regards the pleasant life of the immoral and suffering of the virtuous; the ends to which these circumstances would be inappropriate means must be the rule of universal felicity, morality, and justice. As regards morality and justice in particular, both have only an importance from the point of view of individuation, *i.e.*, they belong only to the world of appearance, not to its essence. Individuation requires as fundamental instinct for the preservation of individuals, thus as fundamental condition of their possibility, *egoism; without* egoism no individuation; *with* egoism necessarily direct injury of another for one's own advantage, *i.e.*, wrong, wickedness, immorality, &c. All this is therefore a necessary unavoidable evil for the sake of individuation, as I have already shown in Chap. viii. A., vol. i. p. 190, in the department of organic arrangements, that certain inevitable evil conditions must be borne in spite of their inappropriateness for *certain* ends, because their avoidance would be inappropriate for still *more important* ends.

The wisdom of the Unconscious is therefore only to be admired, which, in the first place, has placed in the human breast as counterpoise to the necessary egoism those other instincts like compassion, benevolence, gratitude, feeling of approval and instinct of retaliation, which serve for the averting of much wrong and production of positive benefits, and of which the retaliatory instinct and the feeling of approval in conjunction with the instinct to form communities produce, after the transference of retribution to the state, the idea of justice, which now on its part makes the desistance from wrong by prospective punishment an affair of egoism, so that this annuls itself by its own excesses.

But quite apart from this admirable arrangement morality and justice are always only ideas, which have a significance *merely* in regard to the behaviour of *individuals to one another*, or to the corporations formed of individuals, but applied to the *inner being* of the individuals, *i.e.*, to the One Unconscious—*apart* from the form of its manifestation—become *meaningless*. But now, since the All-One can in the last resort only be so far *interested* in the world as it takes part in it, inheres in it with its *essence*, and since the *form of the manifestation* is indeed an important point of transition, but apart from its reaction on the Essential Being itself cannot possibly be a final end; so will also morality and justice as *formal* ideas only be capable of estimation in regard to their teleological value for the Unconscious, according to that standard which exclusively regards their effect on its *essence*.

This, however, is only given by the sum of *pleasure and pain* produced by morality and immorality, by justice and injustice, in all the participating individuals acting or suffering, for these only are altogether *real*, not like morality and justice, *mere ideas of consciousness*, and the Unconscious is the *common subject*, which feels them in all the different consciousnesses. Thus not *in itself* can moral action have a value for the Unconscious, but only so far as it lessens the sum of the sorrow to be felt by it; not in itself, also not for the sake of morality can justice have a worth, but only so far as it diminishes the woe to be felt by diminution of immoral action. Although, therefore, morality and justice, *as such*, cannot be ends in the world-process, they might well *be so for the sake of happiness*, if this, as an object directly concerning the essence of the Unconscious, may be regarded as end, which might well be supposed. As ends in such relative sense, however, morality and justice may certainly be regarded without being contradicted by the facts, since, indeed, the already mentioned instincts, but especially the ever-improving administration of justice, must be recognised as means to the diminution of immoral and unjust action. They must, however, entirely lay aside their claims to absolute validity, and content themselves with a very subordinate relative importance, to which is to be added that, as immorality is an unavoidable evil, without which no individuation is possible, so the demand for a direct divine administration of justice is a piece of theological unreason, which for the sake of an extremely small utility would continually put the laws of the world out of joint. Of happiness, *i.e.*, the greatest possible diminution of pain and the greatest possible enhancement of pleasure, one would certainly think that it must be something affecting the essence of the Unconscious itself, altogether real, *eo ipso* end, especially *since there is no other subject for the feeling* of pain and pleasure than the one Unconscious; in conformity with this we do also, in fact, see a number of preparations taken for the warding off of pain and the enhancement of pleasure.

Just as little can we deny that on the supposition of

individuation and of the egoism connected therewith, the inevitable *necessity* of pain in the struggle for existence and in the death of the individual is given; yet we find a number of facts that appear *inappropriate* as regards happiness, and only become intelligible when the other ends which they serve, *e.g.*, perfection of consciousness, &c., are more important than happiness; nay, this is even the case with individuation itself. But now we cannot at all understand how there should be an end that could take precedence of happiness, since nothing could more immediately affect the essence of the Unconscious than this. We cannot comprehend how there could be anything that would reward a *sacrifice* of happiness except the prospect of a *higher* happiness, or that could repay the taking on oneself of a pain except the prospect and avoidance of a greater pain; otherwise it would only be *driving the teeth into one's own flesh.* If then happiness is actually to be the supreme end, there can be only such sufferings as are unavoidable, in order to attain on another side, or in a later stage of the process, a so much higher happiness, or at least to obviate still greater, more extensive, or more protracted sufferings. But if there were no prospect of this, the existence of a world-process, or of a world at all, would not be rationally intelligible, and the attainment of God knows what *other ends* could afford no rational ground for the assumption of a pain exceeding the pleasure.

Here now is the point where we again come back to Leibniz, for it would indeed be too surprising if the confusion of ideas between the perfect world as *best possible*, and the perfect world as *altogether good and faultless*, had not, in the case of so fine a mind as Leibniz, a hidden support justifying the drift of the "Theodicy" in a certain fashion. This, however, is certainly discoverable; for not, as is asserted, to show the supreme excellence of the world did Leibniz seek to enhance its worth by the privative character of evil and the bad, but to justify the Creator *on account of his creation.*

To wit, under *all possible worlds* the case is not included that *no* world be created, just because *no* world is also no *world*, thus also *no one* of possible *worlds;* should it now turn out that the existing *world* is *worse than none*, the reproach would fall on the Creator why he *at all* created it, since it would indeed have been more rational to create none. Then would the creation as such, altogether apart from *how* it turned out, owe its origin to an *irrational* act, and one would have then the choice *either* to assume that the Reason of the Creator had no part in this irrational act, and that only the task fell to it to continue and carry out in the best possible manner the original decision made without its participation; *or*, however, to grant that the Wisdom of the Creator, unquestionable in details, committed on the large scale a fundamental error, and consequently became perfectly unfaithful to itself, namely, if one wishes to sustain the assertion that in that original act the *totality* of the Creator participated, thus also his *reason*. The *second* hypothesis is too monstrous; how could the Supreme Wisdom be so faithless to itself as just to be guilty of the greatest unreason at the most important moment? But Leibniz would and could *just as little* have adopted the *first* supposition, because he recognised no plurality of attributes in God. Consequently it only remained for him to secure himself *in advance* against the *possibility* that this world could have turned out *worse than none*, and *for this purpose* he invented the theory of the privative character of evil.

We, who seek before all to maintain an unprejudiced attitude in this inquiry, shall in the next chapter try to solve the question *empirically* whether this world is to be preferred or postponed to its non-existence. Should then the latter be the result, we shall not seek to evade the consequence that the existence of the world owes its origin to an *irrational* act, shall however not assume that *Reason itself has suddenly* become *irrational* in this one point, but that this act was only consummated *without* reason, because

Reason had *no part* in it. This is possible to us, because we recognise *two* activities in the Unconscious, of which the one, the will, is just the inherently illogical (not *anti*-logical, but *a*-logical), irrational. As we have already found that all real existence owes its origin to the will, it would, even *a priori*, be only wonderful if this existence were *not* as such irrational.

But whatever the decision may be, in no case can an objection be drawn from it to the *all-wisdom* of the Unconscious, and to the proposition *that of all possible worlds the existing one is the best.*

END OF VOL. II.

www.ingramcontent.com/pod-product-compliance
Lightning Source LLC
Chambersburg PA
CBHW030346230426
43664CB00007BB/552